Emma Bielecki

The Collector in Nineteenth-Century French Literature

Representation, Identity, Knowledge

PETER LANG

Oxford · Bern · Berlin · Bruxelles · Frankfurt am Main · New York · Wien

Bibliographic information published by Die Deutsche Nationalbibliothek
Die Deutsche Nationalbibliothek lists this publication in the Deutsche National-
bibliografie; detailed bibliographic data is available on the Internet at
http://dnb.d-nb.de.

A catalogue record for this book is available from the British Library.

Library of Congress Cataloging-in-Publication Data:

Bielecki, Emma, 1981-
   The collector in nineteenth-century French literature :
representation, identity, knowledge / Emma Bielecki.
       p. cm. – (French studies of the eighteenth and nineteenth
centuries ; 32)
   Includes bibliographical references and index.
   ISBN 978-3-0343-0757-4 (alk. paper)
   1. French literature–19th century–History and criticism. 2.
Collectors and collecting in literature. I. Title.
   PQ292.B47 2011
   840.9'39–dc23

                                     2011037897

ISSN   1422-7320
ISBN   978-3-0343-0757-4

© Peter Lang AG, European Academic Publishers, Bern 2012
Hochfeldstrasse 32, CH-3012 Bern, Switzerland
info@peterlang.com, www.peterlang.com, www.peterlang.net

Printed in Germany

The Collector in Nineteenth-Century French Literature

FRENCH STUDIES

of the Eighteenth and Nineteenth Centuries

Edited by Robin Howells, Emeritus Professor of French
at Birkbeck, University of London, and James Kearns,
Emeritus Professor of French at the University of Exeter

PETER LANG
Oxford · Bern · Berlin · Bruxelles · Frankfurt am Main · New York · Wien

Contents

Introduction

'La collection', according to the 1869 article on the *collectionneur* in the Larousse *Grand Dictionnaire*, 'est un des goûts qui sont appelés à caractériser plus spécialement ce siècle'.[1] Certainly nineteenth-century French literature is crammed with collectors: from the sketch-writing of the 1830s to the late-nineteenth-century decadent fictions of Jean Lorrain, from Balzac's Cousin Pons to Proust's Charles Swann, from Captain Nemo to Arsène Lupin, via Bouvard, Pécuchet and Des Esseintes, from matchbox enthusiasts to mineralogists, bell collectors to bibliophiles, the literature of the period abounds in examples of men (and occasionally women) afflicted with what the *Grand Dictionnaire* termed 'collectionnomanie'.[2] This profusion of fictional collectors reflects the growing number of real collectors in nineteenth-century France, as a new culture of collecting emerged during the July Monarchy, and continued to develop over the course of the century.

1   'Collectionneur', in *Grand Dictionnaire universel du XIXe siècle français, historique, géographique, bibliographique, littéraire, artistique, scientifique etc.*, ed. by Pierre Larousse, 17 vols (Paris: Librairie classique Larousse et Boyer, 1866–77), IV (1869), 601–2 (p. 601).
2   'Collectionneur', *Grand Dictionnaire*, p. 601. Anatole France's first novel, *Le Crime de Sylvestre Bonnard* [in *Œuvres*, ed. by Marie-Claire Bancquart, Bibliothèque de la Pléiade, 4 vols (Paris: Gallimard, 1984–1991), I, 149–313] features a Russian prince who travels the world in search of matchboxes. A character in his 1894 novel *Le Lys Rouge* [also in *Œuvres*, II (1987), 329–562] has an equally eccentric passion for bells. For perhaps the most famous nineteenth-century fictional mineralogist, Professor Lidenbrock, see Jules Verne, *Voyage au centre de la terre* (Paris: Hetzel, 1864).

From the *Curieux* to the *Collectionneur*

The emergence of a new culture of collecting is signalled by the invention of a new word, 'collectionneur'. The *Grand Larousse de la langue française* identifies the first recorded use of this word as occurring in 1839, in a Balzac sketch, 'Monographie du rentier', in which he identifies the 'collectionneur' as a distinct sub-species of *rentier*.[3] The first use of the verb 'collectionner' is identified as occurring a year later, in Horace de Viel-Castel's sketch of the collector for *Les Français peints par eux-mêmes*.[4] The introduction of these new words signals a break with the pre-Revolutionary culture of curiosity. In particular, there are four important differences between the old culture of curiosity and the modern culture of collecting.

The first obvious distinction between the two is that curiosity is a broader concept than collecting. Furetière's dictionary (1690) attaches to the word 'curieux' several inter-related meanings. The first meaning is 'Celuy qui veut tout sçavoir, et tout apprendre.'[5] This is followed by the secondary meaning: 'celuy qui a desir [sic] d'apprendre, de voir les bonnes choses, les merveilles de l'art et de la nature'. The third meaning is 'celuy qui a ramassé les choses les plus rares, les plus belles et les plus extraordinaires qu'il a pu trouver tant dans les arts que dans la nature'. Thus the word 'curieux' could be applied to a collector, but it could equally apply

---

3   See Honoré de Balzac, 'Monographie du rentier', in *Les Français peints par eux-mêmes*, 8 vols (Paris: Curmer, 1840–1842), III (1841), 1–16 (p. 14). In Charles de Lovenjoul's 1888 bibliography of Balzac, it is stated that this article first appeared in 1840. See Charles de Spoelberch de Lovenjoul, *Histoire des œuvres de Honoré de Balzac: troisième édition entièrement revue et corrigée à nouveau* (Geneva: Slatkine Reprints, 1968), p. 240.

4   Horace de Viel-Castel, 'Les Collectionneurs' in *Les Français peints par eux-mêmes*, 8 vols (Paris: Curmer, 1840–1842), I, 121–8.

5   The definition from Furetière's dictionary, and that from the dictionary of the Académie, are cited in Krzysztof Pomian, *Collectionneurs, Amateurs et Curieux: Paris, Venise: XVIe – XVIIIe siècle* (Paris: Gallimard, 1987), pp. 71 and 72. Pomian has researched the early modern culture of curiosity extensively, and it is his analysis of that culture that I follow here. See Pomian, *Collectionneurs*, pp. 30–62.

to someone who simply wanted to 'tout sçavoir, et tout apprendre'. In the entry for 'curieux' in the dictionary of the Académie française (1694), this idea is stated even more strongly. As an adjective, 'curieux' is defined as meaning: 'Qui a beaucoup d'envie et de soin d'apprendre, de voir, de posséder des choses nouvelles, rares, excellentes etc.'. The entry further notes that the word 's'emploie aussi quelquefois dans le subst. et alors il signifie, Celuy qui prend plaisir à faire amas des choses curieuses et rares ou celuy qui a une grande connoissance de ces sortes des choses'. Thus it is possible to be a *curieux* without having a *cabinet de curiosité*, a collection of rare, strange or skilfully wrought things. Indeed, the entry for 'curieux' offered in the *Grand Dictionnaire* picks up on this, as the author suggests that the *curieux* 'peut n'avoir ni cabinet ni collection d'aucune sorte'.[6] This is one of the ways in which the *curieux* is distinguished from the *collectionneur*, for the notion of material possession is absolutely central to the culture of collecting. Writing in 1867, Champfleury, himself a keen collector, described the *collectionneur* as motivated by 'une des passions les plus tyranniques, celle de la possession'.[7] The importance of the concept of material possession in the discourse around collecting meant that throughout the nineteenth century the collector was perceived, as we shall see throughout this book, as having a privileged relationship with material culture.

The increased importance of the fact of material possession in the discourse of collecting in the nineteenth century is a function of a broader shift away from the culture of curiosity. It is clear from the dictionary definitions cited above that the culture of curiosity was a culture of knowledge. Indeed, as the art historian Krzysztof Pomian shows, in his authoritative work on early modern collecting, the notion of curiosity was tied up in

---

6   'Curieux', in *Grand Dictionnaire universel du XIXe siècle français, historique, géographique, bibliographique, littéraire, artistique, scientifique etc.*, ed. by Pierre Larousse, 17 vols (Paris: Librairie classique Larousse et Boyer, 1866–1877), V (1869), 679–80 (p. 680).

7   Champfleury, *L'Hôtel des commissaires-priseurs* (Paris: Dentu, 1867), p. xii.

a problematic of licit and illicit knowledge, the Faustian theme.[8] The *curieux* was thus potentially a dangerous figure. The collector, too, was a dangerous figure, but for rather different reasons. Nineteenth-century collecting was conceived of much less as a heuristic device, and much more as a fundamentally irrational urge. Certainly, much of the discourse around collecting generated by the practice of collecting itself – in guides, handbooks, and specialist periodicals – claimed an intellectual justification for collecting. Thus in *Collections et collectionneurs*, an 1885 collection of essays dealing with different branches of collecting by the journalist Paul Eudel, a man very much immersed in the collecting world, stamp-collecting is praised as a knowledge-producing exercise: 'La timbromanie touche à l'art, à l'histoire, à la diplomatie et à beaucoup d'autres sciences très longues à énumérer'.[9] For this reason it is presented as particularly useful for boys; it produces 'des géographes précoces', as well as acting as 'un cours d'histoire'.[10] Eudel stresses the pedagogic value of stamp-collecting precisely to defend it against the charge of being a 'manie frivole'.[11] For if collectors claimed an intellectual justification for their activities, the uninitiated who looked in on the world of collecting from the outside tended to treat such claims with extreme skepticism (as indicated by the frequent use of the suffix '-manie' throughout the nineteenth century to describe different kinds of collecting: *timbromanie, tableaumanie, bricabracomanie, bibliomanie* etc.). By the time Eudel was writing there was a well-established tradition of treating stamp-collecting with ridicule (a tradition which continues to this day). Thus the *Grand Dictionnaire* article on the 'collectionneur' mocked the specialist periodical, *Collectionneur de timbres-poste*, in the following terms:

8   Pomian, 'Collectionneurs', pp. 75–80. Pomian suggests that disapproval of curiosity, grounded in a religious morality, was on the wane throughout the eighteenth century.

9   Paul Eudel, *Collections et collectionneurs* (Paris: Charpentier, 1885), p. 165.

10   Eudel, *Collections et collectionneurs*, p. 165.

11   Eudel, *Collections et collectionneurs*, p. 165.

Ce singulier moniteur de la plus singulière des collectionnomanies, parfois sati-
rique sans le savoir, donnait un jour ce curieux spécimen de sa rédaction *timbrée*:
'Moldovalachie. Le prince Couza vient d'être déposé. A bientôt une nouvelle série
de timbres!' Ainsi une révolution se fait, un peuple chasse son souverain, le collectionneur se frotte les mains: 'A bientôt une nouvelle série de timbres'.[12]

If for Eudel stamp-collecting provides a course in geo-politics, the article
in the *Grand Dictionnaire* presents the stamp-collector as so obsessed with
the new set of stamps that he brackets off all the events surrounding their
issue. Stamp-collecting, rather than expanding his intellectual horizons,
shrinks them.

The collector is here presented as a species of monomaniac, in the grip
of an implacable *idée fixe*. Elsewhere too the idea that collecting can be
motivated by intellectual curiosity is presented as a specious justification
for an irrational impulse. In Alphonse Daudet's 1880 novel, *L'Immortel*,
the central character, Léonard Astier, is an Academician, historian, and
autograph collector, who has nearly bankrupted himself indulging his particular brand of collectomania. When his wife suggests that he sell some of
his collection to ease their straitened financial circumstances:

> Le bonhomme éclata comme un coup de mine. [...] Il frappait sur la table, très pale,
> la bouche en avant, maniaque et féroce; un Astier-Réhu extraordinaire que sa femme
> ne connaissait pas. [...] Presque aussitôt, redevenu très calme, l'académicien s'expli-
> qua, un peu honteux; ces documents lui étaient indispensables pour la confection
> de ses livres.[13]

Here the justification offered by Astier to explain his violent opposition
to his wife's suggestion is presented as an afterthought and an alibi, an
attempt to rationalize something fundamentally irrational. The text later
confirms this, when the narrator notes of Léonard: 'Au fond, quoi qu'il
se dît pour endormir sa conscience, dans ces prodigalités que personne
ne soupçonnait encore autour de lui, l'historien avait moins de part que

---

12   'Collectionneur', in *Grand Dictionnaire*, p. 601.
13   Alphonse Daudet, *L'Immortel*, in *Œuvres*, ed. by Roger Ripoll, Bibliothèque de la
      Pléiade, 3 vols (Paris: Gallimard, 1986–1994), III, 682–845 (p. 700).

le collectionneur'.[14] A similar idea is expressed in France's 1881 novel, *Le Crime de Sylvestre Bonnard*. The eponymous hero is also an Academician and historian, and a passionate bibliophile. Far from presenting Bonnard's passion for old books and manuscripts as ancillary to his historical interests, the text suggests that in fact his historical interest is a smoke screen for a kind of deep-rooted fetishistic impulse. Bonnard himself compares his passionate desire to acquire a certain book to his craving, as a small boy, for a doll he once saw in a shop window, a craving that is presented in the text as completely inexplicable.[15] When Bonnard travels to Sicily to acquire this book, he meets a matchbox collector, and recognizes their kinship: 'Sans doute j'eusse préféré voir M. et Mme Trépof receuillir en Sicilie des marbres antiques, des vases peints ou des médailles. [...] Mais enfin ils faisaient de la collection, ils étaient de la confrérie'.[16] Thus Bonnard is willing to acknowledge that his supposedly erudite and serious collecting may in fact be a simple mania.

Collecting was often presented as an activity belonging to the domain of abnormal psychology. Edmond Bonnaffé, the art critic, historian and collector, active in the Third Republic, affectionately addressed his fellow collectors thus:

> Collectionneurs, mes confrères, soyez modestes. L'historien passera encore à côté de vous sans vous apercevoir, le philosophe haussera les épaules, l'artiste vous traitera de bourgeois spéculateurs, l'homme du monde de *bibelotiers*; seul, le médecin vous tirera son chapeau ... espérant bien avoir prochainement votre clientèle.[17]

This address to collectors was published in 1878, and in its representation of the collector as a marginal and eccentric figure it belongs to what was by then a well-established discursive tradition. In fact, by 1878 Bonnaffé's sketch of the collector may have appeared a little old-fashioned. Dominique Pety, in an article tracing the evolution of the figure of the collector over the

14   Daudet, p. 797.
15   France, *Sylvestre Bonnard*, p. 163.
16   France, *Sylvestre Bonnard*, p. 182.
17   Edmond Bonnaffé, *Causeries sur l'art et la curiosité* (Paris: Quantin, 1878), p. 9.

course of the nineteenth century, argues that after 1870 collecting became a more mainstream, more fashionable pastime. As a result the collector qua discursive construct passed 'du marginal, au physique et au costume disgraciés, au mondain ou à l'aristocratie'.[18] Pety's argument implies that Bonnaffé's suggestion that the collector and 'l'homme du monde' were mutually exclusive categories was dismantled in the last years of the nineteenth century.

Although the scruffy, perennially impecunious, monomaniacal collector became a rather old-fashioned image towards the end of the century, replaced by a more elegant and sophisticated figure, collecting continued to be presented as a pathology, most obviously in the literature of the fin-de-siècle, where fashionable young men invariably collect something. Max Nordau identified a passion for bric-a-brac as one of the symptoms of degeneration, and throughout the literature of the fin-de-siècle a collection of some sort is presented as an essential accessory for decadent heroes.[19] Collecting thus became part and parcel of a lifestyle that systematically rejected bourgeois mores. If collecting became a more fashionable activity, this was perhaps because of rather than despite its louche and seedy connotations.

The monomaniacal nature of the modern collector also marks a third significant shift between the pre-Revolutionary culture of curiosity and the nineteenth-century culture of collecting. The favoured mode of the cabinet of curiosity was eclecticism, which reflected the encyclopaedic aspirations of the *curieux*, 'celuy qui veut tout sçavoir, et tout apprendre'. The *Grand Dictionnaire* describes the *curieux* as someone who, 's'occupe de tous les monuments de l'activité humaine: épigraphie, philologie, manuscrits et lettres autographes, bibliographie, paléontologie, ethnographie, sciences de toute sorte, aussi bien que les statues, les tableaux, les bronzes, les ivoires, les émaux, les tapis, les armes etc., tout sert de matière à ses recherches'.[20]

---

18   Dominique Pety, 'Le Personnage du collectionneur au XIXe siècle: de l'excentrique à l'amateur distingué', *Romantisme* 112 (2001), 71–81 (p. 71).
19   See Max Nordau, *Degeneration* (London: Heinemann, 1895), pp. 10–11.
20   'Curieux', in *Grand Dictionnaire*, p. 680. On the theme of totality in the discourse of curiosity see also Pomian, *Collectionneurs*, pp. 68–75.

The collector, on the other hand, is typically concerned with one class of objects to the exclusion of all others: 'Il ne fait point d'infidélité à son idée fixe. Le beau, le bien, le vrai, c'est sa collection: tout le reste est chimère. S'il a entrepris de rassembler des coquillages, ne venez pas lui parler d'une terre cuite de Clodion, d'une aiguière de Benvenuto ou d'un diptyque de Van Eyck; il vous recevrait avec dédain'.[21] In contrast to the pre-Revolutionary *curieux*, whose intellectual disposition was a catholic one, the intellectual disposition of the *collectionneur* is a narrow one, geared towards seriality. Where the cabinet of curiosities functioned as a microscosm of the universe, the collection – of shells, stamps or snuff-boxes – is concerned only with a small corner of the universe.[22] Over the course of the nineteenth century, there was a profusion of different kinds of collector. The article on the *collectionneur* in the *Grand Dictionnaire* alludes to this profusion when it concludes a list of different types of collector by noting that: 'Arrêtons-nous. Nous n'en finirons pas si nous voulions passer en revue toutes les variétés, toutes les audaces, toutes les singularités de la *collectionnomanie*'.[23] The article offers not a totalizing vision of the world, but rather a frac-tionalizing one, in which it is broken up into small fragments which do not add up to a coherent, complete whole, but are simply piled on top of each other in a potentially infinite arrangement. The discourse around collecting is therefore structured by notions of partiality, fragmentation, seriality and incompleteness that are among the hallmarks of the experi-ence of modernity.

The profusion of different kinds of collector in the nineteenth century is part and parcel of the increased popularity of collecting in the period, which marks a fourth major difference between the old culture of curiosity and the new culture of collecting. By the 1880s it seemed that everyone in France was a collector.[24] This increased popularity inflected the discourse of

---

21   'Curieux', in *Grand Dictionnaire*, p. 679.

22   On the idea of the microcosm, see Pomian, *Collectionneurs*, pp. 85–95.

23   'Collectionneur', in *Grand Dictionnaire*, p. 601.

24   For this claim see: Edmond de Goncourt, *La Maison d'un artiste*, 2 vols (Paris: Charpentier, 1881), I, 3; Guy de Maupassant, 'Bibelot', *Le Gaulois*, 22 March 1883, reprinted in *Chroniques inédites*, ed. by Pascal Pia, 2 vols (Paris: Maurice Gonon,

collecting, as the collector came to be a less marginal and eccentric figure, and a more mainstream and fashionable one. For many commentators, as we shall see, the democratization of collecting was also a decline, as it shifted from being the preserve of a cultural elite to a mass-market phenomenon. Certainly the increased popularity of collecting was at least partly a function of the development of industrialization, and the advent of the regimes of mass production and mass consumption. It was the age of the *bibelot*, and the accumulation of objects in the late-nineteenth-century domestic interior, crammed full of knickknacks and trinkets, bore witness to the ever-accelerating production of commodities under capitalism. It also blurred the line between collecting and mere accumulation, and risked turning collecting from a practice to a style of interior design. The democratization of collecting also meant that whereas *curieux* were a relatively homogenous group, and the world of curiosity a closed and bounded one, the world of collecting was a multifarious one, marked by diversity and heterogeneity, with unstable and constantly shifting borders.

From this multifarious culture of collecting emerged a new discourse of collecting, at the centre of which stands the figure of the collector, the hero of this book. This discourse comprises not only texts generated from within the world of collecting, secreted by the practice of collecting itself (handbooks, guides, catalogues, reference works for collectors), but also literary and paraliterary texts. Representations of the collector in these literary and paraliterary texts are the main focus of this book, but throughout they are integrated into a broader discourse of collecting. If rather disparate texts are often brought into contact, this is with the aim of providing both a novel framework within which to consider them and a deeper understanding of the culture of collecting in nineteenth-century France, a culture which has received relatively little critical attention. Nonetheless, before going on to adumbrate the argument of this book, it is necessary to review the scholarship which provided its foundations.

1979), II, 27–32 (p. 27); Paul Bourget, 'Edmond et Jules de Goncourt', in *Essais de psychologie contemporaine* (Paris: Plon, 1899), pp. 373–407 (p. 380).

Collecting Studies and Literary Criticism: Established Critical Parameters

Collecting is a widespread cultural phenomenon with an extremely long history, and the question of what kind of psychological, social, and cultural meanings can be ascribed to the behaviour of collectors is one that has received growing scholarly attention in recent years. The museologist Susan M. Pearce, in her wide-ranging book, *On Collecting: An Investigation into Collecting in the European Tradition*, traces the way in which collecting studies has undergone something of a paradigm shift in recent years. Traditional collection studies, she notes:

> have always and still do, concentrate on the material perceived as 'high culture', and its intellectual coherence is derived from the place it occupies in what gradually, in modernist Europe, emerges [sic] as the main disciplines – very broadly those of natural science, academic history, archaeology, anthropology and the history of art (which includes what museums frequently call decorative or applied art). [...] Work within them has concentrated upon the meaning of individual items or groups of collected material rather than upon the significance of the collecting process. Attention concentrated upon typologies and taxonomies, and an interest in period, schools and studios. [...]
> Equally characteristic, too, is the production of a very considerable volume of published work about individual collections and collectors, and similar studies of the history of public or semi-public collections of the world's great museums.[25]

In the final third of the twentieth century, however, a new kind of collecting studies developed, which was concerned with collecting as a process. Pearce traces in detail how developments across the humanities and social sciences have led to a complete reconfiguration of this field of scholarship.[26] She examines the way in which the development of post-Freudian psychology, post-Marxist critiques of ideology and the production of knowledge, a new

---

25 Susan M. Pearce, *On Collecting: An Investigation into Collecting in the European Tradition* (London: Routledge, 1995), p. 6.

26 See Pearce, pp. 3–35.

conception of the importance of material culture in social practice, and the increasing self-reflexivity of an ethnography concerned with interrogating its own epistemological assumptions have all led to new perspectives on collecting. Important contributions to the critical literature on the subject have come from a number of scholars working in different disciplines: Baudrillard, who has provided a psychoanalytically-inflected account of the behaviour of the collector; James A. Clifford, who, in his seminal essay 'On Collecting Art and Culture', describes the subject-object relations inscribed in collecting; the sociologist Russell Belk, who has sought to theorize the relationship between consumption and collecting, and Mieke Bal, who has examined collecting from the point of view of structuralist and post-structuralist theories of narrative.[27] These scholars have contributed to a bourgeoning interest in issues such as how people interact with things, how collecting can contribute to the creation of identity, and how it can create patterns of otherness, dominance and subservience.

Pearce also offers as evidence of a widespread contemporary fascination with collecting, 'the quite amazing extent to which collecting now appears as a major theme in what we might call serious fiction'.[28] The novels of collecting she cites extend from Balzac's *Le Cousin Pons* (1847) to Byatt's *Possession* (1990), via Henry James' *The Spoils of Poynton* (1897), Joyce's *Finnegans Wake* (1937), John Fowles' *The Collector* (1967), and Umberto Eco's *Foucault's Pendulum* (1990). According to Pearce, 'this signals a willingness on the part of the writing and reading public to see collecting as an adequate metaphor for large parts of experience'.[29] The rich metaphorical potential of collecting is highlighted by John Elsner and Roger Cardinal in their introduction to *The Cultures of Collecting*, an edited volume that

27 See Jean Baudrillard, *Le Système des objets* (Paris: Gallimard, 1968), pp. 120–50; James Clifford, *The Predicament of Culture: Twentieth-Century Ethnography, Literature, and Art* (Cambridge, MA: Harvard University Press, 1988), pp. 215–51; Russell W. Belk, *Collecting in a Consumer Society* (London: Routledge, 1995), and Mieke Bal, 'A Narrative Perspective on Collecting', in *The Cultures of Collecting*, ed. by John Elsner and Roger Cardinal (London: Reaktion, 1994), pp. 97–115.
28 Pearce, pp. 12–13.
29 Pearce, p. 13.

brings together a number of important essays on the theory and practice of collecting. Elsner and Cardinal use collecting in an unconventionally elastic sense, expanding the concept to cover all kinds of areas of human experience. Thus they write: 'Empire is a collection of countries and of populations; a country is a collection of regions and peoples; each given people is a collection of individuals, divided into governed and governors – that is, collectables and collectors'.[30] As Elsner and Cardinal understand it, the history of collecting must be understood in much broader terms than heretofore. They point out that no history of collecting has yet included the Nazi genocide, but that 'the Holocaust can be seen as a collection of Jews, gypsies, homosexuals, the insane and other "vermin", differentiated by a specious scientific classification that was then corroborated by a zealous bureaucracy'.[31]

Elsner and Cardinal thus seek to make the reader think about collecting in much broader terms than usual. The usefulness of using such a capacious notion of the collection has been called into question. Thus Bernard Vouilloux, in his article, 'Le Discours sur la collection', writes:

> Parler de collections d'idées, de sentiments ou de sensations [...], de collections de rêves, de lapsus, de symptômes [...], de collections d'aphorismes [...], ou encore de collections de femmes [...], loin de contribuer à la clarté de l'analyse, ne fait qu'en opacifier les enjeux: que l'on puisse collectionner des pensées ou des formules, des succès ou des échecs, des femmes ou des hommes ne nous apprend pas grand-chose sur l'activité qui consiste à collectionner des tableaux, des timbres-poste ou des tuyaux de pipe.[32]

It is partly with Vouilloux's warning in mind that I have chosen here to focus on the figure of the private collector, rather than the concept of the collection. An investigation into the concept of the collection in nineteenth-century French literature would be a vast undertaking. It would

---

30   John Elsner and Roger Cardinal, 'Introduction', in *The Cultures of Collecting*, ed. by John Elsner and Roger Cardinal (London: Reaktion, 1994), pp. 1–6 (p. 2).
31   Elsner and Cardinal, p. 4.
32   Bernard Vouilloux, 'Le Discours sur la collection', *Romantisme* 112 (2001), 95–108 (pp. 96–7).

involve thinking about collecting as a linguistic and literary process, about collections of words and ideas, such as dictionaries and encyclopædias, and about the text as an exhibition space. Such work is being undertaken by other scholars with other competences.[33] The aim of this book is to focus on representations of the collector in nineteenth-century French literature. This topic presents a double interest. On the one hand, the discourse surrounding the collector can deepen our understanding of the relationship between people and things in the period. On the other hand, however, it is because collecting has such wide-ranging metaphorical resonance, because writing about collecting can so easily become a way of writing about other aspects of life, that the discourse surrounding the figure of the collector is such a fascinating one. It is because writing about collecting can so easily become a way of writing about writing that it is fascinating for the literary scholar in particular.

Walter Benjamin's work on the collector offers an example of the double interest presented by the figure of the collector.[34] On the one hand, Benjamin qua cultural historian took the collector as an object of study.

33   On the text as exhibition space see Philippe Hamon, *Expositions: littérature et architecture au XIX*^e *siècle* (Paris: José Corti, 1989). The Cambridge Centre for Research in the Arts, Social Sciences and Humanities last year hosted a conference on collections and compilations that brought together a number of scholars currently working on these ideas, not so much as represented activities but as linguistic and literary processes. See <http://www.crassh.cam.ac.uk/page/235/march-collections--compilations.htm>. As mentioned in the conference report, plans are underway to publish the proceedings in what will no doubt be a fascinating volume.

34   Throughout his work, Benjamin returned again and again to the figure of the collector. On the psychology of collecting, see his lovely essay, 'Unpacking my Library: A Talk about Book Collecting', in *Illuminations*, ed. by Hannah Arendt, trans. by Harry Zorn (London: Pimlico, 1999), pp. 61–9. For collecting in nineteenth-century France, see 'Paris, the Capital of the Nineteenth Century: Exposé of 1935', in *The Arcades Project*, trans. by Howard Eiland and Kevin McLaughlin (Cambridge, MA: Belknap, 1999), pp. 3–13 (pp. 8–9); 'Paris, Capital of the Nineteenth Century: Exposé of 1939', in *The Arcades Project*, pp. 14–26, and 'Convolute H: The Collector', in *The Arcades Project*, pp. 203–27. For the collector as a historical materialist see 'Eduard Fuchs: Collector and Historian', in *The Essential Frankfurt School Reader*, ed. by Andrew Arato and Eike Gebhardt (New York: Urizen Books, 1978), pp. 225–53.

Thus in 'Paris: Capital of the Nineteenth Century', and in the section of *The Arcades Project* dedicated to the figure of the collector, Benjamin examined collecting in nineteenth-century France as a historical phenomenon, and in relation to consumption, commodity culture, and the rise of the private sphere. As we shall see in chapter one, for Benjamin the collector is essentially an ambivalent figure, both a commodity fetishist and a figure of resistance to universal commodification. At the same time, however, as Benjamin explored the discourse around collecting in nineteenth-century France, he was concerned with how collecting related to his own practice as a historian. Thus in 'Eduard Fuchs: Collector and Historian', Benjamin defends his understanding of historical materialism through considering the collecting practices of Fuchs. Moreover, *The Arcades Project* in its final, admittedly unfinished, form is essentially a collection of quotations, which further invites us to read Benjamin's presentation of the collector as a commentary on his own work.[35] Benjamin approaches the figure of the collector from a double perspective, not only studying collecting as a historical phenomenon with specific social and cultural meaning, but also using the idea of collecting to figure his own work as a scholar. In this respect, as we shall see, Benjamin follows in the wake of many nineteenth-century writers, who use the figure of the collector self-reflexively.

In fact, Benjamin's allegorical use of the figure of the collector has proved more influential than his suggestion that the collector was one of the major figures inhabiting the nineteenth-century French cultural imagination. If we turn to consider the field of nineteenth-century French studies, it is striking how little critical attention the figure of the collector has received. Certainly, there are works that fall into the category of 'traditional collecting studies', as designated by Pearce, such as Maurice Rheims'

---

35   On Benjamin's conception of the collector, and how his representation of this figure is also a self-representation, see: Michael P. Steinberg, 'The Collector as Allegorist: Goods, Gods, and the Objects of History', in *Walter Benjamin and the Demands of History*, ed. by Michael P. Steinberg (Ithaca: Cornell University Press, 1996), pp. 88–118; Irving Wohlfarth, 'Et Cetera? The Historian as Chiffonnier', *New German Critique* 39 (1986), 142–68, and Ackbar Abbas, 'Walter Benjamin's Collector: The Fate of Modern Experience', *New Literary History* 20 (1988), 217–37.

La Vie étrange des objets: histoire de la curiosité, a veritable treasure trove
of information and anecdote about the art market through the ages,[36] or
Pierre Cabanne's *Les Grands Collectionneurs*, which provides a series of
biographical sketches of collectors through the ages.[37] These books have
an art historical remit, and are concerned only with one kind of collecting,
albeit the most prestigious kind. From a scholarly point of view, little has
been written about more popular kinds of collecting.

The proliferation of different kinds of collector in the nineteenth
century perhaps explains the absence of any systematic study of collecting practices in France in that period. To undertake such a task would be
an enormous project. The fragmentary nature of the critical literature on
this subject reflects the fragmentary nature of the nineteenth-century discourse around collecting itself. A 2001 issue of *Romantisme*, dedicated to
'La Collection', contains essays which approach the issue from a number
of different perspectives (as well as an invaluable bibliography which lists
both nineteenth-century specialist periodicals and literary texts which
feature collectors, as well as important critical work on the subject). Apart
from articles which consider the idea of collecting in relation to specific
authors, or which are concerned essentially with literature and the visual
arts, there are three essays that provide a useful introduction to the discourse of collecting as a whole, by Krzysztof Pomian, Dominique Pety,
and Françoise Hamon. Pomian, in his article, 'Collections: une typologie
historique', provides an overview of the evolution of collecting practices
in the period. His concern is first and foremost with real collections and
the behaviour of real collectors. Dominque Pety and Françoise Hamon,
on the other hand, are both concerned with the collector as a discursive
construct, the former looking at literary representations of the collector
across the century, and the latter considering how collecting is presented
in relevant dictionary definitions in the period.

36   Maurice Rheims, *La Vie étrange des objets: histoire de la curiosité* (Paris: Plon,
     1959).
37   Pierre Cabanne, *Les Grands Collectionneurs*, 2 vols (Paris: Editions de l'amateur,
     2003–2004).

Collectively these essays adumbrate some of the major shifts in the discourse of collecting in the period. Both Pomian and Hamon discuss the impact that the rise of the public museum had on the fate of the private collector,[38] an impact I consider in some detail in relation to Balzac's great novel of collecting, *Le Cousin Pons*, in chapter two. On the other hand Pety, as already mentioned, argues that collecting became increasingly popular towards the end of the century, and that thus: 'Du sceau négatif univoque, la collection est devenu système de signes polysémiques invitant à un décodage sociologique avant la lettre, et le discours critique aura pour objet de révéler les différentes stratégies sociales dissimulées sous cette pratique généralisée.'[39] Pety thus suggests that the discourse surrounding the collector could encode broader social concerns, with particular implications for how identity is constructed within a specific social formation. Excavating some of these concerns, and seeing how the discourse of collecting is tied to the production of identity, is one of the chief purposes of this book. Moreover, Pety's discussion links the history of collecting into the history of consumption. Reading this alongside Pomian's article, written from an art historical perspective, enables us to map the broad terrain occupied by the nineteenth-century collector, a terrain that extended from the museum to the market-place.

In addition to work on the figure of the collector, I have also been influenced by recent scholarship on material culture, interest in which has waxed considerably among literary scholars in recent years.[40] One recent

---

38   See Krzysztof Pomian, 'Collections: une typologie historique', *Romantisme* 112 (2001), 9–22 (p. 18), and Françoise Hamon, 'Collections: ce que disent les dictionnaires', *Romantisme* 112 (2001), 55–70 (pp. 58–9).

39   Pety, 'Le Personnage du collectionneur au XIX^c siècle', p. 76.

40   For an excellent study of material culture in the Victorian novel, which brilliantly examines how to read things in texts, see Elaine Freedgood, *The Ideas in Things: Fugitive Meaning in the Victorian Novel* (Chicago: University of Chicago Press, 2006). Part of Freedgood's argument is precisely that the Victorian novel bears witness to a 'Thing culture' not reducible to 'commodity culture'. Useful too is *Things*, ed. by Bill Brown, *Critical Inquiry* 28 (2001), which approaches the intersection between literary and material culture from a number of different perspectives. More directly relevant to the concerns of this book is Didier Maleuvre's marvelous book,

and valuable contribution in the field of nineteenth-century French studies has been Janell Watson's book, *Literature and Material Culture from Balzac to Proust: the Collection and Consumption of Curiosities*, a study of the *bibelot* in nineteenth-century French literature. The argument of this book mobilizes and builds on Watson's book in two principal ways. First, Watson is concerned with how material culture influences literary aesthetics in the nineteenth century, and this too is one of the central concerns of my own research. One of the questions structuring Watson's book is how objects can variously elicit and obstruct narrative in literary texts.[41] Asking this question in relation to representations of collecting, rather than representations of the *bibelot*, opens up wide new avenues of enquiry, allowing us to consider how collecting gives rise to a certain experience of time, and a certain sense of history. Moreover, while the *bibelot* has a privileged relationship with decadence and aestheticism, considering the discourse of collecting provides us with a different prism through which to view nineteenth-century literature, which foregrounds other literary forms such as sketch-writing and naturalism. Secondly, and more specifically, Watson's work is centrally concerned with emergent mass consumption, and she examines the ways in which the democratization of collecting – as more and more people collected more and more things – threatened a cultural elite who defined themselves as connoisseurs. The story she tells is one in which the popularization of collecting is often experienced as a vulgarization in the most pejorative sense of the word, and this narrative of decline, in which a lost golden age of collecting is contrasted with a degraded and venal present, is one that we will encounter in our study of the discourse surrounding collecting. The discourse of collecting is not, however, isomorphic with the discourse of the *bibelot*, and, as we shall see over the course of this study, studying the former enables us to map other

---

Museum Memories: History, Technology, Art (Stanford: Stanford University Press, 1999), which explores in detail the relationship between materiality and textuality.

41   See Janell Waston, *Literature and Material Culture from Balzac to Proust: the Collection and Consumption of Curiosities* (Cambridge: Cambridge University Press, 1999), especially pp. 109–42, in which she discusses the catalogue as a literary form, asking why it has been denigrated by modernist critics and celebrated by postmodernists.

historical changes in nineteenth-century France, connected to psychology and epistemology as well as to the history of consumption and the art-market. Nineteenth-century collectors did not only collect *bibelots*, but also, *inter alia*, fossils, butterflies, archaeological finds, and books. Examining the discourse of collecting enables us to explore the many different kinds of meaning that objects bore for nineteenth-century citizens, and consider not only the sociological and aesthetic significance of collecting, but also its epistemological dimension.

One aspect of the broad question of how people relate to things, central to the discourse of collecting, has received considerable attention in the context of nineteenth-century French studies, and this is the concept of fetishism.[42] From its inception in the 1880s, at the same time as collectors proliferated in the pages of novels, the fetishism diagnosis has provided a useful conceptual framework within which to read narratives of collecting.[43] Indeed, within collecting studies psychoanalytic accounts of collecting have proliferated.[44] One of the most famous is Jean Baudrillard's essay on the subject in *Le Système des objets*, which mobilizes the conceptual apparatus of classical psychoanalysis to present collecting as a form of narcissistic regression. Baudrillard's account gives a specifically psychoanalytic twist

42 See Emily Apter and William Pietz, eds, *Fetishism as Cultural Discourse* (Ithaca: Cornell University Press, 1993), for a number of important essays that consider the concept of fetishism from both Marxist and Freudian perspectives, and in relation to various different cultural products.

43 For the history of fetishism as a psychiatric concept, see Robert A. Nye, 'The Medical Origins of Sexual Fetishism', in *Fetishism as Cultural Discourse*, ed. by Emily Apter and William Pietz (Ithaca: Cornell University Press, 1993), pp. 13–30. In her book, *Feminizing the Fetish: Psychoanalysis and Narrative Obsession in Turn-of-the-Century France* (Ithaca: Cornell University Press, 1991), Emily Apter examines how the concept of fetishism developed in literature and psychoanalysis around the turn of the century, and notes the significant interchanges between literature and psychoanalysis in this period.

44 On this, see Pearce, pp. 6–7. For a book-length study of collecting from a psycho-analytic perspective, including a case-study of Balzac, see Werner Muensterberger, *Collecting: An Unruly Passion. Pyschological Perspectives* (Princeton: Princeton University Press, 1994).

to the widespread, popular perception of collectors as pathetically defective figures, a perception which has been present since the collector's first appearance in the 1830s.

This book is in part concerned with excavating that very discursive tradition. Indeed, I shall argue that writing about collecting in the nineteenth century was a way of exploring the operation of desire, and the interplay between desire and lack.[45] In the twentieth century, the most eloquent discourse on desire, lack, and the relationship between the two has been developed by psychoanalysts. The success with which many late-nineteenth-century narratives of collecting have been analysed using a psychoanalytic apparatus, most notably perhaps by Emily Apter in *Feminizing the Fetish: Psychoanalysis and Narrative Obsession in Turn-of-the-Century France*, demonstrates how closely the concerns of psychoanalysis map on to the concerns that haunt the discourse of collecting.[46] The danger of psychoanalytic accounts of narratives of collecting, however, is that they tend to overlook the historicity of collecting practices, and to reduce the category of collecting to the category of fetishism. In translating the discourse of collecting into the language of psychoanalysis, much may be gained, but something might also be lost. This book looks at some of those texts that are habitually read through the prism of fetishism, notably *A Rebours*, but seeks to locate them within a longer tradition of writing about collecting.

But the discourse around collecting does not only engage questions pertaining to material culture or subject-object relations. It also poses questions that are of specific interest to the literary scholar. In this book I

45   See below, pp. 88–136.
46   Charles Bernheimer, in 'Fetishism and Decadence: Salomé's Severed Heads' [in *Fetishism as Cultural Discourse*, ed. by Emily Apter and William Pietz (Ithaca: Cornell University Press), pp. 62–83], discusses the way in which fetishism is central to decadent aesthetics, as exemplified in *A Rebours*, one of the canonical novels of collecting, where narrative so often yields to inventory. See also Renée A. Kingcaid, *Neurosis and Narrative: The Decadent Short Fiction of Proust, Lorrain, and Rachilde* (Carbondale: Southern Illinois University Press, 1992) and Amanda Fernbach, *Fantasies of Fetishism: from Decadence to the Post-Human* (Edinburgh: Edinburgh University Press, 2002), for examples of a critical tradition which uses the concept of fetishism to discuss representations of collecting.

am concerned with how collecting practices relate to specific textual practices. This enquiry takes various forms. On the one hand, I am concerned
with how certain kinds of text – especially physiologies, *feuilleton* novels
and historical writing – use the figure of the collector self-reflexively to
figure their own operations. At the same time, representations of collecting frequently elicit structures that are enumerative, rather than narrative
(the list, the inventory, the catalogue) and that block or disrupt the flow
of narrative texts.[47] In addition to thinking about how representations of
collecting function at this microtextual level, the book also attempts to map
very broad aesthetic changes in the nineteenth century through exploring
shifts in the discourse surrounding collecting.

Representations of the Collector from Balzac to Proust: An Outline

This study of the discourse surrounding the figure of the collector is thus
organized around three axes. First, it seeks to examine what this discourse
tells us about the ways in which the relationship between people and objects
changed in the nineteenth century. In the second place, it is concerned
with how the discourse around the figure of the collector was a vehicle for
exploring questions of identity and selfhood. Third, it examines the relationship between collecting and textuality. These three axes of enquiry cut
across the book as a whole, and are present in differing degrees throughout
all the chapters.

    The first chapter looks at representations of the collector in physi-
ological and topographical sketch-writing. It was in such texts that the
collector first emerged as a discursive construct, and reading them enables
us to reconstruct the physiology of the nineteenth-century *collectionneur*.
It also enables us to consider the relationship between the collector and

---

47   On the inventory as a specific form of writing, see Maleuvre, pp. 113–87.

commodity culture. Drawing on Walter Benjamin's work, I read the collector as an ambivalent figure, whose activity is made possible by the rise of commodity culture, but equally implies resistance to the processes of commodification. In addition, I consider how the figure of the collector functions self-reflexively in sketch-writing to figure the work of the physiologist, in a self-contestatory fashion that in fact subverts physiological discourse. The second chapter examines Balzac's seminal novel, *Le Cousin Pons* (1847). The first major text about collecting, it presents it as already obsolescent. It is often read as suggesting that the collector, as the embodiment of opposition to the priority of exchange value, had no place in a July Monarchy where everything was monetized. In addition to exploring these ideas, I consider a less well-recognized, but equally important, aspect of the text, which is the representation therein of the public museum. I argue that the public museum can be read as a figure for the text itself, and that the novel ultimately rejects the Pons paradigm of private collecting in favour of the public museum.

The first two chapters are very much concerned with the fate of objects within a commodity culture. Of course the existence of objects implies a subject (and vice versa) and this is the concern of the third chapter, which focuses on collecting and selfhood. First, I examine how collecting functioned in the nineteenth century as a means of self-fashioning, through which an individual could emerge as a self-determining, self-determined, male subject. Alongside this, I examine a tradition in which collecting was presented as a symptom of lack. Central here is a comparison of two decadent texts, Huysmans' *A Rebours* (1884) and Jean Lorrain's *Monsieur de Phocas* (1900). The latter is often regarded as a second-rate rehash of the former, since it also features a morbidly neurotic, aristocratic collector as its central character. I argue, however, that Lorrain's and Huysmans' novels, through their treatment of collecting, constellate death, desire and narrativity in very different ways, and that Lorrain's reconfiguration of topoi found in Huysmans' text points to anxieties surrounding the idea of selfhood in late-nineteenth-century France.

If chapter three is concerned with how collecting is a process through which individuals could fashion a specific identity, then chapter four is concerned with the construction of identity at a national level, as it explores the discourse surrounding historical collecting in the nineteenth century, a practice that was shaped by the experience of the Revolution. This chapter reads the discourse surrounding historical collecting alongside Pierre Nora's distinction between Memory and History, and shows how such a distinction unravels in Edmond de Goncourt's *La Maison d'un artiste* (1881), a reading of which problematizes Nora's association of embodied memory with a relationship to objects based on production and use rather than consumption and display. Chapter five is concerned with another specific kind of collecting, in this case natural history collecting. It offers a reading of four texts that deal with natural history collecting: Flaubert's *Bouvard et Pécuchet* (1883), Verne's *Vingt mille lieues sous les mers* (1869), Loti's *Le Roman d'un enfant* (1890), and Maupassant's short article, 'Au Muséum d'histoire naturelle' (1881). All four texts call into question the epistemological claims of taxonomical science, but also pose problems about the relationship between words and things.

Throughout all these chapters a recurrent concern is with how texts that represent the collector also use the idea of collecting self-reflexively, inviting us to read the collector as a figure for the author. The final chapter focuses on the relationship between collecting and writing at a different level, by exploring the relationship between collecting and creativity. From *Le Cousin Pons* to Proust, the collector has been placed in opposition to the creative artist. This chapter explores what is at stake in this opposition, before examining two moments at which it seems to break down – in the mid-nineteenth century, with the emergence of anti-idealist realism, and in the late nineteenth century, where concerns about creative exhaustion were linked to the emergence of certain textual practices.

CHAPTER 1

The Physiology of the Collector

Larousse's *Grand Dictionnaire universel du XIXe siècle* begins its entry on the *collectionneur* by asking: 'Qui de nous n'a ri de bon cœur à la vue de ce personnage à mine pointue, bizarre, fantasque, désagréable, qui se complaît dans la poussière et la vieillerie, parmi les tessons séculaires et le ferblanterie moyen âge, et que l'on appelle un *collectionneur*?'.[1] By 1869, therefore, the shabby, eccentric, risible figure of the collector was established as a recognized type. He had first emerged as such over twenty years earlier, in the sketch-writing of the July Monarchy, featuring, for example, in one of the better-known examples of the genre, *Les Français peints par eux-mêmes*. This self-styled 'encyclopédie morale du dix-neuvième siècle'[2] consisted of a series of sketches of different social types and purported, through establishing a comprehensive taxonomic system, to render intelligible to its readers contemporary social reality. Other examples of sketch-writing were structured not physiologically, as a series of descriptions of different types, but topographically, as a series of descriptions of different urban sites, within which the behaviour of the various species populating the new urban habitat could be observed. In *La Grande Ville*, for example, edited by Paul de Kock, the reader is taken on a virtual tour of Paris, stopping off along the way at the *hôtel des commissaires-priseurs*,[3] the public auction house which, when *La Grande Ville* was published, had two branches, one at the rue des Jeûners and the other at the place de la Bourse, although from 1852

---

1   'Collectionneur', in *Grand Dictionnaire*, p. 601.
2   This appears as a subtitle on the frontispiece of *Les Français peints par eux-mêmes*, 8 vols (Paris: Curmer, 1840–1842).
3   See Charles Ballard, 'L'Hôtel des commissaires-priseurs' in *La Grande Ville*, ed. by Paul de Kock, 2 vols (Paris: Marescq, 1844), II, 275–92.

onwards it would occupy a spacious building on the rue Drouot, becoming
known simply as the *hôtel Drouot*. Whether organized topographically or
physiologically, however, sketch-writing worked to establish a repertory of
social types, among them the figure of the collector. This chapter will trace
the contours of that figure as sketched in a variety of such texts produced
over the course of the nineteenth century. In considering representations
of the collector in physiological and topographical texts two questions
present themselves. The first is what kind of social concerns they encode
through their ascription of certain normative characteristics to the figure
of the collector, and the second is how the practices of collecting relate to
the textual practices of this kind of writing.[4]

'Ces apôtres de bric-à-brac':
Representations of the Collector in Sketch-Writing

The collector can collect anything – shoes or sea shells, pottery or painting, mummies or musical instruments. These texts approach the collector
as a vehicle for the exploration of a certain mode of consumption, and
the article being consumed is of only incidental importance. This mode
of consumption is presented in texts produced under the July Monarchy
and during the Second Empire as being a distinctly modern phenomenon;
as noted in the introduction, the *Grand Dictionnaire* claims that, 'la collection est un des goûts qui sont appelés à caractériser plus spécialement

---

4   For a comprehensive study of sketch-writing in France, Britain, Germany, and Austria
     see Martina Lauster, *Sketches of the Nineteenth Century: European Journalism and its
     Physiologies* (Basingstoke: Palgrave Macmillan, 2007). Sketch-writing has received
     relatively little sustained critical attention, perhaps because of the dominance of a
     Benjaminian critical tradition which, Lauster argues, has tended to reduce it to 'part
     and parcel of a middle-class attempt to gain control over a threatening social body'
     (p. 3).

ce siècle'.[5] Balzac, in his article on the *rentier* in *Les Français*, which first introduced the figure of the *collectionneur*, describes him as a specifically urban figure.[6] Champfleury, in his 1867 study *L'Hôtel des commissaires-priseurs*, implies as much when he diagnoses a mania for collecting as a symptom of contemporary social reality, and links the collector to the development of consumer capital in Second Empire Paris: 'Si la fièvre continue, Paris ne sera plus qu'un grand bazar.'[7] According to Champfleury, it is the passion for collecting which has turned Paris into a giant market, but descriptions of the collector also point to the converse conclusion: that the expansion of the market, the availability of ever more goods for sale, is itself productive of the figure of the collector. One of the keynotes of descriptions of the hôtel Drouot in the period is the heterogeneity of the merchandise on offer. Thus in his article on the collector in *Les Français*, Horace de Viel-Castel observes that in the public auction house, 'tout se vend, depuis les berlines de voyages jusqu'à des lettres autographes de Ninon de Lenclos'.[8] Champfleury echoed this a generation later when he wrote that 'ici, tout est à vendre: meubles, bijoux, tableaux, vins, médailles, dentelles, animaux'.[9] Both quotations draw attention not simply to the fact that all kinds of different things can be bought and sold in Paris, but, more dramatically, that anything and everything can be bought and sold. From this perspective there is no longer any ontological difference between a carriage and a courtesan's letters; both are goods for sale. It is this annihilation of ontological difference between different kinds of objects, for example paintings and empty wine bottles, that allows the collector to emerge as a type, precisely because the choice of collectable is seen as being of secondary importance to the fact of collecting, and the analysis of the mode of consumption is foregrounded rather than a discussion of the objects consumed.

5   'Collectionneur', in *Grand Dictionnaire*, p. 601.
6   Balzac, 'Monographie', p. 14.
7   Champfleury, *L'Hôtel*, p. 5.
8   Viel-Castel, p. 121.
9   Champfleury, *L'Hôtel*, p. ii.

Thus the collector who emerged in the July Monarchy and Second Empire was a distinctly modern figure, in a distinctly modern kind of literature. At the same time, however, the collector is presented as being antipathetic to contemporary reality. Viel-Castel's M. de Menussard, who collects only pre-revolutionary porcelain, is 'furieux [...], contre le siècle tout entier'.[10] Although the Larousse definition of the collector acknowledges that anything can be collected, in its opening sentence it presents the typical collector as an antiquarian, 'qui se complaît dans la poussière et la vieillerie'.[11] Even in the case of those collectors who are not concerned with antiques, however, collecting is presented as being a retreat from the world. In the chapter on the collector, tellingly entitled 'Les Tribulations d'un homme de goût qui n'en avait pas', in Albert Robida's 1888 book, *Le XIXᵉ Siècle*, the narrator's uncle, a keen collector, lives as a recluse.[12] The narrator's father takes his son, as a child, to visit this uncle, precisely to show him what worldly failure means. The father's plan backfires, however, when the narrator, as an adult, inspired by his uncle's example, himself takes up collecting to enjoy 'les joies calmes et reposantes du foyer',[13] and because it seems the most obvious option for somebody 'à la tête de 70 mille livres de rente, d'une remarquable inaptitude commerciale, d'une forte tendance à l'ennui et d'un mauvais estomac'.[14] The collector here is presented as sickly, nervous, and deficient in the qualities needed to be a worldly success.

Robida's text belongs to a discursive tradition that characterized the collector as an inadequate, marginal, and eccentric figure. In Balzac's description of *collectionneurs* in his 'Monographie du rentier', he writes: 'Ils

10   Viel-Castel, p. 123.
11   'Collectionneur', in *Grand Dictionnaire*, p. 601.
12   Although sketch-writing, and the idea of the type on which it depends, flourished in the middle decades of the nineteenth century, it endured to the fin-de-siècle. For the survival of the type as a conceptual and iconographic category, see Luce Abélès, 'La Fin du siècle', in *Les Français peints par eux-mêmes: panorama social du XIXᵉ siècle*, ed. by Ségolène Le Men and Luce Abélès (Paris: Editions de la Réunion des musées nationaux, 1993), pp. 68–83.
13   Albert Robida, *Le XIXᵉ Siècle* (Paris: Decaux, 1888), pp. 228 and 232.
14   Robida, p. 227.

n'appartiennent ni à la Tribu remuante des Artistes, ni à celle des Savants, ni à celle des Écrivains, mais ils tiennent de tous. Ils sont *toqués*, disent leurs voisins'.[15] Balzac's description defines the collector in negative terms; they are neither one thing nor the other. He presents them as interstitial beings, existing in the gaps between different, clearly defined social groups. They are both eccentric and ex-centric characters. This idea is echoed by Champfleury, who writes in *L'Hôtel des commissaires-priseurs* that: 'Le *toqué* et le *rêveur* sont deux variétés d'amateurs entre lesquelles il n'existe que de faibles différences; toutefois la création du mot *rêveur* en matière des beaux-arts est plus délicate que celle de *toqué*, qui appartient à l'argot parisien'.[16] Here the collector is presented as a figure who straddles two worlds, those of art and of commerce, but is considered eccentric in both, either a *toqué* or a *rêveur*. The collector is thus a doubly marginalized figure.

As noted in the introduction, however, from 1870 onwards collecting became a popular pastime, and the collector became a less marginal and more respectable figure.[17] Whereas for Champfleury and Viel-Castel the hôtel Drouot was a place within which the normative social hierarchy was disrupted, where 'sont reconnu ni rang, ni condition',[18] for Paul Eudel, in an article published in the 1897 topographical coffee-table book, *Balades dans Paris*, the hôtel Drouot offers a microcosm of Parisian society. The spatial organization of the hôtel enables Eudel to present it allegorically. In the courtyard into which the narrator and his companion first penetrate they find for sale, 'les débris du mobilier des malheureux, dépouilles opimes de la veuve et de l'orphelin que l'huissier a mis sur le pavé'.[19] Going up the stairs into the slightly shabby sales rooms on the ground floor they encounter 'un entassement de meubles de la vie bourgeoise'.[20] On the first floor the

---

15   Balzac, 'Monographie', p. 14.
16   Champfleury, *L'Hôtel*, p. 64.
17   See Pety, 'Le Personnage du collectionneur au XIXe siècle'.
18   Champfleury, *L'Hôtel*, p. viii.
19   Paul Eudel, 'A l'Hôtel Drouot', in *Balades dans Paris*, by E. R., Paul Eudel, B-H. Gausseron, and Adolphe Rette (Paris: Société des Bibliophiles Contemporains, 1897), pp. 33–70 (p. 37).
20   Eudel, 'A l'Hôtel Drouot', p. 43.

more elegant items are sold, and here an important sale attracts the 'grand
monde', the same audience as would attend a play.[21] The microcosmic
character of the hôtel Drouot is also emphasized in the preface that Jules
Clarétie contributed to Eudel's chronicle of the hôtel Drouot (published
in nine volumes between 1881 and 1891), in which he suggested that the
value of the book lay in the fact that it provided an account of the mores
of the period, and would allow future historians to write the social history
of the late nineteenth century.[22] The collecting world is thus presented as
having a representative value: writing about collecting is a means of writing about society.

In contrast to this, there existed another discourse surrounding the
hôtel Drouot, one with a rather different emphasis, in which the collecting world was presented as interesting because it existed as a sort of secret
society, designated by Champfleury 'la francmaçonnerie du bric-à-brac'.[23]
In the preface to L'Hôtel des commissaires-priseurs, Champfleury presents
himself as a traveller returning from a distant land, the Marco Polo of
curiosity: 'Si je ne rapporte pas de ce pays nouveau les types curieux que
le public est en droit d'attendre, on me saura peut-être gré d'avoir indiqué
un endroit fertile en aventures.'[24] Thus he presents the collecting world as
a mysterious and exotic one, to which few of his readers will ever travel. It
is also a world characterized by trickery and deceit, by all manner of snares
and stratagems. It is through detailing the wheeling and dealing that took
place at the hôtel Drouot that Champfleury's text, like many others, generates entertainment value.

Thus descriptions of the hôtel Drouot can present it either as a microcosm of society, or as a strange and mysterious realm accessible only to ini-
tiates. Although, as suggested above, the latter tendency is more marked in
earlier accounts, in many cases these two tendencies co-exist within a single
text. This is particularly clear in Henri Rochefort's 1862 book, Les Petits

21 Eudel, 'A l'Hôtel Drouot', p. 50.
22 Jules Clarétie, 'Préface', in L'Hôtel Drouot en 1881, by Paul Eudel (Paris: Charpentier,
    1882), pp. vii–xv (p. xiv).
23 Champfleury, L'Hôtel, p. viii.
24 Champfleury, L'Hôtel, p. xii.

Mystères de l'hôtel des ventes. As the title suggests, the book presents the collecting world in the first instance as a distinct realm, governed by its own particular laws, but its purpose is precisely to initiate readers into this realm. It purports to elucidate the eponymous mysteries for its readers, and aims to warn them about the various abusive practices they will encounter at the hôtel Drouot. To this end it contains a catalogue of complaints about the sales practices institutionalized at the public auction house, thus incorporating a consumer watchdog discourse.[25] Eudel's account of the hôtel Drouot, written over thirty years later, functions in a similar way. Early on in the text the narrator advises his companion against buying anything at auction: 'Vous n'êtes pas au courant des ficelles, retours et détours de l'hôtel. Vous n'achèterez rien ici ou vous achèterez mal'.[26] Later on in the text, however, we find a list of complaints similar to that included in Rochefort's book, with various suggestions for reform.[27] Both Rochefort's and Eudel's texts, therefore, have an explicitly monitory function. They assume that their readers, *qua* consumers, have a stake in what happens at the hôtel Drouot. They thus address their readers as potential collectors.

The work of Edmond Bonnaffé, the Third Republican art historian, critic, and connoisseur, offers a further example of an attempt to present collecting as a mainstream activity. In his 1881 *Physiologie du curieux*, he adopts in relation to the culture of collecting the same mock-ethnographic pose as Champfleury, but in a far more extravagant fashion:

> Je connais une contrée pittoresque et charmante, peuplée de castels gothiques, de villas italiennes, d'alcazars moresque, de bastides provençales, de chalets et de cottages, de chaumières et de casinos. Ici les donjons sévères du moyen âge, plus loin les élégants manoirs de la Touraine; l'art classique et l'art libre, tous les styles et toutes les fantaisies: des temples et des mosquées, des chapelles et des pagodes, des huttes et des tentes; des cavernes pour les amateurs.
> [...]

25 Henri Rochefort, *Les Petits Mystères de l'hôtel des ventes* (Paris: Dentu, 1962), pp. 79–107 and pp. 287–92.
26 Eudel, 'A l'Hôtel Drouot', pp. 42–3.
27 Eudel, 'A l'Hôtel Drouot', p. 69.

Les habitants sont en général d'humeur facile et bien élevés; ils accueillent volontiers les étrangers. Ils adorent un grand nombre de dieux auxquels ils donnent des noms bizarres, *le seizième, le quinzième, le dix-huitième*; ils ont un culte, des fétiches, des pontifes. Ils sont grands chasseurs et témoignent un goût prononcé pour le commerce. Des voyageurs assurent qu'ils pratiquent l'anthropophagie, mais entre eux-mêmes seulement; on les a vus dévorer leurs semblables en intimité.[28]

Bonnaffé here clearly delights in presenting the collecting world as a distant and fantastical land, peopled by cannibals and fetishists. At the same time, however, his text is very much concerned with rehabilitating the figure of the collector. According to Bonnaffé, far from being consigned to the fringes of society, inhabiting a bizarre subculture, the collector has a clearly defined and important social role as guardian of the nation's cultural patrimony. Commenting on La Bruyère's rather unsympathetic view of the collector, Bonnaffé writes:

Je suppose que La Bruyère revienne au monde. Il se promène dans nos musées, dans nos bibliothèques, aux expositions, il visite les cabinets des amateurs; il contemple avec étonnement les débris de l'ancien temps sauvés de la ruine et servant de leçon à l'avenir; il assiste au prodigieux mouvement de l'école moderne, remuant, déblayant le passé, refaisant à nouveau l'histoire nationale sur des preuves authentiques, reconstituant la vie privée de nos aïeux, créant des industries nouvelles, ressuscitant des industries mortes, réformant le goût public, instruisant l'ouvrier, l'artiste, l'homme du monde.[29]

Bonnaffé here seeks to dispel the idea of the collector as a shabby, shambling eccentric through emphasizing the knowledge-producing aspect of collecting. His collector is far from useless; on the contrary, his activity contributes not only to the great nation-building project at the heart of the Third Republic, but also to the economic life of France. It is telling that Bonnaffé should choose to use the word 'curieux' rather than 'collectionneur'. Such usage asserts a continuity between the early modern culture of curiosity and the nineteenth-century culture of collecting, presenting the latter as part of a tradition. At the same time, as noted in the introduction, within

28   Edmond Bonnaffé, *Physiologie du curieux* (Paris: Jules Martin, 1881), pp. 12–13.
29   Bonnaffé, *Physiologie*, p. 8.

the culture of curiosity collecting was a technology of knowledge, which is how Bonnaffé too conceives of it. Moreover curiosity, unlike modern collecting, connotes not self-centredness and retreat from the world, but active engagement with it. For Bonnaffé, the collector is not an isolated individual, but one with an important social role.

Bonnaffé's voice is a marginal one in this respect, however; most representations of the collector stress the uselessness of the activity in which he is engaged. Viel-Castel describes pure collectors such as M. de Menussard as useless; those who collect to make money, *les collectionneurs-brocanteurs*, he views as actively pernicious, cultural vandals who, far from preserving, contribute to the destruction of France's cultural patrimony. The *collectionneur-brocanteur* 'dépouillera les églises de leurs reliquaires et de leur verrières, les bibliothèques de leurs manuscrits et les arsenaux de leurs armes; il pillera sans pitié toutes les collections publiques; il achèvera de jeter à terre de vénérables ruines pour en emporter quelques clous'.[30] The collector is at best pathetic, at worst a public menace, and Viel-Castel ends his piece by suggesting a *projet de loi* consisting of a sole article: 'Tout collectionneur est soumis à perpétuité à la surveillance de la haute police.'[31]

The article on the collector in the *Grand Dictionnaire* is more charitable. It assumes that uselessness is one of the attributes conventionally ascribed to the collector, but goes on to question this:

> Lorsque, rentré chez lui, il classe, étudie, numérote, étiquette le produit de sa chasse, n'est il donc qu'un faible d'esprit, qu'un maniaque imbécile qu'il faut prendre en pitié et à qui des hochets sont indispensables pour terminer ses jours inutiles? Non certes! C'est d'ailleurs une erreur fort grande, hâtons-nous de le dire, que de croire que tout *collectionneur* soit nécessairement un être ridicule et décrépit, laid, radoteur et sale.[32]

Although the writer purports to disavow the negative image of the collector, the accumulation of pejorative epithets tends to reinforce it. The writer concludes that although the collector does fulfil a useful social function,

---

30 Viel-Castel, pp. 127–8.
31 Viel-Castel, p. 128.
32 'Collectionneur', in *Grand Dictionnaire*, p. 601.

he neither seeks to do so nor is necessarily aware of doing so: 'les curieux, fussent-ils seulement amoureux de la curiosité en elle-même, n'eussent-ils point tiré personnellement un parti historique de leurs richesses, ont du moins le mérite de conserver. [...] Ce sont eux, ces apôtres de bric-à-brac, qui ont appris à l'Etat à former des archives, des musées, des dépôts de tout genre.'[33] Here the article points to a distinction between the work of archivists and museum curators, who collect in the service of knowledge, and private collectors, who are driven by their own whims and fancies. In many of the negative representations of the collector, their collections do not follow any rational or intersubjectively valid scheme. Thus Viel-Castel's snuff-box collector divides his collection into three classes: 'les tabatières d'hommes célèbres, les tabatières ornées d'émaux ou de peintures, et les tabatières d'une matière ou d'un travail précieux'.[34] It is not clear how he would cope with finding an enamelled snuff-box that once belonged to a man of note. In Robida's portrait of the collector, the various collections which the narrator assembles are closely bound up with his emotional life and personal circumstances. He obtains his first collection, of *faïence*, as a dowry. His wife subsequently smashes them up, following one of a series of rows, and they are discovered to have been fakes, provoking the narrator to wonder whether his wife was not also 'une imitation frauduleuse d'épouse honnête et tranquille?'.[35] In despair at the state of his marriage, the narrator then begins to collect suits of armour: 'je comptais beaucoup sur la fréquentation de ces hommes de fer pour m'endurcir dans les luttes de vie conjugale.'[36] His wife, meanwhile, collects Louis XV objects, but this only contributes to the disintegration of their marriage by acting adversely on her personality, until one day he realizes that 'ma femme était tout à fait Louis XV'.[37] Here therefore the collection is presented as remoulding the collector in its own image. Collecting is thus closely tied to the

33 'Collectionneur', in *Grand Dictionnaire*, p. 602.
34 Viel-Castel, pp. 125–6.
35 Robida, p. 233.
36 Robida, p. 234.
37 Robida, p. 236.

production of subjectivity, but at the same time the collection is an objective corollary of the collector's own personal circumstances. In either case, it is clear that the narrator's collecting is not guided by any intersubjectively valid schema.

It is also worth noting that Robida's collector, although initially he sees the acquisition of a collection and of a wife as part and parcel of the same enterprise – to secure for himself 'les joies calmes et reposantes du foyer'[38] – finds that Champfleury was correct when he wrote: 'La femme ou la collection. La femme *et* la collection, deux rivales, feraient de l'intérieur conjugal un enfer.'[39] Robida's collector, like most examples of the species, ends his days as a childless bachelor. Understood in the context of the way in which collecting was a gendered practice in nineteenth-century France, it becomes clear that the failure to produce heirs and the failure to produce useful knowledge are closely linked.

Leora Auslander has argued that in the nineteenth century, collecting, often figured through the language of duelling, hunting, and war, was conceptualized as a masculine mode of consumption. Auslander writes:

> Appropriate consumption for bourgeois men was deemed to be highly individual, often authenticity-based, creative, self-producing, order-making activity – all best enacted in collecting. The sites at which collectors consumed offer insights into the differences between masculine and feminine consumption. In Balzac's and others' fantasies, rather than shopping in the banal department stores and specialty or custom shops frequented by female consumers, collectors were – with great ingenuity and intrepidness – to hunt down and uncover unexpected, unrecognized treasures at auctions, flea markets, and in antique stores. Finding and acquiring the object of one's desire in each of these places was understood to require different talents. Buying at auction required persistence, guile, quickness, and a willingness to take risks, as did sifting through flea markets, characterized as exotic and dangerous places, to uncover treasures amidst heaps of junk, stolen objects, and dubious characters. Buying furniture from antique dealers also required the pitting of wits, where the collector by bluff would try to persuade the dealer that an object was worth less that it was. Many of the innovations of the department and specialized stores, developed

---

38   Robida, p. 228.
39   Champfleury, *L'Hôtel*, p. 264.

simultaneously with the elaboration of bourgeois women's role as consumers were absent here – there were no fixed prices, and advice represented as 'expert' was often as much challenge as help.[40]

Indeed, many of the sketches of the collector stress that it is almost impossible for women to be successful collectors. Maupassant offered a pithy explanation of this fact, consistently treated as self-evident, when he wrote: 'les femmes surtout sont des collectionneurs inérrablement ridicules, car tout leur manque pour ce métier: la science profonde, la possibilité de voyager à pied, de logis en logis, par les pays peu connus, l'archarnement dans la passion.'[41] Maupassant suggests that women are doubly disabled from being collectors. Both innate qualities (the absence of 'l'archarnement dans la passion') and socio-economic factors (the impossibility of travelling independently) make it impossible for them to enjoy success as connoisseurs. Bonnaffé offered a still more lapidary critique of female collectors when he noted that women, when confronted with a collection of art objects, are quite simply incapable of any response more sophisticated than 'Charmant! Charmant! Charmant!'.[42]

Collecting was, therefore, considered to be a masculine form of consumption, because it required courage and audacity, and because it could be conceptualized as rational, order-making and knowledge-producing. For men, it functioned as a means of self-fashioning. Auslander writes: 'While bourgeois wives and mothers were to make families through their activities as consumers, bourgeois men were to make themselves individuated men through theirs.'[43] But, as Auslander goes on to argue, men too were expected

40   Leora Auslander, *Taste and Power: Furnishing Modern France* (Berkeley: University of California Press, 1996), p. 298. For examples of how the language of masculine activities such as duelling and war was used to describe collecting in the nineteenth century, see Champfleury, *L'Hôtel*, pp. vi–xi. This language continued to permeate representations of collecting in the twentieth century, as for example in Walter Benjamin's 'Unpacking My Library'. Antiques programmes on television today consistently stress the thrill of the auction room, its dangerous unpredictability.
41   Maupassant, 'Bibelot', pp. 27–8.
42   Bonnaffé, *Phyisologie*, p. 24.
43   Auslander, p. 296.

to make families, to secure the perpetuation of the family name through the production of heirs.[44] The collection could threaten this project, usurping wife and child in the collector's affections. Indeed, throughout the nineteenth century, the collection is presented as a potential rival to the family.[45] Thus, according to Charles Roehn, in his 1841 *Physiologie du commerce des arts*, 'un amateur en jupons' is 'le plus souvent une vieille fille qui ne s'étant pas senti une vocation bien décidée pour être dévote, a reporté toutes ses affections sur les ventes publiques'.[46] For an unmarried woman, the collection could act as a focus for her emotional life, in lieu of the family, but a corollary of this was that for a man it could prevent him assuming his proper role as *pater familias*. This is the unfortunate fate of Robida's collector, who suffers from an excessive affective investment in his collection. When the collector's investment in his collection is emotional rather than intellectual, it fails not only to be conceptualized as a rational project, but also as one compatible with assuming a properly masculine role. Robida's collector never manages to write his projected monograph on warming pans, of which he has a fine collection of eighteenth-century examples, because plunging into a work of history 'me rappelait ma femme et les malheurs conjugaux que je devais à l'influence dévergondante du XVIIIe siècle'.[47]

---

44   See Auslander, p. 300.

45   See, for example, Champfleury's novella, *Le Violon de faïence* (Paris: Hetzel, 1862). In this text, the protagonist, a collector of *faïence*, finally abandons his collection and marries: 'Les enfants ne manquèrent pas à cette union, et Dalègre, attendri en regardant l'*émail* des yeux de ces jolis enfants, la transparence de leur teint, le gai *pinkular* de leurs joues, disait à sa femme chérie quelles illusions de bonheur cherchent au milieu des niaiseries du passé les collectionneurs qui se privent des tendresses domestiques' (p. 86). The effect of describing children in terms more normally applied to art objects is ambivalent: on the one hand, it stresses that the family has replaced the collection, but on the other hand it suggests that Dalègre is a crypto-collectomaniac.

46   Charles Roehn, *Physiologie du commerce des arts* (Paris: Lagny, 1841), p. 157. For a more detailed elaboration of the *collectionneuse* as a frustrated spinster, see the J.-H. Rosny novel, *Le Testament volé* (Paris: Fontemoing, 1905).

47   Robida, p. 240.

His failure to produce knowledge is here a function of his failure as husband, and any attempt to extract intellectual profit from his collection is obstructed by a negative cathexis.

The Collector as a Figure for the Sketch-Writer: Undermining the 'Ideology of Visibility'

The idea that collecting can be an order-making, knowledge-producing, rational project, and yet the fact that it rarely attains such a status, generates an instability that resonates through the physiological or topographical texts as a whole, as it undermines the basic premises of such a literature. The collector is an appropriate figure for such texts precisely because they have several features in common with the activity of collecting. Certainly, both sketch-writing and the activity of collecting necessarily involve a taxonomic dimension. Moreover, in their formal qualities such texts tend to lack linear narrative drive; they are anecdotal and descriptive, a hodgepodge of observations. Paul Eudel draws attention in 'A L'Hôtel Drouot' to precisely the way in which the collector can act as a self-reflexive figure in physiological or topographical literature; as his narrator wanders around the upstairs gallery where collectors are examining the paintings, he examines the collectors, noting that the room is 'une galerie d'originaux, où il y a toujours quelques bons portraits à décrocher', and after describing one goes on to say, 'je collectionne en passant un autre type qui est tout à fait opposé'.[48] Richard Sieburth, writing specifically about the *physiologies* produced between 1840 and 1842, but in terms that can be applied to sketch-writing more generally,[49] has also noted the link between the

48   Eudel, 'A l'Hôtel Drouot', pp. 44 and 45.
49   For the differences between the *physiologies* and *Les Français*, see Nathalie Preiss-Basset, 'Les Physiologies, un miroir en miettes', in *Les Français peints par eux-mêmes: panorama social du XIXe siècle*, ed. by Ségolène Le Men and Luce Abélès (Paris:

practices of these texts, themselves marketed as a series to be collected,[50] and the activity of collecting, writing that 'the *physiologies* strip things of their use value in order to insert them into the perfectly closed (and narcissistic) space of a collection.'[51] This is achieved formally, as 'the narrative dimension of these texts is relatively unimportant; the emphasis lies on the organization of its elements into a descriptive system or collection.'[52] He goes on to claim that this functions to suppress history in the texts; both description and collection 'tend [...], to project the axis of selection onto the axis of combination. [...] They remove social types from the order of narrative and, more crucially, from the order of history.'[53] This suppression of history is part of the ideological functioning of the texts, which, according to Sieburth's wider, Benjaminian argument, are part of the 'systematic occultation' of social reality into what Benjamin called 'l'univers d'une fantasmagorie' during the mid-nineteenth century, the transformation of Paris into 'a ghost town populated by phantom figures and phantom desires, an uncanny market place in which all objects, all human relations, have been transformed into commodities.'[54] When Sieburth's argument rests on the conflation of the textual practices of the *physiologies* with collecting practices (without discussing representations of the collector in the literature of the period), it codes collecting negatively as being part of the same story about the rise of commodity culture. The collector col-

Editions de la Réunion des musées nationaux, 1993), pp. 62–7, in which she argues that the physiologies had a more satirical purpose.

50   Jean Baudrillard, writing in *Le Système des objets* in the 1960s, provides an oblique commmentary on the efficacy of this kind of marketing strategy: 'Les enquêtes montrent que les clients des collections de livres (*10/18*, *Que sais-je?*), une fois pris dans la silage de la collection, continuent d'acheter tel ou tel titre qui ne les intéresse pas: la différence dans la série suffit à créer un intérêt formel qui tient lieu d'intérêt réel' (p. 147).

51   Richard Sieburth, 'Same Difference: The French *Physiologies*, 1840–2', *Notebooks in Cultural Analysis*, 1 (1984), 163–200 (p. 184).

52   Sieburth, p. 186.

53   Sieburth, p. 186.

54   Sieburth, p. 173. See Lauster, pp. 3–22, for a critique of this Benjaminian critical tradition.

ludes with the commodity, according to Sieburth's argument, both because
in the collection historicity is suppressed, and because he works to 'strip
things of their use value'.

Sieburth's view of collecting is clearly influenced by Baudrillard's psychoanalytic account of collecting in *Le Système des objets*, where it is presented as a form of narcissistic regression and a strategy for warding off
knowledge of the irreversible slide towards death. In drawing heavily on
Baudrillard, whilst at the same time neglecting to discuss any nineteenth-
century physiological representations of the collector, Sieburth, although
he reproaches the collector for removing objects from the order of time, and
therefore history, might be reproached for being insufficiently historicist
himself. Baudrillard frames his discussion of the collector by suggesting
that there are two different ways the individual can position himself in
relation to an object; he can either make practical use of it, or possess it.
The desire to possess 'relève d'une enterprise de totalisation abstraite du
sujet par lui-même en dehors du monde'.[55] Such an abstraction from the
world is possible, according to Baudrillard, only in the collection, where
each element refers only to other elements in the collection, and, therefore
to the collector, but never to the world. It is this view of collecting that
Sieburth invokes when he describes the collection as a 'perfectly closed (and
narcissistic) space'. In nineteenth-century texts on collecting, however, it
is possible to find the collection being conceptualized in rather a different
way, with an emphasis on its openness rather than its closure. Champfleury
imagines the collection as a site of change and exchange, offering as one
of his axioms for the collector that 'toute collection qui n'offre pas une
sorte de panorama varié et sans cesse renouvelé, fatigue comme une femme
trop fidèle'.[56] Bonnaffé replies to an imaginary interlocutor berating him
for selling off part of his collection that 'l'achat, la vente, l'échange, sont
indispensables de la curiosité active [...]. Vous la rêvez stationnaire, immobile, paralysée; nous l'aimons remuante, vivante et progressive'.[57] Here

---

55   Baudrillard, p. 121.
56   Champfleury, *L'Hôtel*, p. 265.
57   Bonnaffé, *Physiologie*, p. 26.

the membrane between the collection and the world is permeable in both directions; the collector does not hinder the circulation of objects, but acts himself as an agent of that circulation. The collection is thus not the closed space that Baudrillard suggests. In making his second claim, that in entering a collection objects are stripped of their use value, Sieburth recalls Benjamin's comment that the collector 'frees objects from the drudgery of being useful',[58] but he footnotes Baudrillard not Benjamin. Benjamin's own account of collecting in fact offers a rather different perspective. In Benjamin's work the collector, although he strips things of their use value, does not thereby privilege their exchange value; rather for Benjamin the collectible is a magical, nostalgic object whose worth cannot be plotted on the conventional axes of use value and exchange value.[59] The collector resists the commodification of objects by handling them. According to Benjamin the collector is a being with 'tactile instincts'.[60] Thus even if the marks of labour, the traces of the hands that made the object, are effaced in the commodity, the collector can impress on it the marks of his own hands, restoring a human dimension to the object. Collecting emerges in the work of Benjamin as an activity which is enabled by the development of commodity culture, but which also implies resistance thereto.

If the collector is an ambivalent figure in relation to the commodity form, he is also ambivalent in relation to the 'ideology of visibility' Sieburth identifies as underpinning physiological literature, a literature which 'catered to the public's desire to see its social space as a stage or gallery whose intelligibility was guaranteed both by its visibility as image and its legibility as text'.[61] The collector himself is able to apprehend the truth through the eye. As a connoisseur, able to tell a masterpiece by scrutinizing it, he is, according to Benjamin, a 'physiognomist of the world of things'.[62] But, as already noted, the collector is also a being with tactile instincts, and his need to handle objects is part of a broader strategy of resistance to

58 Benjamin, 'Paris, 1939,' p. 19.
59 See Benjamin, 'Unpacking my library', for a meditation on this.
60 Benjamin, *The Arcades Project*, p. 206 [H2,5].
61 Sieburth, p. 166.
62 Benjamin, *The Arcades Project*, p. 207 [H2,7; H2a,1].

the psychological shocks of modernity, a strategy which leads the private individual to turn his apartment into his 'étui':

> It is as if he had made it a point of honour not to allow the traces of his everyday objects and accessories to get lost. Indefatigably, he takes the impression of a host of objects; for his slippers and his watches, his blankets and his umbrellas, he devises coverlets and cases.[63]

Benjamin links this obsession with leaving traces to the rise of detective fiction. The detective is the 'physiognomist of the domestic interior'.[64] In early detective fiction, Benjamin notes, the criminals are 'simple private citizens of the middle class'.[65] There is here a bifurcation in the image of the private citizen: on the one hand, as a collector he is a physiognomist, and therefore close kin to the detective, but on the other hand, as a criminal, he is in a necessarily contestatory and oppositional relationship to authority.

In Benjamin's work, therefore, the collector is an ambivalent figure, and in certain respects a subversive one, and I would suggest that the collector who emerges from nineteenth-century physiological literature is a vehicle for contesting the 'ideology of visibility' which Sieburth identifies as the hallmark of such literature. The collecting world offers a challenge to the desire for intelligibility, precisely because it is one where nothing is as it seems, where everyone is trying to swindle everyone else, where it is difficult to ascribe a fixed value to anything. Part of the interest the collecting world presented to writers was derived from the various scams used by dealers to drive up prices, and by buyers to drive them down. Although the narrators purport to be able to navigate safely between the Scylla of the dealers and the Charybdis of other buyers, this claim to authority is often undermined within the texts themselves. Thus in the article on the public auction house in Kock's *La Grande Ville*, the narrator himself falls prey to an *allumeur*, and in Champfleury's text, the narrator's authority as cicerone is undermined

63   Benjamin, 'Paris, 1939', p. 20.
64   Benjamin, 'Paris, 1939', p. 20.
65   Benjamin, 'Paris, 1939', p. 20.

when he finds himself the victim of a confidence man.[66] Although the texts often claim to be offering practical tips for readers who wish to set themselves up as collectors, this dimension of the texts is frequently ironized. Champfleury, for example, offers his readers 'Un Dictionnaire à l'usage des connaisseurs qui ne s'y connaissent pas'. The dictionary generates part of its humour through pointing towards the denaturing of language within the discourse of art criticism, so that the word 'métatarse', 'représente à volonté le col, ou le mollet, la cuisse ou le nombril'.[67] (The abuse of language is a theme to which Champfleury returns elsewhere, for example in his article on the expert, where he begins with the dictionary definition of the word and then goes on to note that 'les experts de l'hôtel Drouot ne se reconnaîtraient pas dans cette qualification').[68] In any case, since the dictionary is not in alphabetical order it would be impossible to look anything up in it. These texts purport to guarantee to the reader the intelligibility of his social space, but they in fact demonstrate its opacity. This is very clear in Eudel's description of the façade of the hôtel Drouot:

> Au-dessous de la corniche se voient des consoles avec des bouquets de fleurs sur la volute; plus bas, une frise de métopes avec des médaillons encadrant des lyres, des palettes, des sphères, des casques, des livres, des amphores, des pendules Empire et des commodes-tombeaux. L'architecte, dont le nom m'est inconnu, a voulu faire de son œuvre un Panthéon de l'art, de la science et de la poésie. Dans ces symboles significatifs, je regrette de ne point trouver une voiture de transport qui serait venue s'ajouter à ces images sculptées pour indiquer le but pratique de l'hôtel.[69]

Here the very architecture of the hôtel Drouot is presented as misleading. The entire collecting world seems to be based on imposture; it is a world where truth cannot be apprehended through the eye.

One feature of the collecting world which poses a particular challenge to the 'ideology of visibility' is the fake. Fakes became more and more common from the mid-nineteenth century onwards, as the art market,

66 Ballard, p. 286, and Champfleury, *L'Hôtel*, pp. 103–10.
67 Champfleury, *L'Hôtel*, p. 18.
68 Champfleury, *L'Hôtel*, p. 127.
69 Eudel, 'A l'Hôtel Drouot', p. 35.

after a lengthy period of depression, began to flourish.[70] Thus while Viel-Castel, for example, makes no reference to the problem of fakes, from the Second Empire onwards the fake occupies a significant place in the discourse surrounding collecting, and the ability to determine whether an object is authentic or not becomes the acid test of the collector's skill. Both Champfleury and Rochefort consecrate whole chapters to the problem, and in both cases the discourse they develop with regard to the fake serves to suggest that social reality, far from being transparent, and easily navigable, is based around imposture and fraught with peril for those who cannot distinguish the fake from the real. It is in discussing fakes that the tone of Rochefort's book changes, and it goes from being a work of whimsy to one of investigative journalism, as he dons the mantle of the crusader for consumer rights, noting that 'ce grand bazar n'a pas seulement des côtés pittoresques il a aussi des côtés fort abusifs.'[71] In a gesture typical of physiological literature, Rochefort produces a taxonomy of different kinds of fraudster. Thus he discusses not only *les truqueurs* (who manufacture forged objects), but also *les monogrammistes*, who forge signatures on paintings, *les cacheteurs*, who affix ducal or princely seals to the back of canvases in order to suggest they were once part of a prestigious collection, and *les chercheurs d'origine*, who provide false genealogies for paintings.[72] Rochefort notes, with respect to the last, that 'quelquefois il arrive au tableau ce qui arrive aux hommes et aussi aux femmes. Les uns partent de très-bas pour monter très-haut, d'autres partent de très-haut et finissent par tomber très-bas.'[73] Thus Rochefort uses the idea of the falsified object to suggest a society characterized by flux and by imposture. The gesture his book makes, however, in classifying different species of fraudster and displaying examples of their work to the gaze of his readership, suggests that it might be possible for them to learn to distinguish the real from the fake, and successfully to navigate the art world.

70   See Rheims, p. 229.
71   Rochefort, p. 79.
72   See Rochefort, pp. 110–26.
73   Rochefort, p. 118.

Champfleury's account of the forged object is rather more radical in its implications. He is more prepared than Rochefort to see the *truqueur* as being part of the picturesque appeal of the hôtel Drouot. He defuses the culpability of the forger by playfully using a determinist language to suggest that the *truqueur* merely follows his instinct, 'se complaisant dans la ruse comme le poisson dans l'eau'.[74] The *truqueur* is given a voice, and pleads his own innocence by invoking the tenets of physiognomy: 'Les animaux savent reconnaître leurs adversaries et les fuir; pourquoi les hommes ne sont-ils pas assez physionomistes pour voir que mon nez, mes yeux, ma bouche leur crient de prendre garde à moi?'.[75] Champfleury thus ironically makes the forger the spokesperson for the idea that social reality is easily readable, the forger whose work attests to the limitations of such an idea. He generates further paradoxes out of the idea of forgery, referring to the case of a man who fabricated enamels which he sold to the Rothschilds' agent as antiques.[76] Champfleury notes that 'il fut établi aux débats que l'émail était *plus beau* que l'émail ancien'.[77] Here, therefore, it is not the case simply that the fake is so plausible that even the Rothschilds' buyer has been fooled by it; rather the very distinction between original and fake is subverted when the former is superior in quality to the latter. Champfleury undermines the distinction from the other side in the story of M. Levallois, a collector of antiquities who hankers after an obelisk to take pride of place in his courtyard, decorated 'de tronçons de statues, de bas-reliefs frustes, qui pouvaient être pris indifféremment pour des débris d'auges ou de tombeaux'.[78] M. Levallois will finally obtain his obelisk, only to be devastated when he discovers it is a fake. What is striking here, however, is that the authentic pieces he owns, the flotsam and jetsam of antiquity, are also susceptible of being mistaken for something they are not, as indeed they might be either bits of troughs or bits of tombs. It is simply impos-

---

74   Champfleury, *L'Hôtel*, p. 166.
75   Champfleury, *L'Hôtel*, p. 167.
76   Rochefort also refers to the case of a man who sold fake enamels to the Rothschilds, a certain Pierrat (pp. 120–6); presumably they are both alluding to the same case.
77   Champfleury, *L'Hôtel*, p. 181.
78   Champfleury, *L'Hôtel*, p. 177.

sible to tell which. The broken bits of masonry cluttering up M. Levallois'
courtyard testify to the inherent unintelligibility of the world.

At first blush, representations of the collector in physiological and
topographical texts appear extremely repetitious; the same anecdotes are
recounted time and time again, the same practices described, the same
tropes used to figure the behaviour of the collector. On closer reading,
however, it becomes clear that the collector had shifting identities: variously
a producer of knowledge and a victim of monomania, a cultural guardian
and a despoiler, an easy mark for swindlers but no stranger to sharp practice
himself. The shabby, shambling eccentric, the butt of many writers' jokes,
proves to be a more shadowy, elusive figure, and one who inhabits a secret
world, existing in the heart of Paris, contiguous to the workaday world but
given over entirely to consumption rather than production, a topsy-turvy
world in which the physiologist's confidence in his ability to read social
reality correctly is consistently challenged.

CHAPTER 2

Of Money and Museums:
Le Cousin Pons and the Death of the Collector

The collector who emerged from the physiological and topographical texts of which the nineteenth century was so fond was, as we have seen, easily recognisable by his shabby and unkempt appearance. Almost certainly a childless bachelor, living the life of a recluse, he lavished all his affections on his jealously guarded collection. The collector was presented as a monomaniac, albeit a harmless one. It was not only, however, the texts we have considered in the preceding chapter which established this image of the collector; more than any other text, it was Balzac's last novel, *Le Cousin Pons*, that anchored the figure of the collector in the nineteenth-century French cultural imagination.[1] Although the collector was not an *inédit* in French fiction before its publication, *Le Cousin Pons* was the first novel to make a collection not merely part of its furnishing, but part of its architecture; the plot of the entire novel revolves around the Pons collection, famously described at the end of the novel as 'l'héroïne de cette histoire'.[2] From the moment it makes its first entrance into the French

---

1   Pons remained a basic reference point in discussions of collecting for many decades. See, for example, Octave Uzanne, *Les Zigzags d'un curieux: causeries sur l'art des livres et la littérature d'art* (Paris: Quantin, 1888), p. 215, and Robert de Montesquiou, *Les Pas effacés: mémoires*, 3 vols (Paris: Emile-Paul Frères, 1923), II, 92–3. In 1916 an art review was launched entitled simply *Le Cousin Pons* (see Chantal Georgel, 'Moderne ou Ancien: *Le Cousin Pons*', in *Balzac et la peinture*, ed. by Roger Pierrot and Philippe Le Leysour (Tours: Farrago, 1999), pp. 181–5).

2   Honoré de Balzac, *Le Cousin Pons*, in *La Comédie humaine*, ed. by Pierre-Georges Castex, Bibliothèque de la Pléiade, 12 vols (Paris: Gallimard, 1776–1781), VII (1977), 483–794 (p. 763). Sylvain Pons is not, it should be said, the only collector in Balzac's corpus, although *Le Cousin Pons* is the only Balzac novel that can be said to be

novel, however, the collection is a locus of nostalgia, for even as *Le Cousin Pons* was the first novel about collecting it was also a lament for the passing of its golden age. The novel positions Pons' collection in relation to two historical developments that menaced its existence: the commodification of the art object and the development of the public museum. These two issues, explored extensively in *Le Cousin Pons*, would remain of central importance in representations of collecting throughout the nineteenth century. At stake in discussions of money and museums was the status of the art object itself, and ultimately the status of the novel.

Art, Commerce and the Fall of the Collector

Le Cousin Pons is set in a July Monarchy where the priority of exchange value is firmly established. It is a world where everything is monetized, and everything is driven by speculation and greed, including the novel itself. The substance of the plot consists of the attempts of various greedy, grasping, money-grubbing individuals to appropriate to themselves the value of the incomparable collection of seventeenth- and eighteenth-century art objects which the eponymous Pons, a failed musician with a passion for beautiful things, has spent forty years accumulating. There are two distinct cabals ranged against Pons, both speculating on the value of the collection: on the one hand there is his family, the Camusot de Marville clan, bourgeois *arrivistes* whose money is tied up in land and whose political ambitions demand rather greater liquidity than they enjoy, and on the other hand there is a somewhat motley crew of conspirators gathered around Pons'

---

centrally concerned with collecting. For a survey of the various collectors in *La Comédie humaine*, and the significance thereof, see Adrien Goetz, '"De si vives compensations à la gloire": les collectionneurs au centre de *La Comédie Humaine*', in *Balzac et la peinture*, ed. by Roger Pierrot and Philippe Le Leysour (Tours: Farrago, 1999), pp. 187–92.

concierge, Mme. Cibot, including Elie Magus, an art dealer and Pons' chief rival as a collector, and the local *brocanteur*, Rémonencq. The lawyer Fraisier is the liaison between these two groups: engaged by Mme. Cibot to further her interests, he also offers his services to Mme. de Marville. Against these groups Pons, terminally ill, will try to keep his collection intact so that he can bequeath it to his friend, the hopelessly naive Schmucke. He will fail. At the end of the novel, the Camusot clan successfully contest Pons' will, snatching the collection out of the hands of the hapless Schmucke, who quickly follows his friend to the grave. The collection is sold to the Comte Popinot, a connection of the Marville clan, and a man keen to have the reputation of a connoisseur.

Le Cousin Pons is thus about a society ruled by money, but more specifically, through the idea of the collection, it explores the status of the art object in such a society. The novel imagines two possible attitudes towards art on the part of the bourgeoisie. The first is simple philistinism, as incarnated by the response of Pons' and Schmucke's neighbours when the latter plays the piano for his dying friend:

> Intarissable comme le rossignol, sublime comme le ciel sous lequel il chante, varié, feuillu comme la forêt qu'il emplit de ses roulades, il se surpassa, et plongea le vieux musicien qui l'écoutait dans l'extase que Raphaël a peinte, et qu'on va voir à Boulogne. Cette poésie fut interrompue par une affreuse sonnerie. La bonne des locataires du premier étage vint prier Schmucke, de la part de ses maîtres, de finir ce sabbat. Madame, monsieur et mademoiselle Chapoulot étaient éveillés, ne pouvaient plus se rendormir, et faisaient observer que la journée était assez longue pour répéter les musiques de théâtre, et que, dans une maison de Marais, on ne devait pas pianoter pendant la nuit.[3]

Here we are presented with an image of a petty bourgeoisie lacking any faculty for artistic appreciation and apparently entirely acultural. This hostility born of incomprehension is initially shared by Mme. de Marville, who regards a fan given to her by Pons, painted by Watteau and a veritable gem of French craftsmanship, as a 'bêtise'.[4] When told that the fan was

3   Balzac, *Le Cousin Pons*, p. 705.
4   Balzac, *Le Cousin Pons*, p. 508.

expensive, Mme. de Marville tells Pons that he would have done better to invest the money. At this early point in the novel, therefore, she is incapable of imagining that the art object could itself be seen as a financial investment. Her husband later, however, castigates her lack of interest in the arts; in reply to his wife's dismissal of art objects as 'bêtises', Camusot exclaims, 'mais l'État va payer trois cent mille francs la collection de feu monsieur le conseiller du Sommerard, et dépenser, avec la ville de Paris pour moitié, près d'un million en achetant et réparant l'hôtel Cluny pour loger ces petites bêtises-là'.[5] Camusot, therefore, reveals to his wife that art objects can be evaluated in monetary terms. He further informs her that rather than belittle Pons' gift of the Watteau fan, she should have been more appreciative, for Watteau 'est très à la mode'.[6] Mme. Camusot learns through the course of the novel that an ostentatious appreciation of fine art can be socially useful. In the final scene of the novel she is depicted seeking to impress a Russian prince by showing him the Watteau fan, while elegizing her deceased relative: 'Il dînait trois ou quatre fois par semaine chez moi [...], il nous aimait tant! nous savions l'apprécier, les artistes se plaisent avec eux qui goûtent leur esprit'.[7] Through presenting herself as a woman of cultured sensibility and a friend of the arts she is obviously seeking to lay claim to a certain distinction. Thus the novel sketches two possible attitudes towards art in a world ruled by money: blank incomprehension capable of mutating into active hostility, or recognition of the art object as an asset.

In opposition to both these positions stands Pons. A number of critics have suggested that the novel idealizes the collection as a space of pure aesthetic experience radically segregated from the market. Thus Sharon Marcus, in her reading of the novel, argues that Pons embodies opposition to the priority of exchange value. She claims that: 'Pons's collecting short-circuits exchange. [...] The novel glorifies Pons's collecting as an aesthetic

5   Balzac, *Le Cousin Pons*, p. 540.
6   Balzac, *Le Cousin Pons*, p. 541.
7   Balzac, *Le Cousin Pons*, p. 765.

alchemy that endows material objects with transcendent artistic value'.[8]
Thus in Marcus' view, it is by betraying his own values that Pons precipitates his tragic fall; it is his 'uncharacteristic engagement in the world of
heterosexual commerce that proves his downfall as a collector'.[9] Certainly
at several points the novel encourages us to read Pons as standing in opposition to the empire of money. He avoids that 'temple de la spéculation',[10]
the hôtel Drouot: 'Pons se sentait au cœur [...], l'amour de l'amant pour
une belle maîtresse, et la *revente*, dans les salles de la rue des Jeûneurs, aux
coups de marteau des commissaires priseurs [sic] lui semblait un crime de
lèse-Bric-à-Brac'.[11] His discomfort with commerce also means he prefers
to acquire objects through barter rather than sale, taking money out of the
equation. The narrator tells us that Pons shares with Alexandre-Charles
Sauvageot (a celebrated collector of the first half of the nineteenth century whose collection of Renaissance pieces can still be seen in the Louvre
today), 'le même amour de l'art, la même haine contre ces illustres riches qui
se font des cabinets pour faire une habile concurrence aux marchands'.[12]
Pons himself, it is stressed, 'ignorait la valeur vénale de sa collection'.[13]
Pons' cult of beauty is therefore presented as disinterested and gratuitous.
His collecting is not described in the novel simply as a pastime; it has a
far broader resonance, as an act of resistance to the hegemony of money
values in the July Monarchy.[14]

---

8   Sharon Marcus, *Apartment Stories: city and home in nineteenth-century Paris and
    London* (Berkeley: University of California Press, 1999), p. 66. See also Jeannine
    Guichardet, *Balzac: 'Archéologue' de Paris* (Paris: Sedes, 1986), pp. 341–63, for
    another reading that presents the art collecting as a site of resistance to universal
    commodification.
9   Marcus, p. 68.
10 Champfleury, *L'Hôtel*, p. 47.
11 Balzac, *Le Cousin Pons*, p. 491.
12 Balzac, *Le Cousin Pons*, p. 491.
13 Balzac, *Le Cousin Pons*, p. 490.
14 See Pierre Barbéris' discussion of the novel in his *Mythes Balzaciens* [(Paris: Armand
    Colin, 1972), pp. 257–63] for the most exalted account of how the Pons' museum
    enacts a rejection of bourgeois values. Barbéris' account, which suggests that Pons is a
    heroic figure whose actions are glorified by the novel, is problematic in its suggestion

The novel is, however, deeply pessimistic about the possibility of maintaining a space segregated from the market, a space where money values are irrelevant. The novel presents collectors of Pons' ilk as an endangered species. Pons himself is an anachronism. The opening description of him, dressed entirely in Empire fashions, establishes him as a throwback to an earlier age: 'vous n'eussiez pas hésité à nommer ce passant un homme-Empire, comme on dit un meuble-Empire'.[15] Pons is thus presented as himself an antique, and not a very desirable one. In one of the central images of the book, the narrator stresses that Pons, and his friend Schmucke, are both entirely out of place in the world of the July Monarchy:

> Ce qui reste à dire sur le moral de ces deux êtres en est précisément le plus difficile à faire comprendre aux quatre-vingt-dix-neuf centièmes des lecteurs dans la quarante-septième année du dix-neuvième siècle, probablement à cause du prodigieux développement financier produit par l'établissement des chemins de fer. C'est peu de chose et c'est beaucoup. En effet, il s'agit de donner une idée de la délicatesse excessive de ces deux cœurs. Empruntons une image aux railways, ne fût-ce que par façon de remboursement des emprunts qu'ils nous font. Aujourd'hui les convois en brûlant leurs rails y broient d'imperceptibles grains de sable. Introduisez ce grain de sable invisible pour les voyageurs dans leurs reins, ils ressentiront les douleurs de la plus affreuse maladie, la gravelle; on en meurt. Eh! bien, ce qui, pour notre société lancée dans sa voie métallique avec une vitesse de locomotive, est le grain de sable invisible dont elle ne prend nul souci, ce grain incessamment jeté dans les fibres de ces deux êtres, et à tout propos, leur causait comme une gravelle au cœur.[16]

Pons and Schmucke are laggards, unable to keep pace with changes in French society, changes wrought by the locomotive power of finance. If they find themselves out of place in the cut-throat world of the July Monarchy, it is because they are simply not greedy enough to manage. The novel is not merely about the death of a collector, but the demise of the paradigm of collecting embodied by Pons, a model of art appreciation into which

---

that Pons is not merely an art lover but a cultural producer: 'Pons, musicien, est un véritable artiste, et *seulement cela*.' (p. 258). As we shall discuss below, Pons is in fact a failed artist, who eschews creation for consumption, of fine food as well as art.

15   Balzac, *Le Cousin Pons*, p. 484.
16   Balzac, *Le Cousin Pons*, p. 499.

money values have yet to encroach. At the end of the novel, the narrator gloomily concludes that it will soon be impossible to form private collections of the putative significance of the Pons collection, as a result of the inflation of the value of European antiques: 'La bricabracomanie fait rage à Pétersbourg, et par suite du courage naturel à ce peuple, il s'ensuit que les Russes ont causé dans *l'article*, dirait Rémonencq, un renchérissement de prix qui rendra les collections impossibles'.[17] The novel thus laments the passing of one kind of collecting and points to the rise of an ersatz kind of collecting, fashionable collecting, embodied by men such as Popinot who see art as an investment opportunity and the reputation of a connoisseur as a route to social success. Pons is the collector as described by Walter Benjamin, to whom falls 'the Sisyphean task of divesting things of their commodity character by taking possession of them', and who having taken possession of them 'frees them from the drudgery of being useful'.[18] He takes art objects out of circulation and sequesters them in a private space. In opposition to this, the new breed of collectors, the Popinots of the world, both place art under the suzerainty of money and instrumentalize it, flaunting their collections as status symbols.

The relationship between art and commerce is not only probed through the thematics of the collection, however, but is also integral to the very structure of *Le Cousin Pons*, as made clear in the 'avertissement quasi littéraire' which preceded the novel when it was published in *feuilleton* form in *Le Constitutionnel*. According to this preface:

> L'abonné qui subit nos livres, a douze raisons à vingt sous pièce dans la banlieue, quinze dans les départements et vingt à l'étranger, pour vouloir, pendant tout un trimestre, cinquante francs d'esprit, cent francs d'intérêt dramatique et sept francs de style dans le feuilleton. Les écrivains ont imité l'abonné. Tous ceux qui publient leurs ouvrages en feuilleton n'ont plus la liberté de la forme.[19]

---

17 Balzac, *Le Cousin Pons*, p. 764.
18 Walter Benjamin, 'Paris, 1939', p. 19.
19 Balzac, 'L'Avertissement quasi-littéraire', in *La Comédie humaine*, ed. by Pierre-Georges Castex, Bibliothèque de la Pléiade, 12 vols (Paris: Gallimard, 1776–1781), VII (1977), 1388–9 (p. 1388).

The preface to *Le Cousin Pons*, therefore, explicitly draws attention to contemporary changes in the dominant mode of literary production, suggesting that the ascendancy of the *feuilleton* form shackles the novelist's creative freedom. This suggests that *Le Cousin Pons* itself is shaped by commercial demands and unfolds according to a commercial logic. The text itself features many of the generic characteristics of *feuilleton* writing, with its emphasis on the Parisian working classes, crime, and the occult, which obtrudes somewhat unexpectedly into the novel when Mme. Cibot visits a clairvoyant.[20] Thus not only through its exploration of the collection, but also through its insistence on its own conditions of production, *Le Cousin Pons* presents the society within which it was produced as being one within which the market is all-encompassing. Similarly, the novel suggests that it is historically impossible for the collection to exist, as long as it is conceptualized as inhabiting a space radically segregated from the market. One striking feature of *Le Cousin Pons* is that nowhere in the novel is there a full description of its apparent heroine, the collection. The reader is granted partial glimpses of it here and there, and details about its content and organization are scattered through the text, but at no point is there a description of it in its entirety.[21] The collection is constantly discussed, alluded to, and talked about by the various characters, most of whom are speculating on its value, and the reader too is left to speculate, denied an authoritative description of the Pons art trove. The novel can imagine the existence of a space outside the market, but the fact that the collection

20   See Jane A. Nicholson, 'Discourse, Power, and Necessity: Contextualising *Le Cousin Pons*', *Symposium* 42/1 (Spring, 1998), 48–61 for a discussion of the novel as a self-contestatory example of *feuilleton* writing, which opposes not just the new mode of literary production, but the institutions of liberalism more generally.

21   For a detailed reading of those moments where it is partially described, partly through the device of incorporating sections of Pons' own catalogue, see Watson, pp. 129–33. Examining the way in which the catalogue functions in the novel not only as the record of Pons' connoisseurship, but also as a legal document and, indeed, effectively a price-list, Watson concludes that the novel points to the impossibility of keeping the collection out of the marketplace.

remains undescribed suggests that it cannot carve out such a space within itself, as it is too thoroughly imbricated in commerce.

Thus *Le Cousin Pons* is partly a jeremiad against the commodification of art, and a lament for a lost golden age of collecting, before the encroachment of the bourgeoisie. This golden age discourse was echoed by other commentators. For example in his 1842 obituary of the famous collector Du Sommerard (whose collection of mediæval art objects is today housed in the Musée de Cluny), Jules Janin bemoaned the fashion for antiques and the consequent inflation of prices:

> Aujourd'hui, il est vrai, c'est la mode de ramasser çà et là les moindres chiffons des temps écoulés; il n'est pas un honnête bourgeois qui n'ait dans sa maison son bahut gothique, son armoire renaissance ou son canapé Pompadour [...]. Il n'y a rien à faire, sinon attendre; et quand enfin les hommes et les femmes à la mode auront compris que, pour les usages de la vie réelle, une bonne armoire en acajou défend mieux les hardes qu'un bahut en bois de chêne [...], alors l'artiste et l'antiquaire n'auront plus pour concurrents les petites-maîtresses les plus dédaigneuses et les plus riches financières du monde parisien.[22]

The death of Alexandre-Charles Sauvageot provided Clément de Ris with the opportunity to echo these sentiments, elegizing not only his friend and colleague, but the days when the collecting confraternity was a small band widely regarded as maniacs:

> C'était le bon temps! La tempête révolutionnaire avait dispersé aux quatre vents du hasard et jeté au coin de la borne des myriades d'objets [...]. Une caricature du temps représente l'amateur des curiosités sous la figure d'un vieux marquis, culotte courte, bas chinés, souliers à boucles, poudré, et les cheveux tombant derrière le dos et ficelés en queue de rat. Préférer les crédences du seizième siècle, les cabinets du dix-septième siècle, les chantournages du dix-huitième siècle, aux meubles dessinés par David, aux têtes de Sphinx, et à l'acajou, c'était le comble du ridicule et de la démence! [...] Je le répète; c'était le bon temps.[23]

---

22 Jules Janin, 'M. Dusommerard [sic]', *Le Cabinet de l'amateur et de l'antiquaire*, 1 (1842), 324–33 (pp. 326–7).
23 Louis Torterat Clément de Ris, *La Curiosité: collections françaises et étrangères, cabinets d'amateurs, biographies* (Paris: Librairie Ve Jules Renouard, 1864), pp. 277–8.

Clément de Ris draws a contrast between those days and the time in which
he was writing, where money is sovereign, and in which he suggests that
collecting has been reduced to 'une opération financière'.[24] He ascribes to
Sauvageot sentiments which he clearly felt himself:

> La puissance des sacs d'écus le révoltait. Les banquiers, ainsi qu'il appelait tous les
> gens riches, lui agaçaient les nerfs. Ils se refusa à l'idée que cette collection, amassée
> avec tant de soin, caressée avec tant de goût, que toutes ces œuvres dont la réunion
> avait rempli la vie d'un homme, et qu'il aimait comme une mère aime ses enfants, se
> dispersaient aux vents des enchères et s'en iraient orner les vitrines de l'ostentation
> ignorante, n'ayant d'autre droit à un pareil honneur que le hasard de la fortune.[25]

Here Clément de Ris presents the collecting world as having been corrupted
by the influence of money, and rails against those for whom a collection is
simply a status symbol, and who lack true connoisseurship. In this account,
as in Janin's, the collector is placed in opposition to the financier, and collecting is presented not merely as a hobby, but as a means of contesting
the values of the bourgeoisie. Clément de Ris suggests that the art object
cannot be viewed as just another commodity, that the connoisseur has a
different kind of relationship with the art object than the mere purchaser,
an affective relationship of the sort that money cannot buy.

Many nineteenth-century discussions of collecting are centrally concerned with the relationship between art and money. Balzac's short story
Pierre Grassou exposes the ludicrousness of trying to calibrate artistic values
through reference to money values. The eponymous protagonist is a painter
of virtually no talent, who is commissioned by the Vervelle family, solid
bourgeois citizens with pretensions to art appreciation, to paint their portraits. The Vervelles, impressed by Grassou's sober habits, take it upon themselves to act as Grassou's patron, and he achieves success in bourgeois circles,
where his reputation as an artist is founded on the fact that he invests his
money wisely: 'La grande raison des Bourgeois pour employer cet artiste
est celle-ci: "Dites-en ce que vous voulez, il place vingt mille francs par an

24   Clément de Ris, *La Curiosité*, p. 17.
25   Clément de Ris, *La Curiosité*, pp. 284–5.

chez son notaire."[26] The consummation of bourgeois philistinism in the story is represented by M. Vervelle's art collection, celebrated in bourgeois circles, and which Pierre Grassou is privileged to visit. Grassou realizes that the Vervelle collection consists exclusively of fakes, and fakes that he himself unwittingly helped produce. The paintings bought by Vervelle are all works of Pierre's commissioned by Elie Magus, who transformed the painter's *croûtes* into Old Masters and sold them on at a handsome profit. (One such painting, purportedly a Rembrandt, is rather delightfully a portrait of one 'Docteur Tromp'.)[27] Far from being desolate on discovering that he has a collection of worthless fakes, Vervelle is even more impressed by discovering that Grassou is such a capable copier: 'Prouvez-le moi [...] et je double la dot de ma fille, car alors vous êtes Rubens, Rembrandt, Terburg, Titien!'[28] The Vervelle art collection bears gloomy witness to the impossibility of authentic art under a bourgeois regime.

Balzac was not the only writer to use the idea of the fake to probe the relationship between art and commerce. Other writers too used it to suggest precisely that the art object cannot be bought and sold like any other commodity. Thus Bonnaffé speaks in praise of the fake because 'le jour où la curiosité sera réduite à un duel de billets de banque [...], elle sera bien morte'.[29] Here the possibility of forgery introduces into the process of collecting a problem which cannot be resolved by money, but only by flair. True connoisseurship is not something that can be bought and sold. Champfleury also uses the idea of the fake to reflect on the ascendancy of money values and their encroachment into the artistic realm, in his discussion of the figure of the *truqueur*. Champfleury takes a rather indulgent view of the forger, presenting him as a lovable rogue to whom a certain

---

26 Honoré de Balzac, *Pierre Grassou*, in *La Comédie humaine*, ed. by Pierre-Georges Castex, Bibliothèque de la Pléiade, 12 vols (Paris: Gallimard, 1776–1781), VI (1977), 1091–1111 (p. 1111).

27 Balzac, *Pierre Grassou*, p. 1109.

28 Balzac, *Pierre Grassou*, p. 1110.

29 Edmond Bonnaffé, *Causeries*, p. 226. Claims such as this rest on a charismatic ideology of taste, the most devastating critique of which remains Pierre Bourdieu's, *La Distinction: critique sociale du jugement* (Paris: Editions de Minuit, 1979).

measure of admiration is due: 'Il trompe le monde, mais il le trompe avec tant d'imagination!'[30] The *truqueur* is described as being a creature of instinct: 'Se complaisant dans la ruse comme le poisson dans l'eau, tromper est sa suprême jouissance, et il ne trompe pas pour s'enrichir, mais pour se chatouiller le cœur et amener un sourire sur ses lèvres minces.'[31] He is thus presented as largely indifferent to money, and it is precisely this indifference which founds Champfleury's admiration for him: 'J'admire le truqueur, parce qu'il ne travaille point en vue de l'argent.'[32] The forger may be a criminal, but there is nothing venal about his criminality. He emerges from Champfleury's account as a colourful, romantic figure from a bygone era: 'C'est un homme de l'époque des romans picaresques.'[33] He notes that forgers used to be known as 'chevaliers de l'industrie', but that in the nineteenth century 'l'opinion publique [...], a inventé toutes sortes de vilains mots froids et secs, tels que *filou, homme entretenu, grec, escroc,* etc.'.[34] He predicts that the old euphemism 'avant 50 ans aura disparue de la langue; car notre temps ne reconnaît plus guère de *Chevaliers,* et l'*Industrie* est actuellement un titre de noblesse'.[35] Whereas the forger used to be designated by a term that ironically concealed the grubbily commercial nature of his work, Champfleury suggests that in the nineteenth century this term has no meaning, as the value system which underpinned it, within which commerce was treated with suspicion, has crumbled. If the nineteenth century will be less indulgent to forgers than previous epochs, this is the rage of Caliban seeing his own face in a glass.

The contrast Champfleury playfully draws between a nineteenth century ruled by money and an aristocratic never-never land is reworked by other writers in a more frankly reactionary and elitist vein. Maupassant in his writing on the art world developed the idea of an aristocracy of taste, contrasted with a bourgeoisie lacking any aesthetic judgement. Maupassant

---

30   Champfleury, *L'Hôtel,* p. 165.
31   Champfleury, *L'Hôtel,* p. 166.
32   Champfleury, *L'Hôtel,* p. 167.
33   Champfleury, *L'Hôtel,* p. 181.
34   Champfleury, *L'Hôtel,* p. 182.
35   Champfleury, *L'Hôtel,* p. 182.

was distressed by the use of antiques as a status symbol in the late nineteenth century, noting that, 'tout bourgeois ayant gagné 10 mille francs
de rentes dans l'industrie encombre sa salle à manger de ces affreuses assi-
ettes normandes', and that 'tout le monde aujourd'hui collectionne; tout
le monde est ou se croit connaisseur'.[36] According to Maupassant, to be
able to arrogate to oneself the title 'connaisseur' it was sufficient to be able
to gauge the auction value of an object: 'on fait, en un mot, fort bien le
métier de commissaire-priseur'.[37] The capacity for true art appreciation,
in Maupassant's view, is a congenital quality, a 'flair de race'.[38]

The distinction between an aristocratic and a bourgeois model of art
collecting is apparent in the phenomenally popular *Arsène Lupin* stories,
which reworked the archetype of the collector for the *belle époque*. The
universe of the *Arsène Lupin* stories is largely populated by rich bankers on
the one hand and aristocrats living in reduced circumstances on the other.
These two different tribes are presented as having a different relationship
to art objects. A comparison between two of the stories in the first collection of Arsène Lupin adventures published in book form, *Arsène Lupin,
Gentleman-Cambrioleur*, makes this clear.[39] 'Arsène Lupin en prison' pits
Lupin against Baron Cahorn, better known under the soubriquet Baron
Satan, a fabulously wealthy financier and art collector. The Baron lives in
seclusion in the château Malaquis: 'Les seigneurs du Malaquis, ruinés, ont
dû lui vendre, pour un morceau de pain, la demeure de leurs ancêtres.'[40]
The castle houses an enviable art collection containing three Watteaus, two
Rubens, a Jean Goujon sculpture, 'et tant d'autres merveilles arrachées à
coup de billets de banque aux plus riches habitués des ventes publiques.'[41] As
a collector, the Baron relies not on flair but on the simple fact of being able

---

36 Guy de Maupassant, 'Vieux Pots', in *Chroniques inédites*, ed. by Pascal Pia, 2 vols
(Paris: Maurice Gonon, 1979), II, 15–19 (p. 15), and 'Bibelot', p. 27.
37 Maupassant, 'Bibelot', p. 28.
38 Maupassant, 'Bibelot', p. 28, and 'Vieux Pots', p. 16.
39 The first *Arsène Lupin* story appeared in the magazine *Je Sais Tout*, 15 July 1905.
40 Maurice Leblanc, *Arsène Lupin, Gentleman-Cambrioleur* (Paris: Lafitte, 1907),
p. 40.
41 Leblanc, *Gentleman-Cambrioleur*, p. 40.

to outbid anyone else. From a prison cell, Lupin masterminds the burglary of the château Malaquis. When the Baron discovers the burglary, he 'rappelait ses prix d'achat, additionnait les pertes subies, accumulait des chiffres'.[42] Art objects appear to him, therefore, as repositories for his money, little different from safety-deposit boxes. He is thus concerned principally with the exchange value of the objects he buys. As such he is the antitype of the collector as described by Walter Benjamin, to whom 'falls the Sisyphean task of divesting things of their commodity character by taking possession of them. But he bestows on them only connoisseur value, rather than use value'.[43] Thus the collector, in Benjamin's formulation, embodies a protest against the alienated relationship with objects typical of modernity, but although he struggles to liberate objects from the tyranny of exchange value, he does not thereby privilege use value. Rather, as we have already seen, he bestows on his possessions another kind of value altogether, which cannot be plotted on the conventional axes of use and exchange. Of this value Baron Cahorn apparently has little inkling, as the story makes clear that his connoisseurship is not the equal of his purchasing power. Lupin discovers that the Baron has several fakes among his collection. At the end of the story he recovers his collection, sold back to him by Lupin at a very high price. What Lupin knows, however, and the Baron does not, is that much of his collection is fake.

This story invites comparison with 'Le Collier de la Reine', which traces the destiny of the notorious diamond necklace that embroiled Marie-Antoinette in scandal in 1785. In the story this necklace has for several generations been in the possession of an aristocratic family, the Dreux-Soubises, who although they live in increasingly straitened circumstances, have refused to sell their most valuable possession. The necklace is then stolen by the child Lupin to avenge his mother, a country cousin of the Dreux-Soubises, rather ill-treated by them. The crime remains unsolved until the adult Lupin, posing as the Chevalier Floriani, befriends the

42   Leblanc, *Gentleman-Cambrioleur*, p. 53.
43   Walter Benjamin, 'Paris, 1935', p. 9. This comment appears unaltered in the 1939 version of Benjamin's essay.

Count, and at a dinner-party hosted by the latter one evening reveals, in the presence of the guests, how the theft was perpetrated. It is clear to everybody present that the Chevalier Floriani is the thief. There are two final twists in the tale. First, Lupin reveals that the majority of the diamonds in the necklace were fake. The Countess claims that this does not affect the true value of the necklace: 'la monture était l'œuvre essentielle, la création même de l'artiste'.[44] The Countess, therefore, locates the value of the necklace in its workmanship, not simply in the weight of the diamonds. The second twist is that Lupin chooses to restore the setting intact to the Dreux-Soubises. This is apparently in response to a plea made by the Countess, who claims that the necklace 'nous appartient comme notre nom, comme notre honneur'.[45] Lupin, in returning the necklace, seems to endorse this point of view, acknowledging the Dreux-Soubises as the 'légitimes propriétaires'.[46] Their claim to ownership of the necklace is not based on money, but on inheritance. Indeed, the Dreux-Soubises refuse to see the necklace as a solution to their cash-flow problems, and at the end of the story their title to the necklace is apparently vindicated as they are able once more to enter into possession of it, for although it has been stripped of its diamonds, according to the Countess' definition the necklace is still intact. Read alongside each other the two stories point to two different ways of evaluating the art object. On the one hand, the art object can be valued as a symbol of ready money. As such it is a commodity, and it is as a commodity that the financier Baron Satan approaches it. On the other hand, the art object has an aesthetic value which cannot be measured by money. The Dreux-Soubises understand this. In the Lupin universe, buying is presented as a bourgeois mode of acquisition, in contrast to inheritance, understood as an aristocratic mode of acquisition, and the former does not confer title to the object as a work of art. The final story in *Arsène Lupin, Gentleman-Cambrioleur* makes this clear. In this story Lupin burgles Georges Devanne, a rich banker who lives in the château

44 Leblanc, *Gentleman-Cambrioleur*, p. 164.
45 Leblanc, *Gentleman-Cambrioleur*, p. 164.
46 Leblanc, *Gentleman-Cambrioleur*, p. 165.

Thibermesnil, amid 'les incomparables richesses accumulées à travers les siècles par les sires de Thibermesnil'.[47] Lupin is able to commit such a crime because there is an underground tunnel through which it is possible to penetrate the castle from without. The secret of the tunnel, handed down the Thibermesnil family line from father to son, was taken to the grave by the last of the Thibermesnils. Devanne has searched for the tunnel but has been unable to find it. The château withholds its secrets from him, and frustrates his attempts to enter fully into possession of what he has bought; the story suggests that he is a usurper, and that a title based on money alone is not enough.

Of course, inheritance and purchase are not the only modes of acquisition to feature in the Lupin stories. Lupin himself favours theft, which like inheritance neatly bypasses the market, and through which he has accumulated his own private art collection, stealing the great works of European art from the great European galleries and leaving in their places masterfully executed copies. This collection is described in the 1909 novel, *L'Aiguille Creuse*. It is housed in the eponymous needle off the Normandy coast, the hollow interior of which, accessible only through submarine tunnels, was used by the kings of France as a secret hiding place for treasure and arms. According to Lupin, before him 'nul n'avait possédé le secret depuis un siècle, depuis Louis XVI et la Révolution'.[48] Through having discovered the secret of the hollow needle, Lupin claims to have become 'le dernier héritier des rois de la France'.[49] He therefore seeks to inscribe himself in a system of aristocratic values, within which objects are not commodities, and are not acquired through buying and selling. He has contempt for those who privilege exchange value over artistic value. When he invites his nemesis, the adolescent amateur detective Beautrelet, into 'La Salle du Trésor', where he keeps the choicest objects in his collection, Beautrelet is concerned only with whether there is a treasure trove concealed in the room. Lupin castigates Beautrelet for being so money-minded: 'Tous ces chefs-d'œuvre de l'art

---

47   Leblanc, *Gentleman-Cambrioleur*, p. 268.
48   Maurice Leblanc, *L'Aiguille Creuse* (Paris: Lafitte, 1909), p. 308.
49   Leblanc, *L'Aiguille Creuse*, p. 214.

humain, n'est-ce pas? Ça ne vaut pas, pour ta curiosité, la contemplation du trésor ... Et toute la foule sera comme toi'.[50] In fact, of the six treasure chests concealed in the room, five are empty, their resources exhausted by the eighteenth-century kings, but the sixth, a collection of jewellery, is still full: 'Intangible celle-là', claims Lupin, 'nul d'entre eux n'osa jamais y toucher'.[51] Lupin urges Beautrelet to look at the settings of the various pieces, suggesting that their value lies in their workmanship, which cannot be replaced. Like Lupin, the kings of France respected these objects not as a source of wealth, but as art objects. Lupin insistently presents himself as incarnating the aristocratic values of the eighteenth century, as against the commercial values of the nineteenth and twentieth; theft and inheritance are merged together as both are ranged against purchase.

The text, however, again through Lupin's own self-mythologizing, offers us another image of its hero, not as rightful heir but as usurper. When Beautrelet points out that it will one day be discovered that many of the most celebrated paintings hanging in European museums are fakes, Lupin insouciantly replies:

> Un jour ou l'autre, la fraude sera découverte? Eh bien, l'on trouvera ma signature sur chacune des toiles, – par derrière, – et l'on saura que c'est moi qui ai doté mon pays des chefs-d'œuvre originaux. Après tout, je n'ai fait que ce qu'a fait Napoléon en Italie.[52]

Thus Lupin, by his own admission, is as much a Bonaparte as a Bourbon. The paradigm of acquisition of art objects through legitimate inheritance, associated with the *ancien régime*, is not one into which he can comfortably fit. Even as the stories glorify an aristocratic model of collecting in contrast to a bourgeois one, they acknowledge that such a model is impossible. Arsène Lupin himself, unlike Pons, is not a collector who purports to define himself in opposition to merchants. He himself is a merchant, a latter-day Elie Magus. For Lupin is actively involved in what he describes as

50 Leblanc, *L'Aiguille Creuse*, p. 313.
51 Leblanc, *L'Aiguille Creuse*, p. 314.
52 Leblanc, *L'Aiguille Creuse*, p. 310.

'le grand marché de l'art et de l'antiquité, la foire du monde'.[53] Indeed, it is
from 'La Salle du Trésor' that he controls the international fine art market,
and it is his control of the art market that is the source of his power. Lupin
is not a figure who stands outside circuits of exchange and distribution;
it is his imbrication in such circuits that enables him to form a collection,
and to keep it intact. Thus Lupin has an ambivalent relationship with commerce: he can enjoy objects as art, only because he knows how to exploit
them as commodities.

Indeed, it is a feature of the discourse around collecting that although
it constantly asserts an ideal separation of the aesthetic and the commercial,
this distinction is constantly undone. Clément de Ris, whose contempt
for money values is palpable, can finally find no better way to suggest the
significance of Sauvageot's achievement as a collector than to say: 'je ne
serai pas loin de la vérité en affirmant que si cette belle collection était
aujourd'hui soumise aux enchères, elle dépasserait 800,000 francs. Quel
éloge aurait l'éloquence de ces chiffres'.[54] Similarly, Maupassant holds
the Goncourt brothers up as models of true connoisseurs, and points out
that the first Japanese album they had bought for 80 francs could, by the
1880s, command 'des sommes fabuleuses'.[55] The aesthetic is therefore vali-
dated through reference to the commercial. As Octave Uzanne wrote in
a published letter to Eudel, urging the latter to write a history of public
auctions, such a monograph would have 'l'extrême mérite de prouver que
les enchères ont toujours été dans la généralité la pierre de touche de la
valeur réelle des artistes et des écrivains'.[56] This points towards a more
complex understanding of the relationship between the commercial and
the aesthetic than one of simple segregation.

Even within *Le Cousin Pons* itself, the treatment of the relationship
between the aesthetic and the commercial is ambiguous. There is clearly
much in the novel that invites us to read Pons as a figure who stands in

---

53   Leblanc, *L'Aiguille Creuse*, p. 317.
54   Clément de Ris, *La Curiosité*, p. 286.
55   Maupassant, 'Bibelot', p. 30.
56   Uzanne, *Les Zigzags*, p. 250.

opposition to the priority of exchange value. There are also, however, as a number of critics have noted, indications in the text that such a reading needs to be nuanced.[57] Pons does not in fact, despite the narrator's claim to the contrary, behave as if unaware of the exchange value of his collection. When Mme. de Marville tries to humiliate him by offering to pay him back for the fan he has given her, he is quick to tell her that she could not possibly afford to buy the fan at its true price, but adds in self-congratulation: 'soyez tranquille, ma cousine, je n'ai pas payé la centième partie du prix d'art.'[58] At one point Pons devises a plan which would allow him to release the equity in his collection by selling it to Fritz Brunner on condition that the latter take possession of it only after his (Pons') death. Thus he is astute enough to imagine a mechanism through which he can both enjoy his collection and realize its cash value. Sharon Marcus, as we have seen, suggests that when he focuses on the exchange value of his collection, Pons precipitates his own tragic fall. Such a reading represents the novel as idealizing in a straightforward way the segregation of the commercial and the aesthetic towards which it repeatedly gestures. The text easily bears such an interpretation, but it is also possible to argue that Pons' interest in exchange value is not a betrayal of his collection and the principles it enshrines, but that on the contrary he is successful as a collector precisely because he is a shrewd consumer who is more than capable of pulling the wool over art dealers' eyes. Pons himself claims that 'le mérite du collectionneur est de devancer la mode',[59] identifying the ability to realize a return on his investment as the chief characteristic of the collector. There is a constitutive ambiguity in the paradigm of collecting which Pons represents: it is both enabled by commerce and suspicious thereof.

---

57   One of the more compelling readings to address this aspect of the text is Pierre-Marc de Biasi, 'La Collection Pons comme figure du problématique', in *Balzac et les parents pauvres*, ed. by Françoise van Rossum-Guyon and Michiel van Brederode (Paris: Société d'édition d'enseignement supérieur, 1981), pp. 61–73. Eric Bordas also stresses that Pons is an agent of the commodification of art in 'Le rôle de la peinture dans *Le Cousin Pons*', *Australian Journal of French Studies*, 32 (1995), 19–37.

58   Balzac, *Le Cousin Pons*, p. 509.

59   Balzac, *Le Cousin Pons*, p. 511.

Within the novel the collection figures an aspiration towards autonomy from the market, but the text acknowledges the realization of this ambition to be an impossibility. The novel presents this impossibility as historically determined, a function of the grubby venality characteristic of the July Monarchy, where the forces of monetization are ineluctable. Indeed, as we have seen, *Le Cousin Pons* declares itself to have been shaped by such forces, and I suggested earlier that this was the reason the Pons collection is never fully described within the text. Certainly the novel is making a descriptive statement about the relationship between art and commerce in mid-nineteenth-century France. I would further suggest, however, that it also makes a normative claim about the collection, ultimately rejecting the paradigm which Pons represents, and promoting an alternative aesthetics. The collection, as Pons imagines it, remains unrepresented within the novel, I would argue, because it is inherently incompatible with the structuring principles of the realist novel, and this incompatability is twofold. It exists first because the collection gives rise to a certain experience of time which forecloses the possibility of narrative, and second because it embodies a vision of total privacy.

The Private Collection, the Public Museum and the Realist Novel

The Pons collection is described in the text as a space within which linear time is dissolved. Pons 'possédait son musée pour en jouir à toute heure, car les âmes créées pour admirer les grandes œuvres, ont la faculté sublime des vrais amants; ils éprouvent autant de plaisir aujourd'hui qu'hier, ils ne se lassent jamais, et les chefs d'œuvres sont, heureusement, toujours jeunes.'[60] The collection provides an image of plenitude and satiety, of a perpetual desire perpetually fulfilled. The particular experience of time to which the

60   Balzac, *Le Cousin Pons*, p. 491.

collection gives rise, or more accurately the experience of the abolition of time to which it gives rise, is one of the most frequently recurring topoi in discussions of collecting, and it is an issue to which we shall return in the next chapter.[61] Here, however, it is enough to note that the collection is presented as occluding the possibility of change over time, and in so doing it occludes the possibility of narrative development. It is not the collection per se which drives the novel forward. Rather it is Pons' physical appetite, his *gourmandise* that generates narrative, forcing him out into the world, connecting him to those social networks which are the very stuff of *La Comédie humaine*. Greed elicits stories. The substance of the novel consists of the conspirators' various attempts to dissolve the collection. This is highlighted by the odd comment which occurs over halfway through the book, where, following the introduction of Fraisier, the last of the conspirators to appear, the narrator remarks, 'ici commence le drame', describing the preceding part of the book merely as an 'avant-scène'.[62] In so far as it aspires to stasis, the collection thwarts narrative.

The second problem the Pons collection poses for the realist novel is that it is a completely private space. Even fellow-collectors such as Du Sommerard are denied access: 'le prince du Bric-à-Brac mourut sans avoir pu pénétrer dans le musée Pons'.[63] Shabbily treated by the world, for Pons his collection is a private sanctum. The only other person who enjoys unlimited access to the museum is Schmucke, who is almost an extension of Pons. In describing the relationship of Pons and Schmucke the narrator stresses the similarities between the two men. We are told that in 1835 Pons 'épousa un homme, un vieillard, un musicien comme lui'.[64] Furthermore, 'jamais peut-être deux âmes ne se trouvèrent si pareilles dans l'océan humain'.[65] For Schmucke, Pons is 'un autre lui-même'.[66] The novel gestures towards a domestic idyll whereby Pons and Schmucke would live together, each

---

61 See below, pp. 104–10.
62 Balzac, *Le Cousin Pons*, p. 630.
63 Balzac, *Le Cousin Pons*, p. 490.
64 Balzac, *Le Cousin Pons*, p. 496.
65 Balzac, *Le Cousin Pons*, p. 496.
66 Balzac, *Le Cousin Pons*, p. 497.

the image of the other, surrounded by the Pons art trove, an image of its collector. The Pons collection therefore figures an aspiration to a hermetic self-enclosure. The intensely private nature of the collection as Pons conceives of it emerges most forcefully in the text through the allusions to the public museum, which provides an alternative model of art appreciation to the private collection, a model which Pons ultimately rejects. One of the oddities of the text is the inclusion of the sham will, written by Pons purely in order to try and trick Mme. Cibot into revealing her true colours, but reproduced textually, inviting critical reflection.[67] In this will Pons follows Du Sommerard's example and leaves his entire collection to the nation. It allows us to glimpse a possible future for the Pons collection in which the art objects which he has collected, under the protection of the state, are kept out of circuits of distribution and exchange. Pons does not follow this route, however, choosing instead to leave his collection to Schmucke, who is predictably enough divested of his inheritance within a very short space of time and left destitute. The fact that Pons chooses not to implement the plan contained in the first will is something of a puzzle, as the scheme seems to provide an elegant solution to all his problems. It would both guarantee Schmucke an income, and ensure that the collection remain intact, keeping it out of the market. Indeed, the museum would appear to provide the most effective bulwark against the commodification of the art object. This is hinted at in the novel through the somewhat idiosyncratic uses of the words 'collection' and 'musée', both of which are used at various times to describe the ensemble of objects accumulated by Pons. As Sharon Marcus points out, 'collection' is always associated in the text with market value, and 'musée' is used to describe the Pons' art trove as 'an inalienable ensemble inseparable from its location', thus reversing contemporary usage.[68] This reversal neatly encapsulates the problematic of the collection in the text in its double aspect. On the one hand the private

67   The sham will has received, however, little critical scrutiny. For an excellent reading of the novel, from a queer studies perspective, which considers the function of the sham will, see Michael Lucey, *The Misfit of the Family: Balzac and the Social Forms of Sexuality* (Durham, NC: Duke University Press, 2003), pp. 141–54.
68   Marcus, p. 62.

collection does not act as a bulwark against commodification, and cannot resist imbrication in economic circuits. The public collection can provide such a bulwark, and yet Pons finally is unwilling to countenance the idea of his collection entering a museum. In order to understand this, we must examine the representations of the museum in the novel.

There are several allusions in the text to the Louvre and to the Musée de Cluny which allow us to trace the contours of the museum paradigm. As we have already noted, when M. Camusot castigates his wife for not being fashionable enough to know who Watteau is, he points out to her that the state considers antiques sufficiently important to have spent a large amount of money setting up the Musée de Cluny to house the Du Sommerard collection. He goes on to add, somewhat portentously, that antiques 'sont souvent les seuls témoignages qui nous restent de civilisations disparues'.[69] In stressing the historical value of such objects, M. Camusot follows contemporary received wisdom. In the obituary of Du Sommerard published in *L'Artiste*, the famous collector is celebrated for his contribution to historiography; his museum 'est aujourd'hui la dernière trace de sociétés qui ont eu aussi la vie, le bonheur, le drame et la puissance. Cette religion de souvenirs serait bien digne d'une époque éclairée'.[70] The writer goes on to suggest that Du Sommerard's collecting had a double motivation; it is actuated by a 'passion pour le beau' and 'pour la vieille gloire de sa patrie'.[71] Du Sommerard's collection thus becomes a monument of national history, and Du Sommerard is presented as a great patriot. In the parliamentary report Arago prepared on the question of where best to house the Du Sommerard collection, he proposed that it be incorporated into a 'Musée des monuments nationaux', which would 'combler de grandes lacunes de l'histoire écrite'.[72] Arago cited the example of Lenoir's Musée de la rue des Petits-Augustins, where 'le culte de l'art se mariait à de

---

69   Balzac, *Le Cousin Pons*, p. 540.
70   'M. Du Sommerard', in *L'Artiste: Beaux-Arts et Belles-Lettres*, 3rd Series, vol. 2 (1842–1844), 148–50 (p. 150).
71   'M. Du Sommerard', in *L'Artiste*, p. 150.
72   As cited in an article on 'Musée des Thermes et de l'hôtel de Cluny', in *Le Cabinet de l'amateur et de l'antiquaire*, 2 (1843), 385–99 (p. 390).

vifs sentiments de nationalité'.[73] Thus the collection is presented as part of a national cultural patrimony, the exhibition of which will help forge a sense of national identity. Arago further suggests that contemplation of the collection will have a morally edifying effect:

> Mettre chaque jour à la disposition de la brillante jeunesse qui fréquente ces grandes institutions, dans le quartier même où elle demeure [...], une collection variée [...], ce serait faire concurrence, au profit de la moralité, à des établissements dans lesquels beaucoup d'étudiants, désœuvrés et sans expérience vont puiser le goût de la dissipation.[74]

We saw in the last chapter that collecting could be presented as a respectable pastime only if it was knowledge-producing and order-making.[75] Opened to the public, the Du Sommerard collection is slotted into this paradigm, endowed with a two-fold function, fostering patriotism and channelling young men's energies into harmless activities.

Thus one of the effects of the museum is to transform art appreciation from an end in itself to a means to a social end. This is what Pons resolutely refuses to do. He displays none of the patriotic fervour nor public-spiritedness ascribed to Du Sommerard. Although he is explicitly motivated by a desire to preserve, by a fear of irreparable loss ('Alors on a fabriqué des choses admirables et qu'on ne refera plus!'),[76] his collecting is in fact made possible by the dismantling of France's cultural patrimony. He explains that the fan he gives to Mme. de Marville was acquired, 'chez un brocanteur qui venait de le rapporter d'un château qu'on a dépécé près de Dreux'.[77] This detail recalls Viel-Castel's complaint that private collectors are little more than cultural vandals,[78] a complaint echoed by Jules Clarétie almost half a century later, when he reported the story of the château de Montal, which was dismantled, brought to Paris and sold off bit by bit.

---

73   'Musée des Thermes', in *Le Cabinet*, p. 391.
74   'Musée des Thermes', in *Le Cabinet*, p. 397.
75   See above, pp. 37–44.
76   Balzac, *Le Cousin Pons*, p. 512.
77   Balzac, *Le Cousin Pons*, p. 510.
78   Viel-Castel, pp. 127–8.

Clarétie remarks that, 'si les chemins de fer et les amateurs d'art avaient existé depuis les siècles en Grèce, il ne resterait pas debout un seul chef-d'œuvre'.[79] For these writers the private collector is socially irresponsible; their attitude towards art objects and antiques is heavily informed by the idea of a national cultural patrimony, which belongs in the public sphere. Pons is concerned precisely with keeping his objects outside the public sphere; in rejecting the idea of bequeathing them to the nation (choosing instead to leave them to a man whose status as a foreigner is heavily stressed throughout the novel), he reaffirms his commitment to the idea of the collection as a private space.

Pons' commitment to privacy, to keeping his collection a secret, works against the dynamic of the realist novel, which operates through the dissolution of privacy. Balzac's narrator in his novella *La Muse du département* acknowledges that the nineteenth-century novel is committed to making the private public, informing the reader that the story which follows would remain secret, 'si l'avide scalpel du dix-neuvième siècle n'allait pas, conduit par la nécessité de trouver du nouveau, fouiller les coins les plus obscurs du cœur'.[80] Sharon Marcus has argued in her discussion of *Le Cousin Pons* that the reason Mme. Cibot is allowed finally to get away with murder – Mme. Fontaine's predictions of a grisly end notwithstanding – is that she is a figure for the omniscient narrator of the realist novel:

> Throughout *Le Cousin Pons*, Balzac's narrator has dissociated himself from the invasions of privacy required by realist narration by attributing them to the *portière*. Cibot's demonized status as a ubiquitous, all-knowing, meddling woman, compounded by the audacity and cruelty of her intrusions, distracts the reader from her resemblance to the equally omnipresent and omniscient narrator. The narrator, after all, not Cibot, is ultimately responsible for all the characters' fates, and the narrator provides the textual precedents for the acts of spying, inventorying, and tale-telling carried out by Cibot. Yet much as the novel strives to project those acts onto the

79 Jules Clarétie, *La vie à Paris*, 21 vols (Paris: Havard, 1881–1885, 1895–1913), II (1882), 49.

80 Balzac, *La Muse du département*, in *La Comédie humaine*, ed. by Pierre-Georges Castex, Bibliothèque de la Pléiade, 12 vols (Paris: Gallimard, 1776–1781), IV (1976), 629–791 (p. 649).

discredited *portière* and onto the apartment-house network that makes her activities possible, the narrator's investment in realism's publication of private life ultimately impels him to redeem both Cibot and the apartment building.[81]

Following Marcus, we can say that if Pons is killed by Mme. Cibot and her relentless harangues, so the paradigm of the private collection which he represents is destroyed by the logic of the realist novel. Pons imagines himself living in a hall of mirrors, in complete isolation from society, where nothing ever changes, but such an idyll cannot be represented directly in the realist novel, as it would necessarily be compromised were another's gaze – in this case the reader's, via the narrator's – to penetrate it.

Le Cousin Pons is, therefore, structured by the antagonism between the value system inscribed in the Pons collection and that of the realist novel. On the other hand, the museum and the novel belong to the same paradigm. Indeed, *Le Cousin Pons* invites the reader to think of the novel as a portrait gallery. Time and time again, the narrator's descriptions of characters invoke paintings. Thus when Pons is describing to Mme de Marville his triumphant acquisition of the Watteau fan, the narrator notes: 'L'admirable pantomime, la verve du viel artiste qui faisaient de lui, rancontant le triomphe de sa finesse sur l'ignorance du broncanteur, un modèle digne du pinceau hollandais, tout fut perdu pour la présidente et pour sa fille qui se dirent, en échangeant des regards froids et dédaigneux: 'Quel original!'.[82] The reference to Dutch painting here serves a number of purposes.[83] It offers the Dutch painter as a figure for the realist writer. It emphasizes the philistinism of Mme de Marville and her daughter, already

81   Marcus, p. 80.
82   Balzac, *Le Cousin Pons*, p. 514.
83   There is a large body of criticism on painting in Balzac, and the many different aspects of how references to the visual arts function in his novels. See, for example, *Balzac et la peinture*, ed. by Roger Pierrot and Philippe Le Leysour (Tours: Farrago, 1999), for a range of essays on this subject. The broad question of how the visual arts function as a model of representation in Balzac's novels has been most famously treated by Barthes in *S/Z* (Paris: Seuil, 1970), and recently by Diana Knight in *Balzac and the Model of Painting: Artist Stories in 'La Comédie Humaine'* (London: Legenda, 2007).

established as their most salient characteristic, and here highlighted by the fact that they are completely bemused by the spectacle before them, a spectacle compared to a work of fine art. The use of the word 'original' functions ironically in this context, and indicates the absolute chasm in values between Pons and the narrator, connoisseurs both, and the Marvilles. The latter use the word in a pejorative sense to mean 'eccentric', but within the discourse of art collecting that infuses the novel it has another meaning entirely, which locks in to the narrator's description of Pons as 'un modèle digne du pinceau hollandais'. The collector is here assimilated to his collection. Pons' rival collector, Elie Magus, will similarly later be described, in his gallery, as 'un tableaux vivant au milieu de ces tableaux immobiles'.[84] In both cases the art collectors themselves are transformed into art works, exhibited to the reader's gaze. The reference to Dutch painting, acting in lieu of a detailed textual description of the scene, may also serve to evoke for the reader a visual image of the action unfolding; certainly it interpellates the reader as a connoisseur. References to the visual arts that function in a similarly descriptive way are strewn throughout the text. Sometimes, as in those already mentioned, the allusion is a vague one, to a school or genre of painting. Thus the Machiavellian lawyer Fraisier, one of those conspiring to appropriate to themselves the value of the Pons collection, when examining that collection, 'se tenait dans la pose que les peintres prêtent à Méphistophélès'.[85] Sometimes a particular artist is referenced. Thus Mme. Cibot, Pons' concierge and one of the conspirators ranged against him, is likened to 'un modèle de Rubens'.[86] A few lines later we read: 'Si Delacroix avait pu voir Mme Cibot posée fièrement sur son balai, certes il en eût fait une Bellone!'[87] Delacroix's Bellona in *La Liberté guidant le peuple* is inspired by Rubens' image of Bellona in *The Apotheosis of Henri IV*. Thus the reference to Rubens is transformed from a very banal, conventional one, with only an attenuated link to the discourse of painting, into the

---

84 Balzac, *Le Cousin Pons*, p. 598.
85 Balzac, *Le Cousin Pons*, p. 681.
86 Balzac, *Le Cousin Pons*, p. 521.
87 Balzac, *Le Cousin Pons*, p. 521.

witticism of a connoisseur. Elsewhere specific paintings are more explicitly referenced. Thus when the dying Pons listens to his friend Schmucke's
improvisations upon the piano he is plunged 'dans l'extase que Raphaël a
peinte, et qu'on va voir à Boulogne'.[88] Discussing one of the paintings in
the Pons collection, a work by Sebastiano del Piombo, the narrator refers
the reader to another work by the same painter, commenting: 'Aussi peut-
on voir à quelle perfection est arrivé cet homme [...] quand on étudie au
Musée de Paris le portrait de Baccio Bandinelli'.[89]

Collectively, such allusions to painting turn the text itself into an exhibition space, a virtual museum. To function successfully as descriptions,
they require that readers share a common frame of cultural reference; they
require that these works are accessible to the public or that copies circulate
in society. The art object is part of the public sphere, and becomes part of
a dialogue between the reader and the writer, a bridge between self and
other. The Pons model of collecting, where art appreciation is a purely
private and incommunicable experience which locks the individual within
his own subjectivity, is superseded by another model of the collection,
wherein art is socialized.

Le Cousin Pons, therefore, offers the reader an alternative vision of the
collection to that promoted by and defeated with its eponymous protagonist – the text itself, a virtual museum. In this museum, creative labour and
art appreciation are reunited. At the level of its representational content,
Le Cousin Pons is an elegy for the private collector, a figure whose passing
it mourns. But the text at the same time acknowledges the limitations of
the Pons model of collecting. Pons is, after all, a figure of creative sterility,
who sacrificed his career as a musician to his passion for collecting: 'Enfin,
il trouva dans les plaisirs de collectionneur de si vives compensations à la
faillite de la gloire, que s'il lui eût fallu choisir entre la possession de ses
curiosités et le nom de Rossini, le croirait-on? Pons aurait opté pour son
cher cabinet.'[90] In his autobiography, Robert de Montesquiou identified

88   Balzac, *Le Cousin Pons*, p 705.
89   Balzac, *Le Cousin Pons*, p. 612.
90   Balzac, *Le Cousin Pons*, p. 489.

precisely this creative sterility as the defining feature of early-nineteenth-century collectors. Pons and Sauvageot, he writes, 'ne sont que des fureteurs, incapable de donner, à leurs trouvailles, une autre interprétation que le sens immédiat de ces dernières'.[91] Collectors such as himself, however, 'trouvent, pour ses richesses [...], un emploi plus splendide et plus sage; ils les jettent, idéalement, comme faisait réellement Cellini, dans la fournaise de leur pensée, pour accélerer la fonte d'une statue'.[92] Within *Le Cousin Pons* a similar operation is performed, as new meanings are generated through reference to existing works. In Balzac's novel, this is made possible through the paradigm of the museum, where artworks enter the public sphere. And yet the tone of *Le Cousin Pons* is insistently elegiac. In the museum, the pleasure of possession is lost. The idea of a secret, solitary, perfect communion with a work of art remains a potent idea in the text, offering an image of an impossible fulfilment.

91   Montesquiou, II, 92.
92   Montesquiou, II, 92.

CHAPTER 3

Collecting the Self

At one point in Jean Lorrain's 1900 novel *Monsieur de Phocas*, a minor classic of the decadent canon, the protagonist, the Duc de Fréneuse, is invited to a party hosted by the society painter, Claudius Ethal. Ethal lures Fréneuse to his studio by promising him that, 'j'ai tout un lot d'excentriques à vous montrer'.[1] A glance at the guest-list confirms Ethal's claim: an actress and the brother with whom she is incestuously involved, lesbian countesses, an aristocratic dandy, aesthete, and composer of second-rate experimental verse, opium eaters, ether-addicts, and a number of Ethal's compatriots, Englishmen who, in order to establish a reputation in fashionable Parisian society, have set themselves up as collectors. As Ethal explains to Fréneuse: 'Tous collectionnent quelque chose: celui-ci les fourreaux de sabre; celui-là, les boucles de ceintures de la reine Anne; cet autre, les souliers du roi de Rome ou les sabretaches du beau prince Murat; il faut bien faire quelque chose et, sinon s'occuper, occuper le monde de sa petite personne'.[2] Ethal's comments point towards the relationship between collecting and identity that is at the heart of much of the discourse surrounding collecting. For his guests, collecting is intended to function as a means to fashion and display a specific identity. This project does not seem to succeed, however, as none of these English collectors, discussed so contemptuously by Ethal himself, are named in the text; they are merely anonymous extras. In fact, they are presented chiefly as objects in Ethal's own collection of eccentrics, his cabinet of human curiosities, but rather uninteresting objects – part of the background scenery of the novel. Thus far from individuating them as they might hope, their collections serve merely to identify

1   Jean Lorrain, *Monsieur de Phocas* (Paris: La Table Ronde, 1992), p. 100.
2   Lorrain, p. 104.

them all as dedicated followers of a decadent fashion, decadent because the kind of collecting described here involves, as this chapter will argue, a falling away from the values of connoisseur collecting. This falling away operates both at the level of the thematics of the collection, and the level of systematics. First, the nature of the objects being collected – footwear and accoutrements of dress – have little obvious historical importance or even aesthetic value, but are readily recognisable as common fetish objects. Secondly, fashionable collecting, precisely because it is a phenomenon of fashion, undermines one of the major claims subtending much of the writing about collecting, particularly the discourse secreted by the practice itself in handbooks, guides and manuals, which is that collecting operates to produce autonomous and self-reliant subjects. The figure of the collector in the nineteenth century is thus a multivalent one, sometimes a figure of self-control and self-sufficiency, sometimes, as in the case of Ethal's guests, a mere cipher, lacking a will of his own, and sometimes, as we shall see, a figure of self-estrangement and lack. It is this multivalence that this chapter will explore, examining how the discourse surrounding collecting was structured by concerns surrounding identity, and shifting conceptions of selfhood.

Fashionable, Female Collecting in Balzac's
La Muse du département

From its inception in the 1840s the discourse surrounding the collector posited a distinction between what Horace de Viel-Castel called the 'collectionneur pur' and the 'collectionneur *fashionable*'. Viel-Castel deals with the latter only very briefly in his article, describing him as 'un personnage qui n'a ni caractère, ni passion, ni quoi que ce soit, et qui n'est qu'un produit de la mode'.[3] The fashionable collector is thus presented as essentially a

3   Viel-Castel, p. 128.

nullity, a discursive blank. And yet, if collecting was a fashionable pursuit, it was because it allowed individuals to lay claim to a certain distinction. Thus Rochefort, in his taxonomy of the different tribes that congregate at the hôtel Drouot, includes the 'poseurs' who collect 'pour avoir le droit de dire: *Ma galerie!*'.[4] Such collectors 'se recrutent presque toujours parmi les gens très riches qui se font amateurs de tableaux pour être quelque chose'.[5] Collecting allowed individuals with financial capital to accumulate cultural capital; it was a means of presenting oneself as a friend of the arts. Thus Champfleury tells the story of one Désirée Carton, a *demi-mondaine* who collects in order to 'donner à croire au public qu'elle a aussi de nobles passions artistiques'.[6] Champfleury generates ridicule here through baptizing this aspiring *collectionneuse* Désirée Carton, a name which turns her from a collector into a collectable. Not only does her first name identify her as the object of others' desire, but her surname recalls the cartons in which prints are sold. This assimilates her to the merchandise trafficked at the public auction house, but presents her not as a connoisseur piece but an empty receptacle, essentially a piece of disposable waste.

Almost twenty years later, Maupassant employed essentially the same discursive trick to mock fashionable female collectors. In an essay on 'Les Amateurs d'artistes', he uses the word 'amateur' pejoratively to designate those who affect a passion for the arts:

> L'amateur n'aime pas; il pose pour aimer, il se fait gloire d'aimer telle chose, il en tire vanité ou profit [...]. Il a sa galerie, sa collection, ses objets uniques qu'il montre avec orgueil, mais dont il ne se soucie, au fond, qu'en raison du plaisir ou de la réputation d'homme éclairé qu'ils lui donnent.[7]

---

4   Rochefort, p. 25.
5   Rochefort, p. 25.
6   Champfleury, *L'Hôtel*, p. 5.
7   Guy de Maupassant, 'Les Amateurs d'artistes', in *Chroniques inédites*, ed. by Pascal Pia, 2 vols (Paris: Maurice Gonon, 1979), II, 299–304 (p. 299). The article first appeared in *Gil Blas*, on 30 June 1885.

Maupassant goes on to say that such amateurs 'sont généralement des femmes', and notes that 'elles se subdivisent à l'infini'.[8] The main body of the article is dedicated to identifying these various subdivisions, producing a taxonomy of the different kinds of female *amateurs*. Just as Champfleury presented the female collector as a collectable, so Maupassant collects examples of female art lovers. In both cases, therefore, it is suggested that only men can be collectors; women are collected. We saw in chapter one that collecting was gendered as a masculine consumption regime in the nineteenth century, and both Champfleury and Maupassant superimpose on the image of the female collector the features of the fashionable collector, both of them presented as ersatz collectors.[9]

The categories of fashionable collector and female collector were presented as overlapping in one of the earliest novels with a collector as protagonist, Balzac's *La Muse du département*, which first appeared in *feuilleton* form in 1843. The action unfolds in Sancerre and Paris. The eponymous heroine is Dinah, a provincial bluestocking and would-be George Sand, unhappily married to a senescent miser, Polydore de La Baudraye. Polydore's great-grandfather, born the humble Monsieur Milaud, was a Calvinist who converted to Catholicism following the revocation of the Edict of Nantes, and as a result was given a title and lands confiscated from the original de La Baudraye family, who refused to convert. Polydore fears that if he dies without an heir, his lands – which he has considerably extended by purchasing the d'Anzy estate, complete with a magnificent château built by Philibert de L'Orme[10] – will revert to the original de La Baudraye family. Despite his dynastic ambitions, however, his marriage is childless. The crushing boredom of Dinah's married provincial life is alleviated by the homecoming visit of Etienne Lousteau and Horace Bianchon, two Sancerrois who have achieved success and some degree of celebrity in Paris, the former as a journalist and the latter as a physician. Dinah falls in love with Lousteau and, finding herself pregnant, abandons her husband

---

8   Maupassant, 'Les Amateurs', p. 299.
9   On collecting as a gendered form of consumption, see above, pp. 41–4.
10   This château is in fact fictional.

for the literary life in Paris. After having two more children with the perennially impecunious Lousteau, children claimed by Polydore as his own and taken back to Sancerre with him, a disillusioned Dinah returns at the end of the novel to her husband, who has by this time accrued not only heirs, but also a substantial fortune and a peerage. His dynastic ambitions are thus fully realized.

La Muse du département is partly an attack on *Sandisme*, denounced as a 'lèpre sentimentale' which has 'gâté beaucoup de femmes qui, sans leurs prétensions au génie, eussent été charmantes'.[11] In Dinah's case these pretensions find expression not only through the composition of second-rate poetry, the founding of a local literary society and the hosting of a *salon*, but also through collecting antique furniture.[12] In order to give 'des gages visibles de son amour pour les créations les plus remarquables de l'art',[13] Dinah begins by buying 'de fort belles choses en Nivernais et dans la haute-Loire'.[14] In addition, she acquires 'quelques raretés' presented to her by her admirers.[15] These utterly generic references to the objects that form the nucleus of Dinah's collection evince no very great degree of connoisseurship, but after five or six years, her house is crammed with mediæval and Renaissance pieces that function as:

> autant de ressorts qui, sur une question, faisaient jaillir des tirades sur Jean Goujon, sur Michel Columb, sur Germain Pilon, sur Boulle, sur Van Huysium, sur Boucher, ce grand peintre berrichon; sur Clodion le sculpteur en bois, sur les placages vénitiens, sur Brustolone, ténor italien, le Michel-Ange du chêne vert; sur les treizième,

---

11 Balzac, *La Muse*, p. 632.
12 On the sociological significance of antique furniture in the nineteenth century, and the fashion for retro-eclectic interior design, see Watson, pp. 57–82. According to Watson, 'the collection used as decor (in other words, the cultural phenomenon of the bibelot) purportedly originates among the aristocratic and artistic elite [...], then is popularized and vulgarized by the middle classes, and by women' (p. 57). *La Muse* provides an early description of this process of popularization and vulgarization by women.
13 Balzac, *La Muse*, p. 645.
14 Balzac, *La Muse*, p. 645.
15 Balzac, *La Muse*, p. 645.

quatorzième, quinzième, seizième et dix-septième siècles, sur les émaux de Bernard de
Palissy, sur ceux de Petitot, sur les gravures d'Albrecht Dürer (elle prononçait *Dur*),
sur les vélins enluminés, sur le gothique fleuri, flamboyant, orné, pur, à renverser les
vieillards et à enthousiasmer les jeunes gens.[16]

The text here offers us a list, at a moment in the text where we might well
expect to find one. But whereas we might anticipate a partial inventory of
the objects in Dinah's collection, we find instead an enumeration of names
and styles, the subjects on which Dinah has established herself as an expert.
Earlier in the text, the narrator notes that: 'Dans le désir d'entretenir son
intelligence au niveau du mouvement parisien, Mme de La Baudraye ne
souffrit chez personne ni propos vides, ni galanterie arriérée, ni phrases sans
valeur [...]. Aimant à parler des découvertes dans la science ou dans les arts
[...], elle parut remuer des pensées en remuant des mots à la mode'.[17] This
comment presents Dinah as a kind of simulacrum of a thinking subject,
whose words do not express thought but in fact conceal its absence. Dinah's
discourse is presented as basically empty; she operates at the level of the
signifier, a signifier which has split off from its signified. The presentation
of her collection reworks this idea of the free-floating signifier. In place
of a list of objects in Dinah's collection, we have a list of the subjects of
Dinah's 'tirades'. Language here threatens to annihilate objective reality, as
the objects in Dinah's collection disappear behind her discourse. Indeed,
they are presented as interchangeable in so far as they all function as pegs
on which she can hang her own erudition. This attitude is typical of the
fashionable collector rather than the pure collector, for whereas the former
collects in order to lay claim to distinction, the latter is concerned above
all with the quiddity of the object.

The inventory of names and styles that the text offers in place of the
inventory of objects in the collection, is in fact an anti-inventory. Writing
about Balzac's *L'Inventaire de l'Hôtel de la rue Fortunée*, the catalogue of
his own collection, Didier Maleuvre claims:

16   Balzac, *La Muse*, p. 646.
17   Balzac, *La Muse*, p. 641.

In describing his interior, Balzac does not run a survey of exchangeable entities, but recites a roll-call of identities. The intense focus on the object removes its word from the realm of connotation. Balzac's inventory harks back to a utopian language. Thus the word *candélabre* does not generically qualify its bearer – it is not just *a* candelabra – but stands for the particular candelabra set on the Louis XVI cabinet in the green room. [...]
As singularity, the object must remain undescribed. Description is too dialogic and metonymic a process to account for singularity; it always involves a doubling of the object into what it is not, has been, or will be, what surrounds it and what offsets it.
[...] Like an identity card, the inventory designates rather than describes its object.[18]

The representation of Dinah's collection in *La Muse de département* is in stark contrast to the representation of Balzac's collection in *L'Inventaire*, as discussed by Maleuvre. The list of names and styles in the novel betrays the commitment to singularity that is the distinguishing characteristic of the inventory proper. The entire tendency of the list in *La Muse* is away from the singular and towards the generic. Dinah's discourse does not name the objects in her collection; rather the objects simply serve as a signpost to other works, other styles. The entire inventory of names and styles is a function of a metonymic slide away from the objects themselves to the cultural context in which they were produced, and so to other works, other artists. The list itself prompts the reader to make a similar move, through the inclusion of Jean Boucher, whose name inevitably calls to mind that of François Boucher. If the inventory proper functions to identify the object in its uniqueness, the list in *La Muse* refuses to allow the object to reign in splendid isolation, but insists precisely on its context, on 'what it is not, has been, or will be, what surrounds it and what offsets it'. The objects are simply springboards for Dinah to flaunt her art historical knowledge, her connoisseurship. The somewhat chaotic composition of the list itself, in which no consistent taxonomy or organizational principle is readily apparent, serves, however, ironically to undermine Dinah's pretensions in this respect. This unstructured list functions primarily to draw attention to itself

18   Maleuvre, pp. 165–6.

as a list, and almost invites the reader to skip over it, ignoring Dinah's claims on our attention, her claims to be taken seriously as a connoisseur. The use of the word 'ressort' figures Dinah herself as an automaton, a clockwork collector mindlessly regurgitating information.

The use of the word 'ressort' here recalls an earlier reference to Dinah as a mechanized toy: 'Douée d'une belle mémoire, et de ce talent avec lequel certaines femmes se servent du mot propre, elle pouvait parler sur toute chose avec la lucidité d'un style étudié. [...] Ceux qui n'entendaient qu'une seule fois les airs de cette tabatière suisse s'en allaient étourdis.'[19] Here too, Dinah's pretensions to intellectual superiority are ironically undermined. By figuring her as a 'tabatière suisse', a mechanical toy that produces music, the narrator disparages her accomplishments in three distinct ways. First, the metaphor suggests that her intelligence is of a limited, and essentially mechanical nature, more a matter of a good memory than an original mind. Second, by likening her to a toy, the narrator suggests there is something essentially puerile about Dinah's accomplishments. Third, by figuring her conversation as music, the text ascribes to it a certain degree of inanity – it is presented as a mere jingle-jangle of sound. A few lines later the text again uses musical metaphors to describe Dinah's conversation at her salon; it consists of 'une sonate de paroles et des duos de dialectique'.[20] Here the music to which her discourse is compared is more serious that the cheap tinkling of a music box, but the metaphor nonetheless suggests that her conversation, while it may be pleasing to the ear, has no intellectual content. Thus there are two principal and intertwined strands of imagery used to describe Dinah's conversation in the novel, the mechanical and the musical, and both are woven into the discourse of collecting. A few paragraphs after the description of Dinah's collection, the narrator comments on her conversation thus: 'Elle se procura [...] une fort belle collection de phrases et d'idées, soit par ses lectures, soit en s'assimilant les pensées de ses habitués, et devint ainsi une espèce de serinette dont les airs partaient dès

19   Balzac, *La Muse*, p. 644.
20   Balzac, *La Muse*, p. 645.

qu'un accident de la conversation en accrochait la détente'.²¹ This comment once again uses the idea both of music (Dinah as 'espèce de serinette') and mechanism ('la détente') to trope Dinah's conversation, but it also ties these two notions to the idea of collecting, by presenting Dinah's conversation as a collection, patched together out of bits and pieces of other people's discourse. Dinah's collection, it will be remembered, is never inventoried within the text; the objects she acquires disappear behind her commentary on them. In place of Dinah's collection, the text offers the reader an image of Dinah's discourse as a collection, a hodgepodge of phrases and ideas borrowed from other people. Moreover, this is a collection that offers the spectacle of contingency, as Dinah's spurts of conversation are triggered by the 'accidents' of the general conversation. Rather than a well-organized collection, Dinah's collection of phrases has the quality of an accumulation of bric-a-brac. The text thus refuses to accredit Dinah with the title of connoisseur she seeks to claim for herself, using the discourse of collecting instead to figure her own ridiculousness.

If collecting is, on the one hand, associated with Dinah's attempts to claim an intellectual identity, it is also associated with her social ambitions, ambitions shared with Polydore. It is important to note that Dinah, the novel's central character, is not presented simply as a figure of ridicule. Indeed the trajectory of the novel is her passage from third-rate George Sand to 'une femme devenue vraiment supérieure'.²² Her real greatness does not lie in her intellectual efforts; rather, she is 'une femme dont les supériorités apparentes étaient fausses, et dont les supériorités cachées étaient réelles. Dinah, qui se rendait ridicule par les travers de son esprit, était grande par les qualités de son âme'.²³ The narrator acknowledges that it is a 'probité virile et cette force particulière aux ambitieux qui faisait la base de son caractère'.²⁴ Dinah is thus in possession of certain characteristics that are positively coded as masculine, a fact which would seem to

21 Balzac, *La Muse*, p. 644.
22 Balzac, *La Muse*, p. 783.
23 Balzac, *La Muse*, p. 651.
24 Balzac, *La Muse*, p. 753.

dislocate the system of gender dimorphism the text sets up. In order to realize her social goals within a patriarchal system, however, and to regain contact with her children, Dinah must jettison her bluestocking pretensions and confine her energies to acting in the private sphere. The text does not deny that woman can have an intellectual identity, but it denies that a mother and wife can have an intellectual identity. The opportunity for Dinah to become reconciled with Polydore emerges precisely because her husband, 'une fois nommé comte, pair de France et commandeur de la Légion d'honneur, eut la vanité de se faire bien représenter par une femme et une maison bien tenue'.[25] Dinah furnishes the de La Baudraye townhouse in impeccable taste, but at the same time she also refashions her own identity, and recodes her collecting practices. In one of the final scenes in the novel, the couple are shown in this house entertaining various notables, including the Baron de Nuncingen and the Marquis de Montriveau. Both Nuncingen and Montriveau compliment the de La Baudrayes on their fine furniture, and the husbands swap patronising comments about their wives' spending habits. Dinah herself 'fut charmante, spirituelle'.[26] Whereas earlier in the novel Dinah's collection of antique furniture was a springboard for her to display her own learning, at the end of the novel her taste and aesthetic judgement are placed in the service of interior design, a project entirely lacking the intellectual aspect of collecting. Dinah herself is the chief ornament of this interior. She is still identified as a collector, but now by Polydore, who brags that his wife collected antique furniture before it became fashionable: 'vous savez qu'elle a ramassé en 25, 26, et 27 pour plus d'un million de curiosités qui font d'Anzy un musée'.[27] Polydore, a figure distinguished by his miserliness, typically talks about the collection in financial terms, presenting it as a sound investment. More significant is simply the fact that he arrogates to himself the right to talk about it at all, controlling its meaning, and absorbing Dinah into it, putting her on display to his acquaintances.

25   Balzac, *La Muse*, p. 778.
26   Balzac, *La Muse*, p. 783.
27   Balzac, *La Muse*, p. 783.

Dinah herself, therefore, is not finally allowed to be a collector in her own right. The narrator ridicules her aspirations to connoisseurship, and her husband then appropriates to himself her success as a collector, assimilating her to the collection she has established. This transformation of the fashionable, female collector into collectable – a discursive move that, as we have seen, became a staple of the discourse surrounding collecting – highlights the fact that collecting was conceptualized in the nineteenth century as a process through which a particular kind of subjectivity was generated, one characterized by autonomy and self-reliance, and gendered as masculine. Polydore's insistence at the end of *La Muse* that Dinah's collection dates from the late 1820s, before such antique-hunting became fashionable, highlights one of the central paradoxes of fashionable collecting, which is that it was fashionable precisely because it enabled the individual to present himself as capable of exercising independent taste and judgement, as being more than a simple follower of fashion. In the handbooks and manuals for the collector that proliferated in the nineteenth century, collecting is often presented as being valuable precisely because it encourages the individual to rely solely on his own taste.

Collecting as Masculine Self-Fashioning

In a pamphlet entitled *Les Moutons de Panurge* (1861) which addresses the question, 'comment se forme une collection?',[28] Armand-Ambroise Rochoux insists that in acquiring a collection the buyer should be guided by his own preferences; the ideal collector is the man 'qui a su par l'étude acquérir une entière confiance en lui-même'.[29] Rochoux acknowledges

---

28   Armand-Ambroise Rochoux, *Les Moutons de Panurge: chapitres émouvants et dro-latiques sur les estampes, les experts, les catalogues et les collectionneurs* (Paris: Delion, 1861), p. 22.
29   Rochoux, p. 27.

that the novice collector will probably be influenced by fashion, like the eponymous sheep who 'acceptent tout simplement les sentiments, les enthousiasmes qui s'agitent autour d'eux'.[30] Through the process of forming his own collection, however, the collector will achieve independence of judgement; one fine day 'il se prend à admirer tout seul, sans le secours d'autrui'.[31] Collecting is thus presented as a process of individuation. The next generation of collectors would continue to promote the practice in similar terms. Edmond Bonnaffé, for example, writing in 1881, claimed that the aspiring collector must undergo a long apprenticeship 'avant d'être maître de soi', but also that the fully-fledged amateur 'est libre; il ne reconnaît pour juges que son goût et sa conscience',[32] while Spire Blondel, in his 1884 interior design handbook, *L'Art Intime* cites with approval Charles Asselineau's description of a private collection: 'l'âme d'un homme palpite à travers ce charmant chaos, et s'illumine d'une sorte d'éclat domestique et personnel, malgré sa diversité, qui fait voir qu'avant tout il y a là un maître, un libre esprit qui ne relève que de lui-même et de sa fantaisie'.[33] Rochoux, Blondel and Bonnaffé all have recourse to the language of self-mastery and autonomy to describe the collector, presenting it as a means through which a self-determining subject could emerge.

At the same time, in the Asselineau formulation adopted by Blondel, the collection, 'ce charmant chaos', is no longer organized according to any intersubjectively valid taxonomy or historical schema; its principle of coherence lies in the soul of the collector. A similar conception of the collection is apparent in Charles Cousin's *Racontars illustrés d'un vieux collectionneur*. This text is a virtual tour of the writer's collection, the various objects therein each eliciting an anecdote. In the introduction the author inscribes his work in an autobiographical tradition, citing the examples of

30   Rochoux, p. 31.
31   Rochoux, p. 32.
32   Bonnaffé, *Physiologie*, pp. 6 and 27.
33   Spire Blondel, *L'Art intime et le goût en France* (Paris: Rouveyre & Blond, 1884), p. 353. The Asselineau quotation originally appeared in Charles Asselineau, *Mélanges curieux et anecdotiques tirés d'une collection de lettres autographes et de documents historiques* (Paris: Techener, 1861), p. xiii.

Montaigne, Saint-Simon and Rousseau – all those whose subject is always first and foremost 'le moi'.[34] He explicitly warns the reader not to expect 'aucune classification raisonnée des modestes bibelots que reproduisent ces images, et surtout aucune dissertation didactique sur le tableau, le dessin, le faïence, le bouquin'.[35] Rather the book is intended as 'un petit monument' to himself.[36] In this respect, Cousin's book seems to fit into the paradigm of subjective collecting which Krzysztof Pomian has suggested emerged in the nineteenth century as a result of the rise of the public museum: 'les collections particulières sont-elles déchargées de la fonction cognitive s'agissant de tout ce qui est muséalisé [...]. Elles n'ont plus à respecter les impératives d'un classement prétendant à une validité inter-subjective [...]. Chaque collection particulière peut donc devenir, sans réserve, une expression de la personnalité du collectionneur. Elle peut traduire non seulement son savoir et son goût mais aussi ses nostalgies, ses rêves, ses fantasmes. Elle peut être son œuvre, ce qu'il laissera à la postérité'.[37] Within this paradigm of subjective collecting, the collection became a narcissistic space in which the collector could fondly contemplate his own image.

A Rebours: The Monadic Self

The very quintessence of the narcissistic collector is Des Esseintes, the hero of Huysmans' seminal decadent novel, *A Rebours*, first published in 1884. Disgusted by the venality, vulgarity, triviality and hypocrisy of the society in which he lives, Des Esseintes buys a house in Fontenay, where he lives as a recluse. The novel itself is dedicated in large part to the description

---

34 Charles Cousin, *Racontars illustrés d'un vieux collectionneur* (Paris: La Librairie de l'Art, 1887), p. i.
35 Cousin, p. xvi.
36 Cousin, p. vii.
37 Pomian, 'Collections: une typologie historique', p. 18.

of the decor of the house, and the inventory of the various collections Des Esseintes installs therein: books, art, perfumes, and flowers *inter alia*. The retreat to Fontenay is very much a movement of introversion on Des Esseintes' part, a flight from the world to the self. Huysmans' novel can usefully be read alongside a number of texts on interior design produced in the late nineteenth century, which promoted the idea that the private interior should be a space for self-exploration. Henry Havard, whose *L'Art dans la maison* was the official design handbook of the Third Republic, railed against the professionalization of interior decoration, on the basis that the employment of interior designers inevitably meant that the home became a reflection not of the proprietor's tastes but of somebody else's. He also lamented the rise of mass-production, as a result of which everything becomes impregnated with 'ce goût moyen, qui convient à tout le monde et ne satisfait personne'.[38] Octave Uzanne echoed these criticisms in an article on interior design which appeared in 1892 in *L'Art et l'idée*, the symbolist journal he edited, in which he bemoaned the ubiquity of 'des meubles quelconques affreusement fabriqués pour la consommation générale'.[39] The title of this article, 'Notes sur le goût intime et la décoration personnelle de l'Habitation Moderne', is an allusion to Viollet-le-Duc's 1875 manifesto of domestic architecture, *Habitations Modernes*, in which he claimed that one of the defining features of modernity was that 'chacun veut être chez soi', and went on to suggest that:

> quand on a la saine fantaisie d'être chez soi, il faut d'abord savoir ce qu'on est soi-même. [...] L'habitation personnelle peut seule développer l'habitude d'être chez soi, comme l'habitude d'être chez soi impose un caractère particulier à l'habitation: les deux conditions se commandent.[40]

Thus Viollet suggests that private space is instrumental in fashioning the self. This idea parallels those discussions of collecting in which it is conceived

---

38   Henry Havard, *L'Art dans la maison* (Paris: Rouveyre & Blond, 1884), p. 38.

39   Octave Uzanne, 'Notes sur le goût intime et la décoration personnelle de l'Habitation Moderne', *L'Art et l'idée*, 2 (1892), 257–76 (p. 260).

40   Eugène Emmanuel Viollet-le-Duc, *Habitations Modernes*, 2 vols (Paris: Morel, 1875–1877), I, p. 2.

as a process through which the self emerges, and it also forms the basis for Uzanne's ideas on interior design. For Uzanne, the private interior should be a material extension of the self, every nook and cranny filled with the proprietor's own identity. He laments 'l'absence absolu de caractère dans la majorité des installations', a function of the tyranny of mass production, and dreams of writing an interior design book that will be a 'dithyrambe du goût individu'.[41]

Uzanne never wrote such a book, but if he had it would surely have looked very much like *A Rebours*. The rejection of the mass market that Uzanne and Havard promote is enacted by Des Esseintes, who bespeaks all his furnishings, even his books. The house at Fontenay is an extreme example of the subjectivist turn in interior design at the end of the nineteenth century. Ensconsed there, Des Esseintes, living entirely apart from the world, aspires to a wholly self-sufficient identity, untinged with alterity. He adopts a nocturnal lifestyle on the grounds that at night 'on était mieux chez soi, plus seul', and it is therefore possible to experience 'une satisfaction toute singulière, que connaissent les travailleurs attardés alors que, soulevant les rideaux des fenêtres, ils s'aperçoivent autour d'eux que tout est éteint, que tout est muet, que tout est mort'.[42] The fantasy of being the only person left alive in the world indicates the extent of Des Esseintes' solipsism, but in his search for hermetic self-enclosure, Des Esseintes appears typical of the collector described by Jean Baudrillard in *Le Système des objets*.

As discussed in chapter one, Baudrillard begins his account by distinguishing between two ways of relating to objects: practical usage, which 'relève du champ de totalisation pratique du monde par le sujet', and possession, which '[relève] d'une entreprise de totalisation abstraite du sujet par lui-même en dehors du monde'.[43] Possession finds its most

41 Uzanne, 'Notes sur le goût intime', p. 260. On the subjectivist turn in interior design and its relation to both *psychologie nouvelle* and Symbolism, see Debora Silverman, *Art Nouveau in Fin-de-Siècle France: Politics, Psychology, and Style* (Berkeley: University of California Press, 1989), pp. 75–106.

42 Joris-Karl Huysmans, *A Rebours*, ed. by Rose Fortassier (Paris: Imprimerie Nationale, 1981), p. 78.

43 Baudrillard, p. 121.

perfect expression in the collection, where each object, wrenched free of its context of origin, is integrated into a new system, where it refers only to other objects in the collection, and ultimately to the collector himself: 'on se collectionne toujours soi-même'.[44] The house at Fontenay is precisely such a hall of mirrors, reflecting only the collector, Des Esseintes himself. Baudrillard suggests that the principle function of the collection is to obscure our knowledge of the irreversibility of time, 'ce que peut avoir d'angoissant sa continuité et la singularité absolue des évènements'.[45] Organized into a collection, objects function to interpose 'entre le devenir irréversible du monde et nous, un écran discontinu, classifiable, réversible, répétitif à merci, une frange du monde qui nous appartient, docile à la main et à l'esprit'.[46] The collector seeks in his collection a refuge from the agonizing knowledge of his own inevitable slide towards death. Indeed, the retreat to Fontenay is motivated at least in part by Des Esseintes' health problems, and his desire to arrest the progress of a disease that has already wrecked his physical health.

Susan Stewart, in her rich and allusive account of collecting – an account which draws largely on the discourse generated by the activity of collecting in handbooks, guides and catalogues from England and America from the seventeenth to the twentieth centuries – echoes many of Baudrillard's ideas, but translates them to a historicist rather than psychoanalytic register. For Stewart, 'the archetypal collection is Noah's Ark, a world [...] which erases its context of origin'.[47] The defining feature of the collection is its ahistoricism: 'the collection replaces history with *classification*, with

---

44   Baudrillard, p. 128.
45   Baudrillard, p. 132.
46   Baudrillard, p. 132. Baudrillard suggests that collecting in this respect functions in the same way as habit, a claim that resonates with the observation of the nineteenth-century doctor, Jean Baptiste Félix Descuret, who suggests, in his psychosocial treatise *La Médecine des passions* (Paris: Béché jeune et Labé, 1841), that the 'manie des collections' is a variant of the 'manie de l'ordre', which compels people to follow exactly the same routine every day (pp. 741–51).
47   Susan Stewart, *On Longing: Narratives of the Miniature, the Gigantic, the Souvenir, the Collection* (Baltimore: John Hopkins University Press, 1984), p. 152.

order beyond the realm of temporality. In the collection, time is not something to be restored to an origin; rather, all time is made simultaneous or
synchronous within the collector's world'.[48] Many of the texts on which
Stewart draws promote eclecticism in the collection, and this is precisely
because eclecticism 'marks the heterogeneous organization of the self, a
self capable of transcending the accidents and dispersions of historical
reality'.[49] The eclectic collection 'thereby acquires an aura of transcendence and independence that is symptomatic of the middle class's values
regarding personality'.[50] Where Baudrillard suggests that the collection
functions as an immortality fetish, through which the collector disavows
knowledge of death, Stewart suggests that it can function as a means of
fashioning a historically specific form of subjectivity, one that disavows
the subject's historicity.

Stewart's comments can usefully be read alongside the account of Des
Esseintes' collecting habits in *A Rebours*. The house at Fontenay – explicitly figured as a latter-day Noah's Ark: 'une arche immobile et tiède où il
se réfugierait loin de l'incessant déluge de la sottise humaine'[51] – is clearly
designed to create the illusion that its proprietor lives outside history.
Its retro-eclectic furnishings mean that within the house different peri-
ods and different places are juxtaposed, co-existing in a single space. Des
Esseintes does not occupy specific co-ordinates on the axes of history and
geography. His refusal to be tied to history is also apparent in his choice of
specific artworks. The artists he admires above all are Redon and Moreau.
The drawings of the former are described as 'en dehors de tout';[52] they
cannot be historically located. Similarly the work of the latter appeals to
Des Esseintes because of its eclecticism: 'le peintre semblait d'ailleurs avoir
voulu affirmer sa volonté de rester hors des siècles'.[53] As an artist, Moreau

48   Stewart, p. 151.
49   Stewart, p. 158.
50   Stewart, p. 159.
51   Huysmans, p. 72.
52   Huysmans, p. 133.
53   Huysmans, p. 126.

'ne dérivait de personne'.[54] He is self-created, and realizes as an artist Des Esseintes' own aspirations towards an absolute autonomy. In *A Rebours*, therefore, the collection is a space from which history is expelled. Fontenay does nonetheless differ from Noah's ark in one significant respect: Noah has no choice as to what to include in his collection, the inventory of which is drawn up by God, whereas Des Esseintes is wholly free to follow his own fancy. Fontenay is not a space where classification triumphs over history if classification is understood as an objective schema immanent in the world, and not merely something that exists in Des Esseintes' mind. Rather history is displaced by a monadic conception of the self.

The aspiration to escape from the order of time shapes not merely the representational content of Huysmans' novel, however, but also its formal characteristics. *A Rebours* is famously distinguished by an extraordinary priority of description over action; it strains at conventional definitions of the novel by having the barest possible plot. The story of how Des Esseintes came to reject the world is relegated to paratextual status, contained in a 'Notice' which traces Des Esseintes' intellectual development; the novel proper begins once he has retreated to Fontenay, where history is excluded and nothing really happens, where narrative gives way to inventory. Collecting in *A Rebours* obstructs narrative, forcing it to yield to description. Its obsession with detail has led many critics to invoke the figure of the collector's decadent brother, the fetishist, when discussing the novel, diagnosing *A Rebours* a fetishistic text.[55] Françoise Gaillard has usefully used this concept in her reading of the text, '*A Rebours*: une écriture de la crise'. The crisis to which her title alludes is a crisis of nature as a stable referent. She writes of the book that:

---

54   Huysmans, p. 129.
55   See, for example, Fernbach, pp. 48–51. Fernbach discusses the way in which Huysmans' fetishistic aesthetic is used to prop up the discourse of gender difference in the novel. Des Esseintes is thus read as a fetishist in the classical, conservative, Freudian sense, a man who disavows difference, committed to the reproduction of the same. For a more general account of the centrality of fetishism in decadent aesthetics, see Bernheimer.

Levant le voile épais du silence prudent, [*A Rebours*] manifestait qu'il n'y avait rien derrière les signes de la tribu, rien de stable ni d'assuré à quoi ils puissent, comme on le faisait accroire, se rapporter de façon certaine. Rien ne les cautionnait, rien ne se portait leur garant, bref les signes ne renvoyaient qu'à eux-mêmes dans un mouvement circulaire qui excluait toute notion d'extériorité.[56]

Des Esseintes himself, of course, embraces the simulacrum over the genuine article, as when he eschews the opportunity to visit London, preferring simply to pack his bags, buy a guide book, and eat beef in a restaurant in Paris filled with English visitors. But Des Esseintes also goes a step further than this, calling into question the very distinction between the simulacrum and the original, the artificial and the natural, when he chooses for his greenhouse flowers that are natural, but look artificial. Gaillard argues that in this respect, Des Esseintes should be seen not as standing in opposition to the spirit of the age, but as exaggerating to the point of ridicule its fetishistic tendencies: 'C'est par ce passage à la limite qu'*A Rebours* découvraient la vérité encore confuse d'un système fondé sur la fétichisation de ses productions.'[57] Commodity fetishism itself privileges the sign over the referent, and Des Esseintes' actions in the novel merely serve to trace the crisis that unfolds in this situation.

According to Gaillard, this crisis has implications at the level of both society and representation. At the social level, the novel betrays an entropic vision in which the collapse of feudal structures and the dawn of democracy is presented as leading to a gradual dissolution of difference, a homogenizing and levelling-down of society. At the level of representation the triumph of the sign undermines the mimetic postulate on which naturalist writing is based. Hence the strange, hallucinatory style of the text, the most salient characteristic of which are the lengthy inventories:

56 Françoise Gaillard, '*A Rebours*: une écriture de la crise', *Revue des sciences humaines*, 43.170–1 (April–September 1978), 111–22 (p. 112).
57 Gaillard, '*A Rebours*', p. 112.

> Le réel privé [...] de l'exorbitant privilège de se confondre avec l'être, se défait dans
> l'écriture qui le prend en charge; il s'y déconstruit en ses détails, s'y fractionne en ses
> éléments, s'y monnaye dans les signes qui le signifient et ne le représentent plus, s'y
> décline en un paradigme indéfiniment ouvert. Sans chercher par leur addition à en
> produire un équivalent ou un substitut, sans se proposer de rivaliser avec la belle
> unité imaginaire, les fragments s'ajoutent aux fragments, et l'écrivain procède par
> inventaire.[58]

The novel thus enacts a challenge to nature as a stable referent, a guarantee of
authenticity and absolute value, but Gaillard suggests that it also ultimately
stages the triumphant return of nature, as the truth of the flesh, mortality, reasserts itself, and Des Esseintes is forced to abandon Fontenay and
return to Paris. Des Esseintes, although he 'semble aspirer au règne d'une
matière de pure fabrication, qui ne doive rien à la nature',[59] cannot fulfil
such dreams: 'Faute de pouvoir remporter ce triomphe définitif sur la nature
et sur le mal qui l'habite – la mort – il se contente de dénaturer la matière
naturelle jusqu'à sa quasi-désubstantialisation.'[60] Ultimately, therefore, Des
Esseintes reaches a dead end, and the end of the novel, which leaves him on
the cusp of embracing Catholicism, offers religion as a way to escape from
this sterile tyranny of signs. Gaillard thus suggests that the novel contains a
critique of its hero's ideology, and ultimately urges a return to the religious
and feudal values of the Middle Ages, in which a transcendental signified
provided a guarantee of meaning. The novel grounds this critique in the
materiality of the body. It is the frailty of Des Esseintes' body that destroys
the ideal of the monadic self underpinning his project. As a decadent hero,
Des Esseintes valorizes the artificial over the natural, but ultimately his
biological body scuppers his project. His illness forces him to pack up his
collections and return to Paris; his illness elicits the narrative that finally
overcomes description in the novel.

---

58   Gaillard, 'A Rebours', p. 118.
59   Gaillard, 'A Rebours', p. 122.
60   Gaillard, 'A Rebours', p. 122.

Monsieur de Phocas: The Dispersed Self

Quite a different image of the collector is presented in Lorrain's 1900 novel *Monsieur de Phocas*. The protagonist, the Duc de Fréneuse, is a fabulously wealthy and reclusive gemstone collector 'sombré dans l'occultisme et la névrose',[61] and a figure who bears more than a passing resemblance to Des Esseintes. Indeed the novel is clearly heavily indebted to *A Rebours*,[62] but far from being a second-rate rehash of its more famous predecessor, or a mere compendium of decadent clichés, as John R. Reed has suggested,[63] Lorrain's text reconfigures some of the ideas in *A Rebours* in a productive fashion, particularly in its handling of the thematics of the collection. Formally the novel is very different from *A Rebours*, and less startlingly unconventional. The main body of the novel consists of Fréneuse's diaries, which trace the story of his relationship with Claudius Ethal, fashionable society painter and corrupter of souls. This is also the story of the progress of the Duke's neurosis, as Ethal, the evil genius of the novel, claims to be able to cure Fréneuse but in fact delights in exacerbating his illness, a fact which Fréneuse belatedly realizes, finally killing Ethal to escape his maleficent influence. Following his crime he adopts the name Monsieur de Phocas and decides to leave France to travel in North Africa. Prior to his departure, however, he confides his diaries to a journalist, and the encounter between the journalist and M. de Phocas forms the opening chapter of the novel, narrated by the journalist.

61   Lorrain, p. 19.
62   It is also clearly indebted to Wilde's *The Picture of Dorian Gray*. On the relationship between Wilde's novel and *Monsieur de Phocas*, see the excellent article by Michael du Plessis, 'Unspeakable Writing: Jean Lorrain's *Monsieur de Phocas*', *French Forum*, 27 (2002), 65–98, which apporaches the novel from a queer studies perspective. On the treatment of sexuality in the novel, see also Watson, pp. 184–7, in which she suggests that the logic of seriality that animates the collector defies the Œdipal logic of heteronormativity.
63   John R. Reed, *Decadent Style* (Athens, Ohio: Ohio University Press, 1985), pp. 50–4.

The reason Fréneuse-Phocas chooses this particular journalist as his confidant is because both are members of the confraternity of gemstone and jewellery collectors. Collecting is the principle interest in the Duke's life. He tells the journalist:

> Voilà des années que je souffre d'une chose bleue et verte. Lueur de gemme ou regard, je suis amoureux, pis, envoûté, possédé d'une certaine transparence glauque; c'est comme une faim en moi. Cette lueur, je la cherche en vain dans les prunelles et dans les pierres, mais aucun œil humain ne la possède. Parfois, je la trouve dans l'orbite vide d'un œil de statue ou sous les paupières peintes d'un portrait, mais ce n'est qu'un leurre: la clarté s'éteint à peine apparue. Je suis surtout amoureux du passé.[64]

Thus Fréneuse-Phocas is stretched on the rack of a desire he can never satisfy, hunting a chimera. He discusses his inner life in terms of both possession by external, demonic forces, and in terms of emptiness, an unsatisfied, and apparently insatiable hunger. The book thus opens with a statement of desire unfulfilled; before we even start reading the main narrative we know that there will be no satisfying closure, no consummation of this desire for 'une chose bleue et verte' which is a point of continuity between Fréneuse and Phocas. The story of the Duc de Fréneuse, however it may end, does not end because he finds what he is looking for.

What exactly is it that Fréneuse is looking for? As in *A Rebours*, Fréneuse's collecting is closely bound up with the anguish generated by the knowledge of our own mortality. In Fréneuse's case, collecting is closely if obscurely linked to the recurrent homicidal impulses that are prominent in the bundle of symptoms that constitute his illness. In bed with a woman, he is tempted to strangle her: 'la palpitation de la vie m'a toujours rempli d'une étrange rage de destruction, et voilà deux fois que je me surprends des idées de meutre dans l'amour.'[65] The paradox at the heart of his murderous impulses is that he would kill someone because he is horrified at the idea of dying. He wishes to stop his lover breathing because it is her breathing that speaks of her mortality: 'Elle dormait et, de ses lèvres, sortait une petite

64   Lorrain, pp. 18–19.
65   Lorrain, p. 27.

odeur de pourriture'.[66] Everywhere around him Fréneuse sees decay, the slow but ineluctable unfolding of death within life. Death presents itself as an escape from these processes, and our agonized knowledge thereof. Fréneuse's obsession with gemstones – mineral forms that offer a glimpse of immortality – seems a function of this preoccupation with decay. He also frequents museums: 'je suis surtout amoureux du passé'.[67] He spends entire days in the Louvre, and it is in a Roman cameo, or a Greek statue that he finds something that he is looking for: 'Il n'y a de vraiment beaux que les visages des statues. Leur immobilité est autrement vivante que les grimaces de nos physiognomies'.[68] These statues do not belong to the sublunar world; they inhabit eternity. They are precisely '*autrement* vivant': unlike us, their life is not infected by decay, they remain impervious to the action of time.

Thus in both *A Rebours* and *Monsieur de Phocas* collecting is at least partly an attempt to escape from the order of time. In Huysmans' novel, Des Esseintes' flight from history is part and parcel of his flight from the world into the self, a self conceptualized as monadic, bounded and self-sufficient, and figured in the novel through the notion of the collection. This project is sabotaged, however, by Des Esseintes' body, by the undeniable progress of physical decay. The novel thus offers a critique of the monadic conception of selfhood embodied in the triumphant collector, a critique grounded in corporeal reality. In *Monsieur de Phocas*, on the other hand, the discourse of collecting functions quite differently. Whereas in *A Rebours* the collection is always presented as complete (Des Esseintes, having organized his library, notes with apparent satisfaction that 'sa bibliothèque [...] ne s'augmenterait probablement jamais plus'),[69] Lorrain's text is about the impossibility of ever completing the collection. Through his collecting, Fréneuse seeks to fill 'l'irréparable vide qui est en moi',[70] but it is apparent from the opening chapter of the novel that such fulfilment is never found.

66 Lorrain, p. 13.
67 Lorrain, p. 19.
68 Lorrain, p. 24.
69 Huysmans, p. 276.
70 Lorrain, p. 176.

Rather than offering the collection as the image of fulfilment – albeit one shown to be illusory, as in *A Rebours* – *Monsieur de Phocas* explicitly presents collecting as the function of an ontological lack. Rather than a principle of opposition to narrative, collecting in *Monsieur de Phocas* is the very engine of the narrative, driving the plot forward as Fréneuse pursues his quest for 'une chose bleue et verte'.[71] Fréneuse is a figure not of self-mastery, but of self-estrangement and self-loss. If the discourse surrounding collecting traditionally posited the collector as the transcendental signified of the collection, what happens in *Monsieur de Phocas*, I want to suggest, is that the collector is recreated in the image of the collection.

The frame narrative of the novel introduces us to Fréneuse through the journalist, who knows him as a solitary and eccentric gemstone collector, shrouded in mystery, and the object of much rumour, speculation and gossip amongst his peers. He is thought to possess several notable collections:

> Fréneuse possédait, dans l'hôtel de la rue de Varenne, tout un musée secret de pierres dures, célèbres parmi les amateurs et les marchands. Il avait aussi, disait-on, rapporté de l'Orient, des souks de Tunis et des bazars de Smyrne, tout un trésor de bijoux anciens, de tapis précieux, d'armes rares et de poisons violents, mais Fréneuse vivait sans amis, nul n'était admis à visiter l'hôtel familial.[72]

Here we find the familiar discursive move through which the collector and his collection are presented as images of each other. The secret of the museum to which none is granted access figures the secret of Fréneuse's life. The frame narrative thus turns the Duke himself into an object of the reader's curiosity. This curiosity is further piqued in the following chapter, which opens with the transcription of a conversation about Fréneuse. This conversation consists of a number of interlocuters – it is impossible to tell how many – trading bits of gossip and hearsay, speculating as to the Duke's age, his alleged opium addiction, his possible debauchery. The direct speech is quoted without attribution in all but two cases, where

71   Lorrain, p. 18.
72   Lorrain, p. 16.

comments are ascribed to a de Mazel and to a Chameroy, about whom no information is offered and who make no further appearance in the novel. The interlocutors are thus effectively anonymized, and the conversation is presented as merely one example of 'tous ces chuchotements sourds de la médisance et de l'opinion publique intriguée et mystifiée', exemplifying 'toute la sottise des mensonges et des présomptions'.[73] The text offers the reader an image of Fréneuse, but one that is stitched together out of the assorted odds and ends of society tittle-tattle and gossip.

It is also one that is characterized by incoherence and confusion. No solid, totalizing image of the Duke can be gleaned from the conversation about him. Synecdoche structures the description of his physical appearance. The first speaker draws attention to 'la douceur fondante de ses mains toujours glacées'.[74] The second one claims that: 'pour moi, c'est surtout l'œil qui était inquiétant, cet œil pâlement bleu, d'une dureté de pierre dure'.[75] The use of synecdoche here resonates with the journalist's description of Fréneuse in the opening chapter, which focussed on ornamentation and dress – it is the bracelet he wears that first enables the journalist to identify Monsieur de Phocas as the erstwhile Duc de Fréneuse – and on isolated parts of his body: 'ce frêle et blanc poignet de *fin race*', his 'main de princesse et de courtisane'.[76] The Duke's body is fragmented within the text, broken down into various discrete parts. These parts themselves seem to carry contradictory meanings. Thus his age is one of the subjects of debate, with one speaker asserting that he is over forty, another claiming that he looks 28. A third offers an explanation for these two contrasting positions, stating, 'La face est horriblement vieille, le corps est demeuré jeune'.[77] This explanation does not, however, mediate the two views so much as simply restate the issue as an insoluble conundrum. Fréneuse's body appears wholly unnatural, and unreadable.

73   Lorrain, p. 22.
74   Lorrain, p. 20.
75   Lorrain, p. 20.
76   Lorrain, pp. 14 and 15.
77   Lorrain, p. 20.

These motifs are developed in the fullest description of his body, offered by one of the speakers in the following terms: 'Cette pâleur pourrissante, la crispation de ces mains effilés, plus japonaises de formes que des crysanthèmes, ce profil d'arabesque et cette maigreur de vampire, tout cela ne vous a jamais donné à réfléchir?'.[78] This description presents Fréneuse first as an amorphous blob of white, for the adjective 'pourrissante' carries among its connotations the idea of a loss of physical integrity, a process of spreading – oozing, trickling, seeping and leaking – out. Thus the Duke is initially described as colour without form, or more accurately colourlessness without form. The reference to the 'crispation de ces mains effilés', as well as suggesting a nervous disorder through the idea of a perpetual 'crispation', also transforms Fréneuse into one of the myriad Japanese *bibelots* that cluttered the fashionable interiors of the fin-de-siècle. This recalls the journalist's observation in the opening chapter that the Duke had 'une tête semblable à celles que l'on voit, signées Clouet ou Porbus, dans la galerie du Louvre consacrée aux Valois'.[79] In both cases the Duke is presented as an art object, and an artificial creation rather than a natural being. The following reference to 'ce profil d'arabesque' again stresses the unreadability of Fréneuse's physiology. It also involves a sudden leap from Japan to the Arab world, creating an effect of disjunction and discontinuity that strengthens the idea that the Duke is an irreducibly heterogenous being. Finally the reference to the vampire recalls the morbid image of the Duke as a 'pâleur pourrissante', and presents him as an ambivalent being, straddling life and death.

Fréneuse's body is thus presented in the text as thoroughly unnatural. The text itself offers an apt image for its depiction of the Duke's body when, in the main narrative, Fréneuse goes with some acquaintances to see a nightclub singer, and is afflicted with the impression that: 'Je n'écoutais pas chanter une femme vivante, mais un automate aux pièces disparates et montées de bric et de broc, peut-être pis encore, une morte hâtivement reconstituée avec des déchets d'hôpital, quelque macabre fantaisie d'interne

---

78   Lorrain, pp. 21–2.
79   Lorrain, p. 14.

imaginée sur les bancs d'amphithéâtre'.[80] Later, Fréneuse will describe himself as 'un automate, c'est-à-dire un mort',[81] which recalls the description of the nightclub singer. Indeed, the notion of the 'automate aux pièces disparates', a 'macabre fantaisie d'interne' seems applicable to Fréneuse himself, who is a kind of fin-de-siècle Frankenstein's monster, pieced together out of various decadent topoi: vampirism, orientalism, artificiality. Fréneuse the collector is himself a collection of clichés.

The description of Fréneuse offered by one of the speakers in the frame narrative ends with a question, one that seems directed as much towards the reader as to his fellow interlocutors: 'tout cela ne vous a jamais donné à réfléchir?'. The frame narrative thus sets up a basic mystery: who is the Duke de Fréneuse, *really*? The journalist claims to hold the key to this conundrum: 'C'était à moi qu'était échu, de par sa volonté, l'honneur ou la honte de déchiffrer sa vie et d'en connaître enfin l'énigme consignée aux pages d'un manuscrit'.[82] The diaries promise to give us privileged access to Fréneuse's consciousness. In place of the image of the Duke offered in the frame narrative, an image constructed out of bits and pieces, the diaries, 'entièrement écrites de sa main', will, we are lead to expect, offer us the key to the Duke's identity.[83]

In fact, the diaries serve to undermine the notion that Fréneuse has a stable, coherent and unitary identity, and they do so by repeating the discursive moves made in the frame narrative. Thus throughout the main narrative the Duke's body is subject to the same processes of denaturalization and dematerialization as occurred in the frame narrative. In his comments prefacing the diaries, the journalist notes that although entirely written by Fréneuse, the Duke's diaries are 'de diverses écritures (car l'écriture de l'homme change avec ses états d'âme, et le graphologue reconnaît, à un trait de plume, la chute d'un honnête homme devenu un coquin)'.[84] On the one hand, this comment indicates the extent of the Duke's instability,

80 Lorrain, p. 54.
81 Lorrain, p. 177.
82 Lorrain, p. 22.
83 Lorrain, p. 22.
84 Lorrain, p. 22.

but on the other hand it presupposes an intimate connection between the body and the soul, and expresses complete confidence in the hermeneutic powers of the graphologist, who can produce a psychological profile of a man through the traces left by his body. The reader, however, has no access to these traces; when the manuscript is transformed into a book, this evidence disappears. As members of the reading public, the text available to us has been produced by a mechanical press. The Duke's corporeality is lost to us. At the same time, Fréneuse's body, as described within the main narrative, is subject to strange transformations. His hand is first described by the journalist as 'délicieusement pâle et transparente, main de princesse et de courtisane'.[85] This is in stark contrast to the hands of Ethal, another character whose body is similarly dismembered through metonymy. His hairy chest and his hideous hands are the features that fascinate Fréneuse. Listening to Ethal recount the history of one of the wax sculptures he has produced, Fréneuse becomes absorbed by the spectacle of 'l'énorme main aux phalanges velues qu'il crispait, comme une serre [...], en vérité, une serre d'oiseau de proie, dont trois bagues étranges accentuaient encore le caractère féroce et animal'.[86] Later, the image of Ethal's monstrous hand will function metaphorically to describe his relationship with Fréneuse as one of predator and prey: 'Il est le mauvais esprit de ma vie, la main d'ombre étendue sur mes actes et sur mes pensées [...], la serre de proie et d'agonie, qui étreint mon impuissance et, si je ne m'y soustrais, la pousserait au crime.'[87] At the moment towards the end of the novel at which Fréneuse attempts to strangle a prostitute, however (the incident which precipitates the final meeting with and murder of Ethal), he describes his own hands in terms which recall those of Ethal, noting with horror that they have become 'de hideuses mains d'étrangleur, [...] elles sont devenues hideuses, mes mains.'[88] Fréneuse's body thus appears mutable, capable of being remoulded as his psychological state varies. The plasticity of Fréneuse's body, his unnatural,

85   Lorrain, p. 14.
86   Lorrain, p. 90.
87   Lorrain, p. 187.
88   Lorrain, p. 218.

unreadable, protean body, which the text decomposes and recomposes at will, means that the Duke, far from being the source from which the text emanates, appears rather dispersed within it.

The absence of a stable body in the text is closely related to the absence of a stable voice. Fréneuse's first-person narrative never appears univocal. The frame narrative offered an image of the Duke constructed out of bits and pieces of other people's discourse – gossip, rumour, speculation – and the main narrative performs a similar operation through incorporating into the text large amounts of other people's discourse. In his capacity as editor, the journalist informs the reader that the first page of the diaries contained two epigraphs (one from Swinburne, one from Musset), and that after these two quotations, 'les impressions personnelles commençaient.'[89] This seems to relegate quotations to paratextual status, drawing a distinction between the words of other writers and Fréneuse's 'impressions person-nelles'. This distinction proves impossible to sustain, however, as Fréneuse consistently reaches for other people's words to describe his own state of mind, or appears to be little more than a ventriloquist's dummy, voicing other people's ideas. Thus on one occasion early on in the book, Fréneuse, when attending mass one day, tells us that some sacrilegious lines of Remy de Gourmont bubbled up irresistibly to his lips. On another occasion he cites some lines from Charles Vellay, and notes 'je n'ai jamais rien lu qui fût plus près de mon âme et de ma souffrance que les proses de ce Charles Vellay'.[90] Quotations from other writers abound in the text, and collectively these moments create the impression that Fréneuse's discourse is very much stitched together out of bits and pieces of others' writing. Fréneuse's diaries thus have a patchwork quality, as a result of which the collector is himself produced in the image of a collection, a collection which no longer has a stable origin controlling its meaning. There is an odd moment at the beginning of the novel, in the frame narrative, in which the journalist walks into his study to discover Fréneuse leafing through a manuscript on his desk, and is outraged by the impertinence the Duke displays, rifling

89   Lorrain, p. 23.
90   Lorrain, p. 34.

through someone else's papers. The oddity of this is that subsequently we learn that the manuscript Fréneuse was flicking through was his own. This moment of confusion, where authorship is wrongly ascribed to the journalist, resonates through the text, the formal dialogism of which means that Fréneuse's discourse never appears to be flowing from a single unitary source. Fréneuse himself is oddly dispersed throughout the text, called into being by other people.

In particular, Fréneuse is called into being by one man: Claudius Ethal. Ethal is a keen collector, of both objects – masks, wax busts, poisons – and of people: 'il a pour le vice et les aberrations plus qu'une curiosité de dilettante [...]. Il les épie, les recherche et les choie; c'est un collectionneur de fleurs du mal'.[91] We have already seen that the language of curiosity and exhibition is used by Ethal when he invites Fréneuse to the soirée at his studio: 'J'ai tout un lot d'excentriques à vous montrer [...]. Je vous ai promis à leur curiosité, puissent-ils ne pas décevoir la vôtre'.[92] Fréneuse picks up on this language and resents it: 'il m'a promis en exhibition [...]. Suis-je une bête curieuse [...]?'.[93] Just as the frame narrative turns Fréneuse from a *curieux* to a *curiosité* (Porbus portrait, piece of *Japonerie*) so the main narrative repeats this shift, as Fréneuse is absorbed into Ethal's cabinet of curiosities. In the novel it is Claudius Ethal who enjoys the control and mastery that narratives of collecting traditionally ascribe to the collector. But the text suggests a more radically dependent relationship than this. Fréneuse is not merely an object collected by Ethal, but an object created by him. In Ethal's presence, Fréneuse seems incapable of exercising any kind of independent volition, and far from being a self-determined subject, he experiences himself as being Ethal's creation: 'Ce mystérieux causeur me raconte à moi-même [...], *il me parle tout haut, je m'éveille en lui* [...]; ses entretiens m'accouchent de moi-même'.[94] Fréneuse talks about himself principally through object pronouns; he is constructed through another's

91   Lorrain, p. 133.
92   Lorrain, p. 100.
93   Lorrain, pp. 100–1.
94   Lorrain, p. 70.

speech. Although the Duke is the narrator of the novel, he experiences himself as being narrated by Ethal. The painter is the controlling intelligence of the novel, its master subject.

Ethal's power in the book is clearly related to his status as an artist. *Monsieur de Phocas* is a partly a rewriting of Poe's 'The Oval Portrait'. Just as in Poe's short story the woman in the painting dies when the painting is complete, so in *Monsieur de Phocas* those women who sit for Ethal either sicken or die once they have done so. Poe's story is itself a decadent retelling of the Pygmalion myth. Whereas in the myth the statue wakens to life, in Poe's story representation is murder. Art triumphs over life. *Monsieur de Phocas* offers its own version of the Pygmalion myth in a story Ethal tells Fréneuse, the story of the eye of Eboli. This story is about Sarah Lopez, a woman beloved of Phillip II, famous for her bewitching eyes. Although Jewish, the king was sufficiently enamoured to ennoble Lopez, turning her into the Princess of Eboli. One day, Lopez was caught ogling a courtier. Phillip II, in a jealous rage, ripped out one of her eyes, and later 'au regret de la belle prunelle verte qu'il avait gâtée, il fit incruster dans l'orbite vide et saigneuse une superbe émeraude enchâssée d'argent, dont les chirurgiens d'alors firent un semblant de regard'.[95] Unfortunately this operation killed Lopez: 'Tout était barbare, sous ce Philippe II, les façons d'aimer et les chirurgiens'.[96] Philip II seeks to contain Lopez's transgressive sexuality, but his efforts to do so ultimately kill her. Thus the story acts as a kind of reversal of the Pygmalion myth, one with an unhappy ending. In this version, rather than an inanimate object becoming animate, a living woman is treated like a statue and therefore killed.

After the death of Lopez, Phillip II has the emerald set as a ring, and Ethal wears a replica of this ring, filled with poison. Both the Spanish king and Ethal can therefore be read as avatars of Pygmalion. The novel thus presents artistic creation as a fetishistic enterprise, and one fraught with danger. For in *Monsieur de Phocas*, art imperils not only those who model for painters and sculptors, but all those who look at paintings and

95 Lorrain, p. 92.
96 Lorrain, p. 92.

sculptures. Thus Fréneuse writes early on in his journal (before his meeting with Ethal), 'Il n'y a de vrais regards que dans les portraits'.[97] He goes on to apostrophize the eyes in portraits thus:

> Comme vous vivez dans les musées, de quelle vie éternelle, douleureuse et intense vous rayonnez, telles des pierres précieuses enchâssées entre les paupières peintes des chefs-d'œuvres, et comme vous nous troubler au delà du temps et de l'espace, recéleurs que vous êtes du rêve qui vous créa!
> Vous, vous avez des âmes, celles des artistes qui vous voulurent, et c'est pour avoir bu le liquide poison figé dans vos prunelles que je me désespère et que je meurs.[98]

This quotation describes Fréneuse's sense of being annihilated by the powerful gaze of portraits. It also foreshadows the ending of the novel, through the references to 'des pierres précieuses enchâssées entre les paupières peintes des chefs-d'œuvres', which resonates with the Lopez story, and 'le liquide poison figé dans vos prunelles'. The ending of the novel literalizes this image, for Ethal is killed when Fréneuse forces him to drink the poison contained in the emerald ring. When Ethal is murdered by his own creation, we are invited to read this as the basilisk gaze of the painting rebounding on the artist.

Monsieur de Phocas, therefore, initially seems to posit a distinction between the artist, who is granted a kind of demonic power, and the dispersed subject such as Fréneuse. The process of artistic creation, however, is presented as a hazardous one for the artist as well as the model or spectator. When Fréneuse kills Ethal and apparently wrests control of his own narrative, he uses the language of authorship to describe his new found status as an autonomous subject: 'seul auteur de ce crime', he claims after the murder, 'je me suis reconquis and je suis bien moi'.[99] At this point Fréneuse changes his name to Phocas, bequeaths his diaries to the journalist and walks off the page to North Africa. But the reader might well be suspicious of the language of authorship, given the fate of Ethal. Indeed, despite the Duke's claims, there remains something utterly

97   Lorrain, p. 35.
98   Lorrain, pp. 35–6.
99   Lorrain, pp. 239 and 245.

inconclusive about the ending of the novel, as Phocas goes in search of the elusive 'chose bleue et verte' that haunted Fréneuse. Despite Phocas' insistence that he has become an autonomous self-willed subject, the ending of the novel draws the reader's attention to the continuity between Fréneuse and Phocas, both prey to the same compulsion, both searching for something that they cannot find.

The collector in Lorrain's novel is thus a figure of desire unsatisfied, and apparently unsatisfiable. In this respect the novel reconstellates the relationship between collecting, desire and narrative that is found in earlier novels featuring collectors, for example *Le Cousin Pons* and *A Rebours*. In both those novels the space of the collection is a space of plenitude, in which all desire is consummated and from which time is expelled. In both novels, this vision of the collection is set up only to be destroyed: in Balzac's novel, as we have seen, it is the narrative demands of the realist novel that dissolve the space of the collection, and in Huysmans' it is the reality of the mortal body that defeats Des Esseintes. In both texts, collection and narrative are antagonistic principles, and the latter ultimately triumphs over the former. In *Monsieur de Phocas*, on the other hand, as already suggested, collecting elicits narrative. The narrative trajectory of the novel is one of metonymical movement along a signifying chain, as Fréneuse encounters a number of objects all of which approximate to, but none of which are identified with, the object of his desire.[100] Indeed, this metonymic logic is made explicit when, towards the end of the novel and in the hope of finding some respite from his distress, Fréneuse decides to revisit his family estate in Normandy, and recovers memories that explain the origin of his obsession with 'une chose bleue et verte'. As a boy, Fréneuse formed an attachment to a farm labourer on the estate, Jean Destreux, with bright blue eyes: 'Il y avait comme du ciel dans ses prunelles, tant leur eau bleue souriait dans sa face roussie'.[101] He recalls with particular fondness the Sunday afternoons

100   On the significance of metonymy in the work of Lorrain more generally see Kingcaid, pp. 91–103. Du Plessis also addresses the function of metonymy in *Monsieur de Phocas*, arguing that the metonymic structure of the text is symptomatic of the way in which it disavows homosexual desire.

101   Lorrain, p. 184.

spent in a barn with other children from the farm, while Jean Destreux read to them from old almanacs. Those afternoons are presented as a pinnacle of bliss, when the young Fréneuse was immersed in a nature from which he subsequently became alienated. Jean Destreux, however, died in an accident on the farm, witnessed by the young Fréneuse. The death of the labourer is then identified by Fréneuse as the origin of his neurosis:

> Les prunelles d'eau de Jean Destreux! C'est parce que ses yeux-là avait en eux tout ce que je désirais et que j'ai cherché depuis et que je poursuis encore, qu'ils sont demeurés dans mon souvenir. Ils ont été la première révélation d'un impossible bonheur! le bonheur de l'âme! Ce sont les yeux de pureté de mes années d'ignorance, et ce n'est qu'après m'être dépravé et corrompu au contact des hommes, que j'ai convoité follement les yeux verts. La hantise de ces prunelles glauques est déjà une déchéance.[102]

The gemstones and eyes that Fréneuse covets are all substitutes for the original, irretrievably lost object of desire. Whereas in *Le Cousin Pons* and *A Rebours* the space of the collection is a space where all desire is consummated, in *Monsieur de Phocas*, such a space is located in the past, and lost forever. Collecting, far from holding out the promise of fulfilment, is 'déja une déchéance'.

Collecting in *Monsieur de Phocas* is therefore explicitly presented as a decadent, postlapsarian practice that speaks of an irrecoverable loss. I want to argue, however, that this decadent collector was not a product of the fin-de-siècle; rather Lorrain's text can be inscribed in a tradition that dates back to the inception of the modern discourse surrounding collecting, a discourse that was always split. If, as we have already seen, collecting was often presented as a means for the individual to fashion himself as an autonomous subject, if it was often associated with values of mastery and control, the collector was also always a desiring subject.

102   Lorrain, p. 193.

Collecting and Desire: A Never-Ending Story

Viel-Castel, in his seminal sketch of the collector, defines collectors as 'tous ceux que l'amour de la collection, le désir d'amener à l'état de collection un rassemblement plus ou moins considérable de choses œuvrées par l'industrie humaine, ou créées par l'industrie surhumaine du grand Créateur, a lancés dans l'arène où combattent les martyres d'une idée fixe'.[103] The most significant discursive move made in this passage – a seminal move, because it allowed the collector to emerge as a type – is to approach the collector not in relation to a specific collection, but in relation to the desire to collect, foregrounding the psychology of the collector. Anything is susceptible of being collected, but although the object may vary, the mechanism of the collector's desire always operates in the same fashion, and it is this mechanism of desire that Viel-Castel's article, and much of the writing about collecting that came later, explored.

The collector's desire is always already misdirected. The discourse of the collector's desire is haunted by the question of what the collector really desires when he desires an object. In using terms such as 'amour' and 'désir' to describe collecting, in referring to its 'voluptés', Viel-Castel tropes the collector as a lover.[104] In fact, however, the anecdotes he recounts in his article suggest that the relationship between the two is not merely a metaphorical one. The stories of M. Menussard, who talked to his Sèvres porcelain as he would do to his mistresses, and, more suggestively still, of the collector of Egyptian artefacts who falls in love with one of his mummies, only to die of a broken heart after discovering that it was not the princess he assumed but actually a man, both suggest that collecting is a substitute for sexual activity.[105]

Forty years later, Edmond de Goncourt theorized a similar relationship between sexual passion and collecting in the introduction to *La Maison*

---

103   Viel-Castel, p. 123.
104   See Viel-Castel, p. 124.
105   Viel-Castel, pp. 123–5 and pp. 126–7.

d'un artiste, an odd book in which he elegizes his dead younger brother, Jules, through a detailed catalogue of their collections. Attempting to explain why collecting should have become such a widespread pursuit in the nineteenth century, Goncourt suggests that it has something to do with the growth of the private sphere. In the nineteenth century:

> ces habitudes moins mondaines amenaient un amoindrissement du rôle de la femme dans la pensée masculine; [...] et à la suite de cette modification dans les mœurs, il arrivait ceci: c'est que l'intérêt de l'homme, s'en allant de l'être charmant, se reportait en grande partie sur les jolis objets inanimés dont la passion revêt un peu de la nature et du caractère de l'amour.[106]

Here Goncourt suggests simply that male desire has shifted focus; where it was previously directed towards women it is now directed towards *bibelots*. The collector has replaced the lover. But he then goes on to suggest a subtly different relationship between love and collecting: 'Pour notre génération, la *bricabracomanie* n'est qu'un bouche-trou de la femme qui ne possède plus l'imagination de l'homme, et j'ai fait à mon égard cette remarque, que lorsque par hasard mon cœur s'est trouvé occupé, l'objet d'art ne m'était rien.'[107] The use of the word 'bouche-trou' here suggests that the passion for collecting is an ersatz one, which invites us to think of its pleasure as essentially ersatz. Collecting is thus presented as a hollow pursuit.

The idea that collecting is a substitute for sexual activity, and an inadequate one at that, is also voiced by a fictional collector, Proust's Baron de Charlus in *A La Recherche du temps perdu*. Attempting to seduce the narrator, Marcel, Charlus at one point tells him:

> Il n'y a rien de plus agréable que de se donner de l'ennui pour une personne qui en vaille la peine. Pour les meilleurs d'entre nous, l'étude des arts, le goût de la brocante, les collections, les jardins, ne sont que des ersatz, des succédanés, des alibis. Dans le fond de notre tonneau, comme Diogène, nous demandons un homme.[108]

106 Goncourt, *La Maison*, I, 2–3.
107 Goncourt, *La Maison*, I, 3.
108 Marcel Proust, *A La Recherche du temps perdu*, ed. by Jean-Yves Tadié, Bibliothèque de la Pléiade, 4 vols (Paris: Gallimard, 1987–1989), II (1988), 581.

Collecting is an empty pursuit here. The different activities which Charlus enumerates, and which might be thought to form a rather heterogeneous lot (the seriousness of 'l'étude des arts' contrasts with the frivolity of 'le goût des brocantes', giving the sentence a certain bathetic movement), are presented as interchangeable because they are functionally equivalent, drained of any inherent value. Charlus presents collecting as a perversion of a perversion, a function of a sexual desire that, by the standards of heteronormativity, has already been displaced on to an inappropriate object.[109]

Viel-Castel, Goncourt, and Proust all suggest that collecting is a function of sexual desire gone awry, that the collector is a lover in disguise. Other narratives of collecting, however, configure the relationship between the lover and the collector rather differently. Rochoux's 1861 text, *Les Moutons de Panurge*, tells the story of a collector of historical documents, keen to acquire certain important pieces owned by a sexagenarian spinster unwilling to part with them for sentimental reasons. The collector is in despair of ever obtaining the pieces until he remembers that he himself is a bachelor. The ensuing marriage causes quite a stir; most people assume that the spinster must have a secret fortune, but the narrator explains that the collector 'avait tout simplement épousé une épreuve unique, le seul objet de son amour. La lune de miel fut pour lui bien douce; elle se prolongea durant toute sa vie'.[110] The comic effect of the story is, therefore, generated by the conflation of the roles of collector and lover. This is not quite the last word, however, for the final punchline depends on drawing a distinction once more between the pleasures of collecting and the pleasures of

---

109 A link between collecting and homosexuality was suggested by Jean-Martin Charcot and Valentin Magnan in their 1882 essay, 'Inversion du sens génital' [*Archives de Neurologie*, 3:7 (January–February 1882), 53–60 and 4:10 (July 1882), 296–322]. This essay subsumes homosexuality and fetishism within the same category, presenting them as two modalities of a single pathology. Among the case-studies of fetishists they discuss is a man who found *bonnets de nuit* sexually exciting, and who, they note, had long been a keen collector of *bibelots* and *objets d'art*. The border between collecting and fetishism is thus presented as a rather porous one, as it appears in many late-nineteenth-century texts, including *Monsieur de Phocas*.

110 Rochoux, p. 20.

marriage: 'Il n'y a que les pièces uniques pour vous donner de pareilles lunes de miel'.[111] The joys of collecting are here presented as sure and certain, in contrast to the short-lived joys of marriage. Here the collector's passion is primary, and the lover's pleasure presented as an ersatz.

This story bears comparison with one of Champfleury's narratives of collecting, dating from the same decade, 'La Faïence des Médicis'.[112] This story too involves passion feigned in the interests of acquiring a coveted object. In this case the narrator of the story is the private secretary of a famous writer, pursued mercilessly by a *bas-bleu* of mediocre talents who invariably sends him her manuscripts, which he just as invariably returns unread. Having alienated the *bas-bleu*, the famous writer then discovers, much to his chagrin, that she has in her possession a faïence cup which he, a keen collector, has long coveted. The writer hatches a plan to acquire this cup. He tells his private secretary to write a letter to the *bas-bleu*, pretending to be an aspiring poet and admirer of her novels, newly arrived in Paris. She will undoubtedly invite him to call on her at her home, and having thus inveigled his way into the apartment the young man will pretend to fall in love with the *bas-bleu*: 'Vous recevrez en entrant le coup de foudre, ce fameux coup de foudre auquel nulle femme ne résista jamais [...]. Quand on sait jouer du coup de foudre, on conquiert la faïence des Médicis, ou on est un nigaud'.[113] The secretary is persuaded to execute his employer's plan, which proves successful in an unexpected fashion: the famous writer 'voulut connaître dans ses moindres détails l'insensée passion que j'avais été obligé de feindre pour visiter les appartements les plus sacrés du bas-bleu; mais sa joie fut sans bornes quand je lui annonçai l'issue de l'enterprise, c'est-à-dire la découverte de mauvaises tasses de fabrique anglaise moderne sans rapports avec la faïence des Médicis!'.[114] The story does not end so happily for the private secretary: 'Et ainsi je fus chargé d'une délicate et désagréable mission, qui aboutit les jours suivants à des poursuites insen-

111   Rochoux, p. 20.
112   Champfleury, *L'Hôtel*, pp. 41–59.
113   Champfleury, *L'Hôtel*, p. 50.
114   Champfleury, *L'Hôtel*, pp. 58–9.

sées de la dame, voulant entendre répéter l'aveu de ma passion sur tous les tons, sans cesse et toujours.'[115]

Thus in Champfleury's story, as in Rochoux's, the figures of the lover and the collector are strategically conflated as a ruse to enable the collector to acquire a precious object. The comic effect of the stories is at least partly generated by the fact that they rewrite the relationship between the lover and the collector posited by many other writers, in which collecting is a substitute for sexual activity. In response to the question suggested by Viel-Castel, Proust and Goncourt – what does the collector really desire when he desires an object? – these stories offer an ironic riposte, reversing the terms of the question to ask what a collector really desires when he ostensibly desires a woman. The relationship between the lover and the collector thus emerges as a reversible one in the discourse surrounding collecting, as each can be presented as a perverted version of the other, each can signify the other. The discourse around collecting does not provide a definitive answer to the question of what the collector really desires; rather it suggests that desire is always misdirected. The workings of desire elicit a question that can never be answered, but remains always open.

The idea that desire is an open structure is also emphasized in the final world of 'La Faïence des Médicis', as the secretary describes the *bas-bleu* as insatiable, 'voulant entendre répéter l'aveu de ma passion sur tous les tons, sans cesse et toujours'. The link, which the story has already established, between the figures of the collector and the lover, invites us to read this not merely as a comment upon the mechanism of the lover's desire, but also upon the mechanism of the collector's desire. The idea of the constant repetition of the same vow, in a slightly different form, points to the seriality of the collector's desire, and also to its insatiability, ideas which are more fully developed in another story in *L'Hôtel des commissaires-priseurs*, that of 'Le Collectionneur de chaussures'.[116] This story opens with the narrator noting that: 'Chaque jour révèle un nouveau type d'amateurs, et je tracerai en traits rapides le profil du singulier personnage qui a réuni un assem-

115 Champfleury, *L'Hôtel*, p. 59.
116 Champfleury, *L'Hôtel*, pp. 231–5.

blage de souliers'.[117] Thus the story opens by suggesting that the category of collectors is always expanding, as more and more types of collector emerge. This rhetoric of expansion resonates with the story of this eccentric collector, whose collection has developed far beyond 'un assemblage de souliers'. Having begun with collecting shoes, he moves on to collecting shoe-nails: 'Les clous sont trop proches parents du cuir pour que l'amateur n'ait pas ouvert une salle spéciale à la clouterie de chaussures'.[118] From nails he moved on to other artefacts, again those that are the 'proches parents' of shoes. Thus he began to study representations of feet in art: 'Notre homme en arrive à faire mouler des pieds antiques et des pieds modernes; il démontre comment le rude Michel-Ange introduisait de muscles dans les pieds de ses héros, et combien le doux Raphaël en supprimait'.[119] At this point he is forced to rent three more rooms to house his growing collection of paintings, sculptures and casts of feet. Still he keeps collecting, moving on to socks and stockings, walking sticks, and shoe-wax: 'Nécessairement le cirage a appelé sa maîtresse la brosse [...]. Bientôt la maison ne suffit plus. Il faudrait une rue, un quartier, une ville'.[120]

The collection in this story is structured by metonymy. This figure operates in two different ways. First, it is through the work of metonymy that the collection of shoes functions to produce knowledge:

> L'usure des talons ou de la semelle [the narrator explains], la fatigue particulière à certaines parties de la chaussure, suivant que l'homme marche en dedans ou en dehors, ont inspirés à ce collectionneur des mondes de pensées. Il a bâti une théorie à ce sujet: 'Dis-moi comment tu marches, je te dirai qui tu es.' En montrant telle chaussure, il affirme qu'elle n'a pu appartenir qu'à un cagneux. L'état d'un homme qui pense habituellement lui est révélé par des trous bien conformés sous la plante des pieds; à l'entendre, de saines réflexions conduisent à une chaussure sainement usée.[121]

117   Champfleury, L'Hôtel, p. 231.
118   Champfleury, L'Hôtel, p. 232.
119   Champfleury, L'Hôtel, p. 233.
120   Champfleury, L'Hôtel, p. 235.
121   Champfleury, L'Hôtel, p. 232.

Through studying the properties of the shoe, the collector can deduce the characteristics of its wearer. The effects of wear and tear tell a story, and connect the shoe to an entire social context. Champfleury's story resonates with the account of collecting offered by Robert Opie, a packaging collector and the founder of the Museum of Advertising and Packaging in Gloucester, in an interview published in John Elsner and Roger Cardinal's *The Cultures of Collecting*:

> One of my great philosophies is to think about a subject, putting it into an environment, a context, rather than as a defined subject, and that's leading you back to your earlier question about limits. [...] There are no limits, but that doesn't mean I want to save everything – that is the difference between being sane and being mad. If one is sane, one doesn't need to *collect* everything, but one does need to *understand* how everything relates to each other. The trouble is, as soon as I start talking about packaging, I'm talking about brands and products. Packaging is just the evidence that a given product existed [...]. But I'm not just interested in the packaging, I'm interested in the brand, the product, the way it's advertised, what people think about it, how it's marketed, how it's retailed and how it related to all the competition around it, and then the worldwide scenario. What I'm saying is that one has to understand the whole concept.[122]

The collection is here conceptualized as a knowledge-producing technology that operates through a movement from part to whole, from fragment to totality. For both Opie and Champfleury's shoe collector, collecting is very much associated with a totalizing impulse. Within Champfleury's story, however, metonymy also operates in another way, and one that sabotages any totalizing ambition. A metonymical movement propels the collector along the axis of contiguity, from one class of objects to the next. The activity of collecting finally grinds to a halt for purely contingent reasons, when the collector finally runs out of money and auctions his collection at the public auction house, 'ce grand creuset où tout se métamorphose

---

122   "'Unless you do these crazy things ...": An Interview with Robert Opie', in *The Cultures of Collecting*, ed. by John Elsner and Roger Cardinal (London: Reaktion, 1994), pp. 25–48 (pp. 39–40).

et devient utile'.[123] Thus objects are restored to circulation, making of the end of the story also a beginning.

This vision of collecting as being a process of moving along a never-ending chain can be contrasted with La Bruyère's disparaging portrait of the *curieux*. First published in *Les Caractères* in 1688, La Bruyère's critique was often cited in nineteenth-century writings on the collector, in support of the idea that collecting is a a ridiculous pastime. In his discussion of 'la curiosité', La Bruyère's narrator cites a conversation he had with a certain Démocède, who told him about his friend Diognète:

> je le comprends moins que jamais; pensez-vous qu'il cherche à s'instruire par les médailles, et qu'il les regarde comme des preuves parlantes de certains faits, et des monuments fixes et indubitables de l'ancienne histoire? rien moins; vous croyez peut-être que toute la peine qu'il se donne pour recouvrer une *tête*, vient du plaisir qu'il se fait de ne voir pas une suite d'empereurs interrompue? c'est encore moins: Diognète sait d'une médaille le *frust*, le *feloux*, et la *fleur de coin*, il a une tablette dont toute les places sont garnies à l'exception d'une seule, ce vide lui blesse la vue, et c'est précisment et à la lettre pour le remplir, qu'il emploie son bien et sa vie.[124]

Démocède mocks the numismatist for his obsession with filling the one remaining empty space in his display cabinet, but he himself, a collector of Callot engravings, suffers from a similar obsession: 'j'ai tout *Callot* hormis une seule qui n'est pas, à la vérité, de ses bons ouvrages, au contraire c'est un des moindres, mais qui m'achèverait Callot, je travaille depuis vingt ans à recouvrer cette estampe, et je désespère enfin d'y réussir: cela est bien rude'.[125] La Bruyère's collectors are therefore figures of frustrated desire; their collections remain incomplete. If that final space in the cabinet remains unfulfilled, however, this is for contingent reasons; it is nonetheless possible to imagine a collection that would be exhaustive and com-

123 Champfleury, *L'Hôtel*, p. 236.
124 Jean de La Bruyère, *Les Caractères ou les mœurs de ce siècle*, in *Œuvres complètes*, ed. by Julien Benda, Bibliothèque de la Pléiade (Paris: Gallimard, 1951), pp. 59–478 (pp. 387–8).
125 La Bruyère, p. 388.

plete. In Champfleury's text, however, the collection is always necessarily incomplete.

The nineteenth-century discourse of collecting is based not on closed structures, such as Diognète's cabinet, but on open structures, such as Champfleury's always-expanding collection of shoes. This rhetoric of inexhaustibility is at least partly a function of the proliferation of collectors in nineteenth-century France, as the closed world of the connoisseur exploded and gave rise to a mass market in collecting. Thus the article on the *collectionneur* in the *Grand Dictionnaire*, after enumerating various kinds of collector, abandons the attempt to produce an exhaustive taxonomy: 'Arrêtons-nous. Nous ne finirions pas si nous voulions passer en revue toutes les variétés, toutes les audaces, toutes les singularités de la *collectionnomanie*.'[126] The tricolonic structure of this sentence itself points to how collecting in the nineteenth century generated certain kinds of structures, ever-expanding chains, enumerative structures that are presented as incomplete. This is not merely a matter of rhetoric. These structures are the structures of desire itself, and the discourse of the collector emerged as a useful vehicle for exploring the operation of desire. If the collector acted in some texts as a figure for self-mastery, as a figure for the self-determined and self-determining subject, he was also a figure for a desire founded on lack.

126 'Collectionneur', in *Grand Dictionnaire*, p. 601.

CHAPTER 4

(Re)Collecting the Past

As we have already seen, the article on the *collectionneur* in the *Grand Dictionnaire* identifies *collectionnomanie* as a specifically nineteenth-century condition: 'La collection est un des goûts qui sont appelés à caractériser plus spécialement ce siècle; manie charmante du reste [...], et qui est essentiellement propre aux esprits délicats. "Jamais rustre prit-il assez d'intérêt aux menus débris du passé pour les receuillir à grand'peine, dit M Paul Parfait?"'.[1] This observation hinges around an opposition between delicacy and hardiness, the latter quality embodied in the figure of the peasant. The painstaking, pernickety work of the collector ill befits the vigorous and robust country-dweller, but it is, the article suggests, a suitable pursuit for the soft city-dweller. The modernity of collecting is located in the fact that it is an urban phenomenon. The quotation also points towards another idea, however, without explicitly voicing it, which is that the modernity of collecting lay in the specific relationship to the past that such a pursuit implied. For it is not just anything that is being collected here, it is anything old, the 'débris du passé'. It is the modern, urban citizen who is concerned with amassing material relics of the past, a concern described as wholly alien to the country-dweller. The article here brushes, with the lightest of touches, past a set of issues which were of central importance to the discourse around collecting in the nineteenth century, and which present it as closely bound up with an experience of historical disjunction, and, in a more personal register, loss. It is to this set of issues that we shall now turn. The central question to be addressed is what kind of relationship between the past and the present was implied in the collection and display of antique objects.

1   'Collectionneur', in *Grand Dictionnaire*, p. 601.

Pierre Nora, in his famous introductory essay to *Les Lieux de mémoire*, draws a distinction between history and memory. The latter is a relationship to the past that posits an essential continuity between then and now, in which the past infuses the present through myriad traditions, customs, and habits, in which it is seamlessly woven into the lived experience of the present. It is associated with the regime of production, and settles 'dans les métiers où se transmettent les savoirs du silence, dans les savoirs du corps'.[2] Memory is a binding force, unlike the solvent history. History, far from being synonymous with memory, is in Nora's perspective opposed to it in every respect. It is a critical attitude to the past that posits it as radically alien from the present: 'L'histoire est la reconstruction toujours problématique et incomplète de ce qui n'est plus. La mémoire est un phénomène toujours actuel, un lien vécu au présent éternel; l'Histoire, une représentation du passé.'[3] For Nora, there was an age in which history was the servant of memory: 'L'histoire, et plus précisément celle du développement national, a constitué la plus forte de nos traditions collectives; par excellence, notre milieu de mémoire. Des chroniqueurs du Moyen Âge aux historiens contemporains de l'histoire 'totale', toute la tradition historique s'est développée comme l'exercice réglé de la mémoire et son approfondissement spontané, la reconstitution d'un passé sans lacunes et sans faille.'[4] For Nora, the apogee of this tradition was the Third Republic, in which national history was a means of forging a sense of national identity; it was only in the 1930s that the holy Republican trinity of History, Memory and Nation began to split apart. Nora identifies the period in which he was writing (the essay was first published in 1984) as the age of the triumph of history over memory. He describes the 'effondrement central de notre mémoire' as occurring at the end of the *trente glorieuses*, and links it to the final extinction of the peasantry: 'Qu'on songe à cette mutilation sans retour qu'a représentée la fin des paysans, cette collectivité-mémoire par

2   Nora, 'Entre Mémoire et Histoire', in *Les Lieux de mémoire*, ed. by Pierre Nora, 3 vols (Paris: Gallimard, 1984–1992), I, pp. xvii–xlii (p. xxv).
3   Nora, p. xix.
4   Nora, p. xx.

excellence dont la vogue comme objet d'histoire a coincidé avec l'apogée de la croissance industrielle.'⁵ Paradoxically, however, the gradual erosion of memory, by highlighting its fragility, leads to a desire to gather up and safeguard its scraps.

It is at this point that we can return to the Larousse article on the *collectionneur*. Nora suggests that memorial consciousness was the predominant mode of experiencing the past in nineteenth-century France, a consciousness which finds its purest form among the peasantry. The article in the *Grand Dictionnaire* also invokes the figure of the peasant, taking it as axiomatic that the peasant could never be a collector, and conversely that collecting is a mode of consumption only to be found among the modern, urban classes. I wish to argue that Nora's distinction between memory and history resonates in the encounter between the peasant and the collector, as conceptualized in the *Grand Dictionnaire*'s article on the collector, and that if the peasant is the repository of memory, then the collector stands on the side of history. A standard story in the folklore surrounding collecting is that of the collector who goes to rural France, and there uncovers a masterpiece of French craftsmanship in the home of a peasant who has no idea of its true worth, and who has innocently been making use of it, rather than exhibiting it as an antique collectable.⁶ The point of this story is not that the peasant is a philistine, incapable of recognizing an *objet d'art* – although this claim may well be made – but that the peasant does not recognize antiques as being a specific and specifically valuable category of object because, living in memory, he does not experience the need to

---

5   Nora, p. xvii.
6   See, for example, Champfleury, *Le Violon de faïence*, where the collector Gardillane asks his friend in the provinces, Dalègre, to seek out pieces for him in the homes of local peasants, or 'Les Trouvailles de M. Bretoncel' in Champfleury, *L'Hôtel*, pp. 239–54. In this latter story the collector, M. Bretoncel, is swindled by some peasants, who lead him to believe that they are in possession of an antique enamel. Bretoncel lavishes gifts on them in the hope of acquiring the (fictive) enamel at a bargain price. The story thus operates in an ironic mode, but it is nonetheless underpinned by the assumption that the collector and the peasant have a completely different relationship to the material traces of the past.

preserve bits of the past born of the anguished knowledge of loss that is
the hallmark of the historical consciousness. There is a profound ambivalence in the discourse surrounding collecting in the nineteenth century in
terms of how it conceptualizes the relationship between the present and
the past, an ambivalence which Nora's distinction between memory and
history, and their relation to forging a sense of national identity, can help
us to think through, but which also calls into question Nora's distinction.
On the one hand, collecting was closely bound up with an experience of
historical dislocation and irreparable loss, but at the same time narratives
of collecting often tell a story of an essential continuity between past and
present. It is this tension that we shall be exploring here.

Collecting and Post-Revolutionary Historiography

Walter Benjamin speculated that: 'perhaps the most deeply hidden motive
of the person who collects can be described this way: he takes up the
struggle against dispersion. Right from the start, the great collector is
struck by the confusion, by the scatter, in which the things of the world
are found.'[7] Benjamin goes on to link the collector to Baroque allego-
rists, whose world-view was underpinned by this sense of scatter. Unlike
the allegorical dramatists of the German Baroque, however, nineteenth-
century collectors did not perceive scatter as an inherent feature of the
sublunar world, but as a historical phenomenon, a consequence of the
French Revolution, without which the modern collector could not exist.
It was the Revolution that, by liquidating the great noble and ecclesiastical
estates, had flooded the market with antiques and art objects. The collector, although he was called into being by the Revolution, is often presented
as working to reverse its effects. Thus in Jules Janin's 1843 guide-book to

---

7   Benjamin, *The Arcades Project*, p. 211 [H4a,1].

Paris, *The American in Paris*, the narrator-flâneur, wandering past the Gobelins factory, is prompted to the following reflection:

> The carpets of the Gobelins, and the china of Sèvres have, for a long time, answered for all the presents made by the kings of France [...] They reproduced, each in its own way, the most exquisite chefs-d'œuvre. But when the French revolution began to break everything, to destroy books, to cut paintings in pieces with its pitiless hands, to melt gold and silver, and the most costly jewels, to tear laces, to sell – at auction even – the marbles of the tombs [...], – the Revolution, above all, attacked the porcelains of Sèvres. [...] Madmen! they fancied they could annihilate the past, just as they reduced to nothing, [sic] those delicate little chefs-d'œuvre of form and colour. But no! in their terrible anger, they have been unable to annihilate anything, not even the cups and vases and paintings of the ceramic art. In vain did they throw to the winds the ashes of the kings of France; those royal ashes found each other in the air [...]. Everything rises, everything is repaired [...]. In Paris itself, there is a whole army of antiquarians, honest men, whose life and fortune are spent in collecting these scarce remains, in saving from oblivion these precious remembrances, in gathering up this noble dust.[8]

Janin here presents the Revolution as a major historical dislocation, not only because it was a rupture in the smooth continuum of history, but because it sought to deny the past's claims on the present. It was an exercise in willed amnesia, and its vandalism was an essential part of this attempt to forget. The antiquarian, on the other hand, works to preserve the past through the collection and restoration of its artworks.

Janin's denunciation of revolutionary vandalism raises two important points. First, it invites us to think about collecting in relation to the notion of a cultural patrimony, an idea that was itself revolutionary in origin, and rested on the assumption that the cultural value of objects is independent of their political significance. Thus the Abbé Grégoire, denouncing the 'fanatisme' of revolutionary vandals, stated: 'Certainement le temple des Druides à Mont-Morillon, et celui de Diane à Nîmes, n'ont pas été contruits [sic] par la main de la raison; et cependant quel est le véritable

---

8 Jules Janin, *The American in Paris* (London: Longman, Brown, Green and Longmans, 1843), pp. 195–6. This book was first published in translation; there is no French language edition.

ami des arts qui ne desirât les voir subsister dans leur entier! Parce que les pyramides d'Egypte ont été élevées par la tyrannie et pour la tyrannie, faudrait-il démolir ces monumens [sic] antiques.'[9] This discursive move is one that Janin declines to make. In the above quotation he refuses to separate the political significance of the art objects he mentions from their cultural significance, thus conflating political iconoclasm with a more generalized hostility to art. His description of revolutionaries smashing 'those delicate little chefs-d'œuvre of form and colour' that antiquarians cherish tends to imply that they are essentially philistines. The parallel he draws between the restoration of eighteenth-century art objects and the gathering together of the ashes of the kings of France suggests that the former is important essentially as a token of a return to pre-revolutionary political ideals. Janin's reasoning, in its refusal to constitute the cultural as a sphere independent of the political, ironically mirrors that of the revolutionary vandals he attacks. His position can be contrasted with that of the Second Empire writer and collector Charles Blanc, who claimed that art 'est la seule hérédité, la seule légitimité que les révolutions respectent.'[10] For Blanc, the artistic sphere is important because it is sealed off from politics, unaffected by its vicissitudes, and it is therefore possible to find therein a national historical narrative characterized not by cataclysm but by continuity, not by rupture but by unbroken tradition. A much more

9   Henri Grégoire, *Troisième Rapport sur le vandalisme*, in *Œuvres de l'Abbé Grégoire*, 14 vols (Nendeln, Liechtenstein: Kraus-Thomson; Paris: Editions d'Histoire Sociale, 1977), II, 335–57 (p. 352). In his article, 'The Bric-a-Brac of the Old Regime: Collecting and Cultural History in Post-Revolutionary France' [in *French History* 22 (2008), 295–315], which explores how collecting influenced the writing of history in the mid-nineteenth century, Tom Stammers notes that among collectors of Revolutionary memorabilia, 'many owners had no interest in reconstructing political 'traditions' out of their finds' (p. 306), valuing their objects according to formal or historical criteria and bracketing off their ideological significance. He associates this with the emergent values of 'impartiality, comprehensiveness and even 'positivist objectivity' in nineteenth-century historical science (p. 307). It also, of course, testifies to the irrationality, the irreducible mysteriousness, of the collector's motivations.

10   Charles Blanc, *Le Trésor de la curiosité tiré des catalogues de vente avec diverses notes et notices historiques & biographiques etc.* (Paris: Jules Renouard, 1857), p. iv.

developed use of this idea is found in the work of Blanc's contemporary, Clément de Ris, the art critic, curator, and historian of collecting, who found in this history the true and essential history of France itself. It is to this work that I wish now to turn.

In the introductory essay to his 1864 collection of essays and biographical sketches, *La Curiosité: collections françaises et étrangères*, Clément de Ris suggested that the French were defined as a nation by their artistic skill. He wrote:

> Il faut, en vérité, que nous soyons la nation artiste par excellence. Les objets d'art poussent en même temps que le blé, et le laboureur en retournant son sillon se préoccupe autant de le faire bien que de le faire bon. C'est l'irrésistible attrait en même temps que la supériorité de notre pays: *artifex Gallia*.[11]

The artistic temperament of the French makes them not only producers of art objects, however, but also consumers thereof – a nation of collectors, or *curieux* to use the author's preferred, somewhat old-fashioned term:

> le goût de la curiosité n'est pas nouveau chez nous. En cela, comme en tout, nous ne faisons que suivre nos aïeux dans une voie tracée d'avance. Ils ont dû à l'exercice de ce goût bien des heures délicieusement passées, sans compter cette politesse d'esprit, cette vivacité d'intelligence, cette richesse et cette abondance d'imagination, choses légères qui ont assuré la supériorité de la France sur les autres nations.[12]

The passion for collecting is an essential part of French history, but more than this it is a destiny. It is what distinguishes France amongst the nations, and the mainspring of its greatness. These claims are repeated and amplified in his later work, *Les Amateurs d'autrefois* (1877), the introduction to which opens with the somewhat audacious claim that: 'Enumérer les preuves de l'influence exercée par les Amateurs depuis l'origine de la monarchie équivaudrait à raconter l'histoire du goût en France, c'est-à-dire l'histoire même de notre patrie au point de vue intellectuel.'[13] The difference between

---

11 Clément de Ris, *La Curiosité*, p. 16.
12 Clément de Ris, *La Curiosité*, pp. 16–17.
13 Clément de Ris, *Les Amateurs d'autrefois* (Paris: Plon, 1877), p. i.

the claim made in the earlier text and the claim made here is that here all explicit reference to production, to *artifex Gallia*, has been suppressed. It is no longer in craftsmanship that the genius of France, in both its etymological and modern senses, is to be located, but in taste. Through the vicissitudes of France's political history, taste has proved a point of stability and continuity: 'Au milieu des ses malheurs, à la suite de ses revers, c'est au goût qu'elle a dû la consolation de ses tristesses, l'oubli de ses douleurs, le réveil de son activité et de ses espérances.'[14] The story of the history of collecting is the story of 'l'émancipation du goût';[15] initially 'le monopole des classes privilégiées',[16] over the course of the centuries art is made available first to the bourgeoisie and then to the popular classes. Clément de Ris therefore plugs the history of collecting into an accepted historiography charting the emergence of democracy. He concludes his potted history of collecting thus: 'Cette prépondérance [of taste], proclamons-la nous de toutes nos forces, défendons-la de toute notre énergie, contribuons par tous les moyens que Dieu met en notre pouvoir à la maintenir, à la développer, à la consolider, à la faire prospérer et grandir. Tout bien considéré, c'est la part la plus féconde, la seule intacte de l'héritage de nos pères.'[17]

Here the history of collecting is pressed into the service of producing a history of France 'sans lacunes et sans faille', to use Nora's expression,[18] but this is made possible only by the elision of the regimes of production and consumption in the regime of taste. Clément de Ris' vision of historical continuity can usefully be contrasted with the narrative of historical discontinuity elaborated by Edmond Bonnaffé in his *Causeries sur l'art et sur la curiosité*, where discontinuity is located precisely in a split between the regimes of production and consumption. In the *Causeries*, Bonnaffé dwells at length on furniture-making as the art in which Frenchmen have traditionally excelled, and which best expresses the 'génie national'.[19] In

14   Clément de Ris, *Les Amateurs*, pp. i–ii.
15   Clément de Ris, *Les Amateurs*, p. xx.
16   Clément de Ris, *Les Amateurs*, p. xx.
17   Clément de Ris, *Les Amateurs*, p. xxxi.
18   Nora, p. xx.
19   Bonnaffé, *Causeries*, p. 130.

a chapter entitled 'Les Propos de Maître Salebrin', the ghost of a master carpenter from the Renaissance period (for Bonnaffé the greatest period of French craftsmanship, because the period when it was least subject to foreign influences), appears to the narrator, and bemoans the advent of the division of labour and mechanized production. The former 'isole les forces et détruit cette communauté de pensées et d'efforts sans laquelle on ne crée point de belles choses'; the latter can lead only to 'banalité et pacotille'.[20] The problem, as diagnosed by Maître Salebrin, is the loss of traditional skills. In the glory days of French furniture-making, skills were passed down from father to son: 'Les fils de vos menuisiers se font avocats, les nôtres continuaient l'état du père et s'en faisaient gloire'.[21] In the modern world, however, according to Maître Salebrin:

> Vous avez changé tout cela [...] et vous faites de l'art à la nouvelle mode. La tradition ayant déménagé avec tant d'autres vieilleries, il fallait bien la remplacer par quelque chose. On a inventé les académies; on a des savants, des beaux parleurs, des docteurs en esthétique, en métaphysique, en théorique et autres fanfares. Tout cela est fort bien, pourvu qu'on n'en abuse pas. Jean de Connet, peintre-verrier, était aussi un parleur excellent sur les choses de son art; seulement, comme il avait l'haleine punaise (c'est Maître Palissy qui en fait l'histoire), les couleurs se décomposaient sous son pinceau, et il ne produisait rien qui vaille.[22]

Thus Maître Salebrin is concerned that skills are no longer transmitted from generation to generation. Following his diatribe about modern furniture production, he dispenses to the narrator some advice about how the defects of modern furniture could be corrected, but he is interrupted when the narrator's son wakes his father up from his dream. The story finishes with the narrator urging his son to take a cigar and listen to him recount his dream. Thus the story ends with knowledge being transmitted from father to son, but in a parody of the transmission of craft skills, all the narrator can bequeath his son is the knowledge of the loss of those skills. Collectors, connoisseurs, and *curieux* are the custodians of the national patrimony, but

---

20 Bonnaffé, *Causeries*, pp. 47 and 49.
21 Bonnaffé, *Causeries*, p. 51.
22 Bonnaffé, *Causeries*, p. 52.

they are consumers not producers, curators rather than creators. In locating a moment of historical disjunction in the advent of mass-production, Bonnaffé points to a connection between alienated labour and alienated memory, which resonates with Nora's own association of memory with the regime of production.[23]

Deracinated Art, Deracinated Subjects

In addition to inviting us to think about the notion of an artistic heritage, Janin's comments in praise of antiquarians raise a second question, which concerns the fate of the objects they preserve and restore: who will lay claim to them, and where will they be housed? Although restored to their original condition, such objects could not return to their original homes. Rather they could look forward to a future in either a private collection or a public museum. By passing over the fate of the restored objects in silence, Janin can avoid some of the debates central to discussions of collecting. Although he places the antiquarian in opposition to the vandal, for other writers the collector was himself a species of vandal, actively involved in dismantling the national cultural patrimony, not through destruction, but through displacement, through taking objects out of the public sphere and sequestering them in private collections. Such criticisms became more and more frequent over the course of the nineteenth century, partly as a result of the development of the public museum. Françoise Hamon has examined representations of the private collector in the specialist art magazine, L'Artiste, established in 1831, and found that although early editions of the magazine spoke enthusiastically about private art collections in Paris, as time went by this enthusiasm waned dramatically, to be replaced with a

---

23   On the link between the nineteenth-century memory crisis and the commodity function, see Richard Terdiman, *Present Past: Modernity and the Memory Crisis* (Ithaca: Cornell University Press, 1993), pp. 10–13.

rather censorious attitude: 'En l'espace de quelques années, *L'Artiste* est donc passé de la découverte éblouie des trésors méconnus à une mise en cause générale de ces accumulations éphémères de pièces parfois douteuses et qui finiront par quitter la France à l'occasion de ventes publiques'.[24] Hamon goes on to suggest that the increasingly negative representations of the collector were a function of the rise of the public museum: 'Le mécène municipal, bienfaiteur de la collectivité, devient alors la figure emblématique du citoyen éclairé qui se substitue à celle du collectionneur solitaire'.[25] The development of the public museum made collectors' claims to be guardians of national treasures appear increasingly specious.

There was, however, another, more fundamental issue at stake for those who criticized the activities of the collector, one that cut across the public museum/private collection distinction to tar both with the same brush, and this was the fact that in entering the collection or the museum, objects were ripped out of their original contexts. Quatremère de Quincy, in his vigorous polemics against the museum, inaugurated a long tradition of opposition to such institutions, an opposition rooted in anxieties about deracinated art.[26] Quatremère was writing in the context of Napoleonic art confiscations and against the vision of the Musée Napoléon, which was intended not as a national but rather as a universal museum, and which obviously posed the problem of deracinated art in a particularly acute form. Dominique Poulot has shown, however, that similar anxieties were also aroused by Alexandre Lenoir's Musée des monuments français, housed in the Petits-Augustins from 1795 to 1816 (when it was forced to close, partly due to the inveterate hostility of Quatremère), on which the Musée de Cluny was modelled. Lenoir's museum was immensely popular, but

---

24 Françoise Hamon, p. 58.
25 Françoise Hamon, p. 59.
26 See Antoine-Chrysostome Quatremère de Quincy, *Considérations morales sur la destination des ouvrages d'art* (Paris: Fayard, 1989) and the *Lettres à Miranda sur le déplacement des monuments de l'art et de l'Italie*, ed. by Edward Pommier (Paris: Macula, 1989). For debates about the art museum in revolutionary France see Pommier's postface to Jean-Baptiste-Pierre Le Brun, *Réflexions sur le Muséum national: 14 janvier 1793* (Paris: Réunion des musées nationaux, 1992), pp. 51–94.

was not greeted with universal enthusiasm. The removal of tombs from their original setting was particularly contentious, and the museum was seen by some at the time (as well as by some historians writing about it subsequently) not as a bulwark against but as an example of revolutionary vandalism. Of this strand of discourse, Poulot writes:

> Les Petits-Augustins apparaissent [...] comme le lieu de la perte du souvenir [...]. Les monuments ont été conservés, non leur fonction de repères; la mémoire, qui est savoir des lieux et de leurs relations, s'évanouit. Ces 'restes', privés des liens du sens, ne sont plus que des signes mutilés que l'institution organise différemment dans un discours étranger.[27]

Thus this early example of a national museum was a controversial one. In chapter two we saw that one of the arguments urged in favour of establishing the Musée de Cluny was that it would foster patriotism, and Lenoir's museum was cited as a successful example of how a museum could do so. Some who visited Lenoir's museum, however, evidently emerged not with a sense of being heirs to the national past, but of being disinherited from that past.

This view of the museum as a locus of dispossession continues to recur in accounts of the museum throughout the nineteenth century and beyond, accounts which present the museum experience as being characterized by a sense of confusion, disorientation and deracination.[28] Paul Bourget, in his hostile but perceptive essay on the Goncourt brothers, discusses the museum in precisely these terms. Bourget's central argument is that the Goncourts' collectomania, the fact that they lived always in a museum, was

---

27   Dominique Poulot, 'Alexandre Lenoir et les musées des monuments français', in *Les Lieux de mémoire*, ed. by Pierre Nora, 3 vols (Paris: Gallimard, 1984–1992), II(2) (1986), 497–531 (p. 513).

28   On this see François Dagognet, *Le Musée sans fin* (Lyon: Champ Vallon, 1984). The first part of this book consists of an essay denouncing the modern museum, picking up on many of the topoi we have already encountered. The second part of the book features an anthology of anti-museum discourse, with extracts from Quatremère de Quincy and Valéry *inter alia*.

the principle factor in the evolution of their literary style.[29] (Bourget does not distinguish between the private collection and the public museum; this distinction is, as should become apparent, irrelevant to his argument.) The essay posits two distinct ways of experiencing art. The first experience is that of a devout Catholic seeing a religious painting in the chapel for which it was painted, in which everything harmonizes, everything belongs together. It is an organic aesthetic experience, the keynote of which is coherence. The second kind of aesthetic experience is that of seeing a painting in a museum:

> L'œuvre d'art est ici comme détachée du coin spécial, comme déracinée du monde pour lequel l'artiste l'avait conçue et créée. [...] Entre les baguettes d'un cadre tient le raccourci de tout un Idéal, une conception complète, systématique et distincte, d'un certain ordre de choses du cœur. Ces conceptions se battent sur les murs, se disputent l'esprit du visiteur [...]. Au lieu que l'œuvre d'art devienne un prétexte au développement de sa personnalité particulière, elle n'est plus pour lui qu'un moyen d'entrée dans des personnalités étrangères. Il la comprend, comme une langue qu'il ne parle pas, au lieu de penser par elle comme dans sa langue maternelle.[30]

Bourget here stresses the sense of dislocation experienced by the museum visitor, wandering around surrounded by objects that are alien to him. Such a characterization of the museum experience is similar to those recorded by Poulot in his article on Lenoir's museum, with the difference that Lenoir's museum was explicitly engaged with issues of tradition, with the transmission of a collective cultural memory, and in the negative responses to his museum it is precisely a sense of historical dislocation that is at stake. In Bourget's article, which is not concerned with a national history museum, this same sense of dislocation is generalized. The trope of the 'langue maternelle' suggests both a displacement in space, the experience of exile, and deracination, a disconnection from one's origins.

Bourget then goes on to discuss the relationship between the Goncourts' work as historians and their work as novelists, and in doing so he again

---

29 For a discussion of Bourget's essay in the context of late-nineteenth-century dilettantism and aestheticism more generally, see Watson, pp. 21–6.

30 Bourget, p. 379.

obliquely raises the question of how the display of antique objects can influence historical consciousness. Bourget recalls to the reader's mind the fact that the Goncourt brothers were historians before they were novelists, and that their work as historians grew out of their collecting: 'Quand on examine habituellement et par le menu les meubles et les costumes, les dessins et les tapisseries d'un temps [...], on est bien tenté [...] de se représenter ces hommes et ces femmes.'[31] Since they could not be sure of the accuracy of their representations of the past, however, they switched to writing about the present. In Bourget's view what unites the Goncourt brothers' practice as historians and their practice as novelists is the emphasis on *les mœurs*. It is because they are first and foremost concerned with *les mœurs* that their books lack drama: 'l'action n'est jamais un très bon signe des mœurs.'[32] Bourget claims that the Goncourts' novels lack plot and narrative drive; that they privilege description over action. We might add that this is also true of their historical works, which are primarily concerned not with marking change over time, or with causality, but with the lived experience of the past. Their first book as historians was not a 'History of the French Revolution', but an *Histoire de la société française pendant la Révolution*. The preface describes this work as 'un essai de reconstruction d'une société',[33] and although the book does chart the progress of the revolution, it is not so much concerned with establishing its whys and wherefores as with recovering the texture of everyday life under the Revolution. Thus there are sections on interior design, costume, duelling, cafés, and courting. In suggesting that it was through their collecting that the Goncourts became historians of *mœurs*, Bourget repeats an argument often made by antiquarian collectors earlier in the nineteenth century. Collecting was seen not just as having enriched the study of history, but as having modified it by opening up new areas of historical enquiry. The

31   Bourget, p. 385.
32   Bourget, p. 389.
33   Edmond et Jules de Goncourt, *Histoire de la société française pendant la révolution*, 2nd edn (Paris: Dentu, 1854), p. i.

editorial to the opening number of the specialist periodical, *Le Cabinet de l'amateur et de l'antiquaire*, puts the matter thus:

> Grâce à l'amateur, rien ne s'est perdu dans la défroque que les siècles laissent après eux en tombant sans retour dans le gouffre de l'éternité. L'historien, préoccupé des batailles, des traités et des trois ou quatre personnages qui remplissent une époque de leurs évolutions, a laissé de côté les mœurs domestiques, les usages, la vie intime des générations disparues.[34]

Collecting is therefore associated with a specific historical project, one that was perceived as something of a novelty in the first half of the nineteenth century, the history of everyday life. Through the collection, the past could be resurrected.

This new kind of history, born of collecting, is indicative of a crisis of memory. In 'Entre Mémoire et Histoire', Nora discusses the increasing popularity of attractions that promise to bring the past back to life. Nora writes:

> l'hallucination artificielle du passé n'est concevable, précisément, que dans un régime de discontinuité. Toute la dynamique de notre rapport au passé réside dans ce jeu subtil de l'infranchissable et de l'aboli. Au sens premier du mot, il s'agit d'une représentation, radicalement différente de ce que cherchait l'ancienne résurrection. Si intégrale qu'elle se voulût, la résurrection impliquait en effet une hiérarchie du souvenir habile à ménager les ombres et la lumière pour ordonner la perspective du passé sous le regard d'un présent finalisé. La perte d'un principe explicatif unique nous a précipités dans un univers explosé, en même temps qu'elle a promu tout objet, fût-ce le plus humble, le plus improbable, le plus inaccessible, à la dignité du mystère historique. C'est que nous savions autrefois de qui nous étions les fils, et que nous sommes aujourd'hui les fils de personne et de tout le monde. Nul ne sachant de quoi le passé sera fait, une inquiète incertitude transforme tout en trace, indice possible, soupçon d'histoire dont nous contaminons l'innocence des choses.[35]

These observations are extremely pertinent to the way in which, in the nineteenth century, historical collecting was seen as enabling the resurrec-

---

34   'Introduction', in *Le Cabinet de l'amateur et de l'antiquaire*, I (1842), 5–13 (p. 6).
35   Nora, p. xxxii.

tion of the past. The novelty of the Musée de Cluny was that visitors could there experience the illusion that they had travelled back in time. They were immersed in mediaeval life.[36] The museum did not offer its visitors a narrative of historical progress, it did not tell the story of how the France of yesteryear became the France of today. The kind of history closely tied up with antiquarian collecting was not the kind of history that sought to explain the relationship between the then and the now. It simply aimed at restoring the appearance of the then. Salvaging the material indices of the nation's past spoke of an interest in that past, and a desire to hold on to it, but the exhibition of such relics often served as a reminder of its loss, or of the fact that it was alien to the concerns of the present. But, more fundamentally, the 'inquiète incertitude [qui] transforme tout en trace, en indice possible' was constitutive of the discourse around collecting in the nineteenth century, in which it was axiomatic that anything and everything could be collected. The article on the collector in the *Grand Dictionnaire*, after pointing out that all objects are susceptible of being collected, goes on to claim that 'toutes les collections, quelles qu'elles soient, ont leur côté utile', and cites in support of this an observation of the eminent collector Feuillet de Conches that 'vient-il un jour où les objets les plus indifférents empruntent des circonstances inattendues un certain intérêt.'[37] He goes on to cite a number of examples of apparently innocuous objects that have helped decide historical controversies. It is impossible, he seems to suggest, for the present to judge what the future will find interesting. The safest course is therefore to preserve everything. This reasoning explicitly underpins Paul Eudel's monumental chronicle of the hôtel Drouot, which details all the sales held there between 1881 and 1888. In the preface he contributed to the first volume, Jules Clarétie describes the hôtel Drouot in familiar terms as a space in which anything and everything can be bought and sold, and in which all aspects of life can be observed:

36　On the experience of the Musée de Cluny, as contrasted with Lenoir's museum, see Stephen Bann, *The Clothing of Clio: a study of the representation of history in nineteenth-century Britain and France* (Cambridge: Cambridge University Press, 1984), pp. 77–92.
37　'Collectionneur', *Grand Dictionnaire*, p. 601.

'Tout aboutit à l'hôtel Drouot. C'est le grand collecteur de nos richesses et de nos ruines.'[38] The use of the word 'collecteur' is significant here. The word 'collecte', like the word 'collection', can be translated by the English word 'collection', but it has an instrumental dimension, and is used in the sense of a tax collection, or a charitable collection, or a rubbish collection. Thus Asselineau, in an essay on collecting *lettres autographes*, distinguishes between 'collectionneurs' and the 'collecteur'. The former are 'goulus qui ont une gueule et point de palais', whereas the latter is 'celui qui choisit (legit), qui déguste et qui savoure'.[39] Asselineau's 'collecteur' collects not for the sake of collecting, but in the service of historical science. Clarétie's use of the word resonates with this, as he praises Eudel's project as a useful resource for historians of the future: 'Curieuse aujourd'hui, cette histoire de l'hôtel Drouot sera précieuse pour l'avenir. La collection de dix volumes pareils à celui-ci serait, pour l'étude de nos mœurs, une mine inépuisable.'[40] The cornerstone of Eudel's project as construed by Clarétie, therefore, is its comprehensiveness, and it is this quality that will make it useful as a historical document, as everything is grist to the historian's mill.

Loss, Forgetting and Silence in *La Maison d'un artiste*

Collecting, therefore, contributed to shaping a historical consciousness often characterized by feelings of deracination and dislocation, a sense of being estranged from the past. *La Maison d'un artiste*, written by Edmond de Goncourt after the death of his brother, is a sustained meditation on the idea that in post-revolutionary France it is impossible to fit past, present and future into a coherent narrative, impossible to join the chronological dots, and it probes this issue in relation to the practice of collecting. The text is a

38 Clarétie, 'Préface', p. x.
39 Asselineau, p. iv.
40 Clarétie, 'Préface', p. xiv.

catalogue raisonné of the Goncourt collections. In the preamble, Edmond de Goncourt seeks to explain why collecting should have become such a widespread pastime in the nineteenth century. We have seen elsewhere that he ascribes its popularity in part to changes in sexual mores – the bibelot is 'un bouche-trou de la femme'[41] – but he then subsumes this suggestion within a more general argument:

> Oui, cette passion devenue générale, ce plaisir solitaire, auquel se livre presque toute une nation, doit son développement au vide, à l'ennui du cœur, et aussi, il faut le reconnaître, à la tristesse des jours actuels, à l'incertitude des lendemains, à l'enfantement, les pieds devant, de la société nouvelle, à des soucis et à des préoccupations qui poussent, comme à la veille d'un déluge, les désirs et les envies à se donner la jouissance immédiate de tout ce qui les charme, les séduit, les tente: l'oubli du moment dans l'assouvissement artistique.[42]

Goncourt here suggests that he was living through an age adrift in history, essentially an age of transition, but a transition towards something as yet undefined. The present is cut off from the future. At the same time the text is suffused with nostalgia for a lost past. The house on Boulevard de Montmorency was a little enclave of the Rococo in Haussmann's metropolis, 'un des nids les plus pleins des choses du XVIIIe siècle qui existent à Paris': 'du seuil de la maison, le visiteur est acceuilli par des terres cuites, des bronzes, des dessins, des porcelaines du siècle aimable par excellence, mêlés à des objets de l'Extrême-Orient, qui se trouvaient faire si bon ménage dans les collections de Madame de Pompadour et tous les *curieux* et les *curiolets* du temps'.[43] As this makes clear, Edmond de Goncourt did not collect only eighteenth-century antiques, but also oriental art objects. He does not, however, present these as forming two separate collections. Both materially, in the arrangement of the house at Auteuil, and discursively, in the text of *La Maison d'un artiste*, the different objects on display, of various different sorts, are presented as forming one coherent and harmonious collection, the Japanese swords as much a nod to Rococo design as the

41   Goncourt, *La Maison*, I, 3. See above, pp. 127–8.
42   Goncourt, *La Maison*, I, 3.
43   Goncourt, *La Maison*, I, 1 and 1–2.

Boucher drawings. Both text and house are a monument to the eighteenth century. Thus Goncourt describes his bedroom as 'une chambre du siècle passé', which, 'le matin, lorsque j'ouvre les yeux, me donne l'impression de me réveiller, non dans mon temps que je n'aime pas, mais bien dans le temps qui a été l'objet des études et des amours de ma vie: en quelque chambre d'un château d'une *Belle au Bois dormant* du temps de Louis XV, épargnée par la Révolution et la mode de l'acajou'.[44] Here the reign of Louis XV is not presented as a precisely defined, chronologically delimited epoch in the history of France; rather the 'temps du Louis XV', through the reference to the fairytale princess, is transformed into a Rococo never-never land, a golden age.

Like Never-Never Land, Goncourt's Rococo idyll is closely bound up with the fears and anxieties generated by the knowledge of our own mortality. In his bedroom, Edmond de Goncourt conjures sickness and death: 'à l'heure où l'on devient vieux, malingre, souffreteux, il faut songer à meubler pour la maladie un coquet logis, où elle sera moins laide pour les autres et pour soi-même, et se préparer, au milieu d'élégances, à accueillir la Mort en délicat'.[45] Throughout *La Maison d'un artiste* it is the voice of an old man that we hear. For Goncourt, putting together the catalogue of his collection is first and foremost an exercise in reminiscence. He provided his own epigraph for the text: 'En ce temps où les choses, dont le poète latin a signalé la mélancolique vie latente, sont associées si largement par la description littéraire moderne à l'Histoire de l'Humanité, pourquoi n'écrirait-on pas les mémoires des choses au milieu desquelles s'est écoulée une existence d'homme?'[46] In this book, description gives rise to narrative, as the process of inventorying the collection unlocks the memories stored in the various objects – a Japanese sword, for example, now hanging in the Petit Salon, elicits an anecdote about the siege of Paris, when it was

44 Goncourt, *La Maison*, II, 200.
45 Goncourt, *La Maison*, II, 204.
46 Goncourt, *La Maison*, I, 'Préface'.

used to kill a chicken.[47] The past, however, is always viewed in the text from the perspective of an impoverished present, marked by loss and grief. Describing the dining-room, Edmond recalls the celebrated dinner-parties he and his brother used to throw, and goes on to say: 'Dans ce temps, il faut le dire, nous étions deux ... Aujourd'hui la salle à manger d'Auteuil n'est plus que la salle à manger d'un vieil homme seul, qui aime mieux la salle à manger des autres'.[48]

La Maison d'un artiste is, therefore, also *Les Mémoires d'un artiste*, but its organization differs from the conventional memoir, as it uses things to elicit anecdote. Objects offer a material support for memory. Edmond stresses the reliquary function of objects when he describes visiting the room where his brother died: 'dans le recuillement de la demi-obscurité, et parmi ce que gardent et vous font retrouver d'un mort bien aimé les choses de sa chambre mortuaire, je me donne la douleureuse jouissance de me ressouvenir'.[49] The paradoxical formulation, 'douleureuse jouissance', suggests the ambivalence of memory, which is both a function of the passage of time and a bulwark, albeit a fragile one, against its corrosive effects. Memory preserves the past from complete oblivion. The text throughout, however, is haunted by the spectre of forgetting, for example in the short account of the art market in the mid-nineteenth century with which Goncourt prefaces the catalogue of eighteenth-century drawings. Edmond looks back on the 1840s and 1850s as a golden age of collecting, when it was possible to pick up Boucher drawings for a song:

> Qui se rappelle aujourd'hui la vieille place du Carrousel avec tous ces cartons bâillant entr'ouverts à la porte de ses centaines d'échoppes? En 1848, j'y achetais, à seize ans, mon premier dessin, une aquarelle de Boucher [...]. Qui se rappelle les cartons bâillant entr'ouverts sous les arcades de l'Institut, et tout le long des quais, et à l'entrée de cet antre s'ouvrant sous un jardin, là où s'élève aujourd'hui le *Journal officiel*? Je trouvai là un jour [...] neuf croquis de Gabriel de Saint-Aubin pour une illustration du *Zadig* de Voltaire [...]. Qui se rappelle les cartons à la porte des bric-à-brac du boulevard

47 Goncourt, *La Maison*, I, 23–4.
48 Goncourt, *La Maison*, I, 21.
49 Goncourt, *La Maison*, II, 370.

Beaumarchais et dans le renfoncement de tous les vieux murs délités et des édifices religieux abandonnés ... ? Là, pour une pièce de trois francs, je devenais possesseur d'un de mes jolis Cochin.[50]

This paragraph, fundamentally concerned with the passage of time and the changes it wrings, is structured by the repetition of the question, 'Qui se rappelle ...?', acting as a refrain. Only an old man can remember the old days, which soon will be lost forever.

This passage, where nostalgia is rooted in an experience of embodied memory recognized as precarious, can usefully be read alongside Nora's account of memory and history. Both Nora and Goncourt are concerned with the imminent disappearance of memory, but Goncourt's account constellates the ideas of memory, consumption and inheritance differently from Nora's, and in so doing disrupts some of the antitheses that Nora's dichotomous system ceaselessly piles on top of each other. In the above passage, Goncourt associates memory not with production, but with consumption. The days that Goncourt happily remembers were days he spent bric-a-brac hunting with his brother, or before that with his aunt. In *La Maison*, Goncourt speculates as to the origin of his collectomania, and – linking it disturbingly to syphilis – wonders whether it was 'un accident, un mal attrapé par hasard, ou si ce n'était pas plutôt une maladie héréditaire'.[51] An investigation into his paternal lineage, however, convinces him that 'le collectionneur chez moi ne doit rien aux ascendances, et qu'il a été créé uniquement par l'influence d'une femme de ma famille'.[52] This woman was not a blood relative but an aunt by marriage. Goncourt thus substitutes an environmental explanation of his 'maladie' for an hereditary one. Although collecting connects him with the past, the French eighteenth century, and with his own childllhood, so many happy hours of which were spent in antiques shops, it does not connect him with his (father's) family's past. Rather collecting appears as a disruption of patrilineal inheritance, and as such, and because it belongs

---

50   Goncourt, *La Maison*, I, 31–2.
51   Goncourt, *La Maison*, I, 354.
52   Goncourt, *La Maison*, I, 355.

to the regime of consumption rather than production, Goncourt's text poses a challenge to Nora's model of memory. Nora presents the regime of production and the regime of memory as parallels, suggesting that, just as the latter involves a 'natural' rather than an estranged relationship with the past, so the former involves a 'natural' rather than an estranged relationship with objects. Goncourt, by associating embodied memory with collecting, calls into question this romanticization of the regime of production. Goncourt's view of memory thus undermines the rhetoric of plenitude that characterizes Nora's descriptions thereof.

The fear of forgetting emerges again in *La Maison d'un artiste*, in the description of the junk-room on the second storey:

> Sur le palier s'ouvrent des chambres inhabitées, ensevelies dans la poussière des caphar-naüms, où tout bibeloteur emmagasine et entasse les choses boiteuses et estropiées, les choses achetées les jours d'erreur, où le goût est *embourgeoisé*, et les choses pour lesquelles une inexplicable indifférence est venue. Il y a là, pêle-mêle, dans le fouillis pittoresque d'un grenier du bric-à-brac, des porcelaines égueulées, des grues de bronze aux frêles et longues pattes cassées par la trépidation du chemin de fer, des cadres dédorés qui doivent aller en visite chez le doreur, des dessins chassés de l'entresol et du premier étage par des acquisitions récentes, des piles de cuirs japonais destinés à fabriquer des reliures de livres orientaux, des objets de toutes sortes et de toutes formes, dont la mémoire est comme perdue, et dont le regard se détourne, ainsi que d'achats dont on rougit [...].
> Au milieu de cet amoncellement de choses, disparates et hétéroclites, des armoires entre-bâillées laissent voir des rangées interminables de livres modernes.[53]

This passage takes up many of the major motifs of *La Maison d'un artiste*, with the junk-room functioning as a negative counterpart to the collection, an anti-collection. First, the objects in the junk-room have been excluded from the collection proper because they appeal to 'le goût ... *embourgeoisé*', in contrast to the *objets d'art* in the rest of the house, which pay tribute to the tastes and mores of the eighteenth-century aristocracy. The assumption that the bourgeoisie were culturally illiterate philistines was, of course, a commonplace of nineteenth-century thought, and we have already encountered

---

53   Goncourt, *La Maison*, II, 359–60.

numerous examples of it, from Balzac to the *Arsène Lupin* stories, but Edmond de Goncourt was particularly insistent in conflating the aristocracy of taste with the aristocracy of birth, promoting a design style that drew inspiration from the court of Louis XV. Goncourt's disrelish for the century in which he lived is apparent throughout the passage, in the 'rangées interminables de livres modernes', where the adjective 'interminables' serves to suggest the boringness of contemporary letters, and in the reference to bronzes damaged during the course of railway journeys, an image of modernity pulverising the past, smashing to pieces those objects that the collector cherishes. The pristine objects in the collection proper, relics of a bygone era, enable the past to survive into the present, but the objects in the junk-room are broken-down and decrepit, ruined objects signifying the destructive, wasteful action of time. The most salient feature of the junk-room, however, is the irreducible heterogeneity of the objects it houses. It is a 'capharnaüm', where oddments that are 'disparates et hétéroclites' lie 'pêle-mêle', an accumulation without order, where the only relationship between the objects is one of physical propinquity.

The Goncourt junk-room is thus governed by 'the logic of juxta-position'[54] that Janell Watson identifies as underpinning the museum display:

> In the museum setting, paintings and artifacts are placed side by side. There is no intrinsic connection among these items, only the external connections of similarity or seriality based on genre, theme, provenance, etc., connections imposed on them by curators, catalogues, or the viewer. Unlike linguistic elements, the material objects possess neither semantic nor syntactic connections, for as one analysis of the museum display puts it, 'The problem with things is that they are dumb. They are not eloquent as some thinkers in art museums claim.' Connections must be added by a narrator figure, either a speaking guide or a text.[55]

Watson's initial claim that the museum display is characterized by a fundamental heterogeneity rests on her second claim, that objects are mute. By distinguishing objects from linguistic units, Watson suggests that by

54 Watson, p. 111.
55 Watson, p. 111.

themselves they cannot signify. This proposition is one that the entire discourse around collecting strenuously denies, which is why in the context
of *La Maison d'un artiste*, the existence of the junk-room is presented as
a scandal. Walter Benjamin, in one of the fragments on the collector prepared for *The Arcades Project*, suggested that the collector is engaged in
an attempt 'to elucidate things through research into their properties and
relations. [...] [He] brings together what belongs together; by keeping in
mind their affinities and their succession in time, he can eventually fur-
nish information about his objects'.[56] Benjamin's comment is the negative
of Watson's characterization of the museum object. For Watson, objects
'possess neither semantic nor syntactic connections'; Benjamin's collector,
on the other hand, is devoted precisely to bringing to light the 'properties
and relations' of the objects he owns. For Benjamin's collector, it is as if over
the lifetime of the object a kernel of meaning and significance has grown
within it, which the collector is able to extract. He clings to the idea that
there is meaning immanent in the world of things. Sylvain Pons similarly
claims that meaning and significance emanate from objects, when he tries
to explain to his uncomprehending cousin, 'Moi, je crois à l'intelligence
des objets d'art, ils connaissent les amateurs, ils les appellent, ils leur font:
"Chit! Chit!"'.[57] Pons ascribes a voice to things, and presents himself as a
kind of Dr. Dolittle of *objets d'art*, his ear attuned to their speech. Germain
the numismatist in Jules Clarétie's novel, *Un Assassin*, prefers medals to
coins because:

> La médaille parle toujours, la monnaie est souvent muette. Moins précieuse comme
> valeur intrinsèque, la médaille vaut davantage; elle vaut surtout par le souvenir. Que
> de fois Germain avait-il regardé ces médailles curieuses qui lui racontait si éloquem-
> ment le passé! Que de fois avait-il expliqué à Henriette [...] ces légendes, ces énigmes,
> ces devises latines, ces rébus presque indéchiffrables.[58]

56   Benjamin, p. 211 [H4a,1].
57   Balzac, *Le Cousin Pons*, p. 512.
58   Jules Clarétie, *Un Assassin* (Paris: Faure, 1866), p. 219.

Germain qua collector values medals over coins because the former speak to him. It is not, however, by virtue of being antique objects, material relics of days gone by, that the medals can speak about the past. The past they recount is not that in which they participated, but that which they commemorate through their inscriptions. It is the bits of text they carry that confer meaning on them. Germain's preference for medals over coins gestures towards the fact that objects are not speaking subjects.

The description of the Goncourt junk-room similarly exposes the muteness of objects. As already noted, the conceit which underpins the text is that it recounts 'la mélancolique vie latente' of the objects in the collection, 'les mémoires des choses'.[59] But the objects in the junk-room are those 'dont la mémoire est comme perdue, dont le regard se détourne.'[60] There is a crucial ambiguity in these words, for they allow for the possibility that the objects are both forgotten and forgetting, and that it is they that are averting their gaze. This ambiguity is closed down by the final clause in the sentence, however, 'ainsi que d'achats dont on rougit', which makes it clear that it is the collector who is doing the forgetting, and the collector who is looking away. Goncourt momentarily ascribes voice and gaze to the objects in the junk-room, but then makes clear that this ascription is illusory. The objects can neither forget nor look away because they can neither look nor remember; they are dead things, and it is only the collector who can breathe life into them, for example by recycling them, using old Japanese leather to bind books. Such recycled objects enter into the collection stripped of their personal histories, with new identity papers created for them by their owner. The fact that the objects in the junk-room might yet find their way back into the collection, that the junk-room is as much a waiting-room as a graveyard, demonstrates that the membrane between the two is not impermeable. The junk-room is both the collection's despised and abject other and its necessary complement. The existence of the junk-room within the house at Auteuil therefore poses a threat to the collection as a whole, by presenting a different ontology of the object.

---

59   Goncourt, *La Maison*, I, 'Préface'.
60   Goncourt, *La Maison*, II, 359.

Materiality and Discursivity in the Bouvard-Pécuchet Museum

The muteness of objects is also encountered by two other famous, in this case fictional, collectors, Flaubert's Bouvard and Pécuchet. After accidentally stumbling across an intriguing sideboard which Gorju, a local carpenter of dubious reputation, assures them is an authentic Renaissance piece (the reader is never given reliable information about the provenance or value of the object) the two retired copy-clerks develop a taste for antiquarian collecting, and consequently, 'leur maison ressemblait à un musée':[61]

> Quand on avait franchi le seuil on se heurtait à une auge de pierre (un sarcophage gallo-romain) puis, les yeux étaient frappés par de la quincaillerie.
> Contre le mur en face, une bassinoire dominait deux chenets et une plaque de foyer, qui représentait un moine caressant une bergère. Sur des planchettes tout autour, on voyait des flambeaux, des serrures, des boulons, des écrous. Le sol disparaissait sous des tessons de tuiles rouges. Une table au milieu exhibait les curiosités les plus rares: la carcasse d'un bonnet de Cauchoise, deux urnes d'argile, des médailles, une fiole de verre opalin. Un fauteuil en tapisserie avait sur son dossier un triangle de guipure. Un morceau de cotte de mailles ornait la cloison à droite; et en dessous, des pointes maintenaient horizontalement une hallebarde, pièce unique.[62]

These opening paragraphs in the lengthy description of the museum establish its salient features. The keynote of the description of the museum is its disorderliness. The objects seem a random accumulation rather than an ordered collection. It is hard to discern any connection between any of the items on display; rather the museum seems to offer a spectacle of contingency. One of the random objects on display is 'l'arbre généalogique de la famille Croixmare'.[63] A family tree normatively functions to knit together past and present, to present different generations as linked together in an unbroken chain. This family tree seems to function almost parodically in

---

61 Gustave Flaubert, *Bouvard et Pécuchet*, in *Œuvres complètes*, ed. by Bernard Masson, 2 vols (Paris: Seuil, 1964), II, 201–301 (p. 232).
62 Flaubert, pp. 232–3.
63 Flaubert, p. 233.

this respect. 'Croixmare' is the name of a Normandy village, located in Seine-Maritime, and the inclusion of the 'l'arbre généaologique de la famille Croixmare' could therefore be seen as a piece of local history, if local is used in a rather expansive sense. Certainly the family tree seems to demand to be read as a symbol of geographical rootedness and historical continuity, but since it belongs to a family whose name is never again mentioned in the text, and who have no obvious link with Chavignolles, it in fact functions more as a symbol of the absence of an authentic connection to past and place.[64] On the reverse of the door on which hangs this arbitrary family tree, 'la figure au pastel d'une dame en costume Louis XV faisait pendant au portrait du père Bouvard [sic]'.[65] This further emphasizes the fact that the museum seems to offer an image of historical disjuncture, as the arrangement of the portraits, by coupling an anonymous woman 'en costume Louis XV' (and it is unclear from this whether the portrait dates from the reign of Louis XV or whether the sitter is simply dressed in Louis XV style) with Bouvard's father, and thus creating another sham genealogy. The Bouvard-Pécuchet museum seems to offer the reader, a virtual visitor, the experience of historical dislocation.

The language used to describe the experience of the museum visitor is the language of assault: 'on se heurtait ...', 'les yeux étaient frappés ...'. This is picked up later, when we learn that visitors to the Bouvard-Pécuchet museum are constantly bumping into and breaking things, much to its curators' annoyance. M. Marescot, the notary, breaks a fragment of chain mail which he had picked up to examine more closely. The image of a chain being broken offers an apt image for the experience of the visitor to the Bouvard-Pécuchet museum, confronted with a spectacle in which nothing seems properly connected to anything else. Later, the Comte de Faverges also causes some damage: 'Jamais pareilles bottes vernies n'avaient craqué

---

64 Flaubert's great-grandfather on his mother's side, Nicolas Cambremer, somewhat speciously styled himself Nicolas Cambremer de Croixmare, in an attempt to fashion a false genealogy that resonates with the representational content of the museum chapter. See Frederick Brown, *Flaubert: A Biography* (Cambridge. MA: Harvard University Press, 2007), p. 18.

65 Flaubert, p. 233.

dans le corridor. Elles se heurtènt contre le sarcophagus. Il faillit même
écraser plusieurs tuiles'.[66] This moment introduces a note of humour in
the text, generated through the shift from a figurative use of 'bottes' in
the first sentence, where they function metonymically to designate their
wearer, to a sudden emphasis on their materiality in the second sentence,
as they crash into the sarcophagus. This shift exemplifies the way in which,
throughout the description of the Bouvard-Pécuchet museum, the materiality of objects seems excessive, hampering the two clerks' attempts to
guide their visitors around the museum, distracting them from the story
they are trying to tell.

  Janell Watson, in her reading of the museum episode in *Bouvard
et Pécuchet*, discusses the nineteenth-century museum in terms of the
Foucauldian distinction between the episteme of Order (dominant,
broadly speaking, in the eighteenth century) and the episteme of History
(dominant in the nineteenth century). For Watson, the nineteenth-century
museum belongs to the latter.[67] In terms of the disciplines of history and
archaeology, those disciplines that shape the public museum, the shift
from the episteme of Order to the episteme of History involved a recon-
sideration of the relationship between discursivity and artefactuality.
Watson writes:

> The old order of history sought meaning by superimposing a layer of discourse on the
> monuments of the past, or artifacts, making them into documents. The new order
> of history, a history which aspires to archaeology, makes the document itself into
> a monument/artifact. Discourse does accompany the deployment of the museum's

66   Flaubert, p. 235.
67   At stake in Watson's discussion of the museum episode are the intellectual claims
     of deconstruction. She reproaches poststructuralist critics such as Eugenio Donato
     for being insufficiently historicist in their reading of the novel, and the museum epi-
     sode in particular, especially in so far as they have sought to claim that the museum
     – understood as an abstract concept – is grounded in the episteme of Order, and
     expresses a will to totalizing knowledge. For such an account of the museum episode,
     see Eugenio Donato, 'The Museum's Furnace: Notes Toward a Contextual Reading of
     Bouvard et Pécuchet', in *Textual Strategies: Perspectives in Post-Structuralist Criticism*,
     ed. by Josué V. Harari (Ithaca: Cornell University Press, 1979), pp. 213–38.

monumentalized documents, discourse in the form of labels, catalogues, voices of tour guides, and comments of visitors. However, the primary aim of the modern museum is not to seek the discourse of history behind or beyond the document, but rather to describe the documents themselves in as much detail as possible. The rise of the modern museum signals that the artifact's materiality has become as significant as its discursivity. For modern archaeology, material culture produces knowledge.[68]

I would suggest, however, the museum episode in *Bouvard et Pécuchet* drives a wedge between discursivity and materiality, and undermines the notion that material culture can produce knowledge. As readers we are guided around the museum twice, first by the narrator, in the opening description, and then again as the visits of various of the novels' characters to the museum are recounted. The initial description inventories the objects on display, limiting description to the material characteristics of the objects; the subsequent account includes Bouvard's and Pécuchet's commentary on the objects, the stories they attach to them. It is only through Bouvard's and Pécuchet's commentary that the objects in the museum come to signify anything other than the fact of their own brute existence. The text insists on the fact that meaning is not immanent in the objects on display in the museum, but projected on to them by the curators. The reference to 'une auge de pierre (un sarcophage gallo-romain)' in the opening passage quoted above operates as a microcosm of the museum episode as a whole. The object is first described through reference to its material and its use value, before its cultural and historical significance is revealed. The transformation of trough into sarcophagus, effected abruptly and parenthetically, appears somewhat arbitrary. The Bouvard-Pécuchet museum makes clear that the notion of the speaking object is a ventriloquist's trick.

The relationship between history and material culture was a vexed one in nineteenth-century France. On the one hand, the collector was often seen as a crucial agent in the formation and transmission of a collective cultural memory, preserving material relics of the past and bringing them into the present, helping to keep craft traditions alive. On the other hand, the collection often seemed to speak not of the survival of the past into the

68   Watson, p. 86.

present, but of its loss. Moreover, at stake in the discourse around historical collecting is the notion that material culture can produce knowledge. This notion that forms the very basis of historical collecting, but was consistently called into question, in texts such as *Bouvard et Pécuchet*, in which the object, in its brute materiality, is dangerously refractory to meaning.

CHAPTER 5

The Poverty of Taxonomy

Nineteenth-century collectomania was not confined to the sphere of *artificialia*; abundant too were collectors of *naturalia*: from mineralogists and paleontologists to lepidopterists and conchologists, professional and amateur natural historians established collections to classify and catalogue the natural world. Indeed, collecting has long been a vital technology of knowledge in the study of the natural world. In its classical paradigm, natural history was concerned with the elaboration of a general taxonomy of all things animal, vegetable and mineral. Collecting was not merely its method, but to a large extent its meaning as well, and natural historians were engaged above all in a work of inventory and classification.[1] Over the course of the nineteenth century, however, this classical natural historical paradigm was dismantled, as comparative anatomy gave birth to modern biology, concerned with physiological functioning, and a preoccupation with taxonomy was displaced by the study of the processes of life.[2] Thus the taxonomical epistemology that underpinned natural history collecting came to be viewed with increasing scepticism. At the same time, as we shall see, taxonomical knowledge was often regarded as arid or sterile, as an intransitive discourse lacking any instrumental dimension, in which

---

1   See Michel Foucault, *Les Mots et les choses: une archéologie des sciences humaines* (Paris: Gallimard, 1966), pp. 137–76.

2   See Foucault, pp. 275–92, and also James A. Secord, 'The Crisis of Nature', in *Cultures of Natural History*, ed. by N. Jardine, J. A. Secord and E. C. Spary (Cambridge: Cambridge University Press, 1996), pp. 227–59, in which Secord examines the breakdown of natural history in the nineteenth century and addresses the question of why sciences of classification have come to be held in such low esteem.

nomenclature had occluded nature and words had split apart from things.[3] Nonetheless natural history collecting remained a popular pastime in the nineteenth century, even as its epistemological foundations crumbled. This chapter will explore the discourse of natural history collecting in four literary or paraliterary texts of the period: Flaubert's *Bouvard et Pécuchet* (1884), Verne's phenomenally successful *Vingt mille lieues sous les mers* (1869), Loti's *Le Roman d'un enfant* (1890), and a short Maupassant article, 'Au Muséum d'histoire naturelle', first published in *Le Gaulois* in 1881. All four texts problematize the activity of natural history collecting. Flaubert and Verne use the notion of natural history collecting to reflect on the relationship between words and things, a concern which Loti ties into a meditation on the morbidity of natural history collecting. This notion of morbidity, linked to the vitalist tendencies in late-nineteenth-century thought which emerged with the new biology, is, as we shall see, central to Maupassant's gothic account of the Muséum d'histoire naturelle as a space haunted by death.

Bouvard And Pécuchet Ask:
Why Is Devonian Rock Not Found Only In Devon?

The Bouvard-Pécuchet museum contains both historical bric-a-brac and *naturalia*: 'Une vieille poutre de bois se dressait dans le vestibule. Les spécimens de géologie encombraient l'escalier; – et une chaîne énorme s'étendait

---

3   Popular works of natural history often seem to assume that readers would find the extensive use of taxonomical discourse either boring or rebarbative and thus sought to minimize its presence in the text. See for example, P. Bernard and Louis Couaillhac, *Le Jardin des plantes: description complète, historique et pittoresque du Muséum d'histoire naturelle, de la ménagerie, des serres, des galeries de minéralogie de d'anatomie* (Paris: Curmer, 1842), which mocks as ersatz those savants, 'créateurs intrépides de mots grecs' (p. 654), who take seriously Voltaire's injunction, 'Si vous ne pensez pas, créez de mots nouveaux' (p. 655).

par terre tout le long du corridor'.[4] These geological specimens are relics of a prior enthusiasm for geology, explored in the chapter immediately preceding the museum episode. The 'chaîne énorme' which lies along the floor, and the presence of which in the museum is mimicked by the presence of the en dash in the text, functioning almost as an ideogram, seems at first blush to point to a link between the disciplines of archaeology and geology: both are after all concerned with excavating origins, and in both collecting is a vital technology of knowledge. In fact, however, although the museum episode follows on directly from the geological episode, the transition from one to another is not presented as being intellectually motivated. After becoming disenchanted with geology, for reasons we shall examine shortly, Bouvard and Pécuchet arrive at the study of archaeology quite by accident, as a result of their chance encounter with a Renaissance *bahut*. It is characteristic of the text that the shift from archaeology to geology, which seem to be kindred disciplines sharing certain fundamental epistemological assumptions, is presented as wholly contingent. (The en dash, often (mis)used as a punctuation mark to denote a relationship of mere parataxis, thus seems particularly appropriate here.) Nonetheless, there are significant parallels between the copy-clerks' adventures in archaeology and geology. In the museum episode, as we have seen in chapter five,[5] collecting is of central importance as a normatively knowledge-producing activity that fails to produce the kind of knowledge that Bouvard and Pécuchet seek, and which Françoise Gaillard has aptly characterized as 'pas le vrai

---

4   Flaubert, p. 232. Franc Schuerewegen notes in his reading of the museum episode that: 'Le manque d'unité est d'autant plus frappant que des outils d'un assemblage virtuel sont exposés à côté de ce qeu ces mêmes outils devraient pouvoir unir [...] Il faut rappeler également la "chaîne énorme" dans le corridor, dont la présence même semble vouloir suggérer l'absurdité de toute opération d'enchaînement' ['*Muséum* ou *Croutéum?* Pons, Bouvard, Pécuchet et la collection', *Romantisme* 55 (1987), 41–84 (p. 43)].
5   See above, pp. 166–71.

mais le *sûr*, the assurance that the meaning is immanent in the world.[6] The geological episode follows a similar trajectory of disillusion.

The first problems that the two bachelors encounter as amateur geologists are in the acquisition of specimens, which involves them in a variety of scrapes, but more radically disenchanting are the difficulties they encounter when they return home:

> Ce n'était pas une mince besogne avant de coller des étiquettes, que de savoir le nom des roches; la variété des couleurs et du grenu leur faisait confondre l'argile avec la marne, le granit et le gneiss, le quartz et le calcaire.
> Et puis la nomenclature les irritait. Pourquoi dévonien, cambrien, jurassique, comme si les terres designées par ces mots n'étaient pas ailleurs qu'en Devonshire, près de Cambridge, et dans le Jura? Impossible de s'y reconnaître! Ce qui est système pour l'un est pour l'autre un étage, pour un troisième une simple assise. Les feuillets de couches s'entremêlent, s'embrouillent; mais Omalius d'Halloy vous prévient qu'il ne faut pas croire aux divisions géologiques.
> Cette déclaration les soulagea.[7]

The first difficulty Bouvard and Pécuchet encounter is in trying to identify their specimens. Material reality proves somewhat resistant to the activity of the novice taxonomists, as different kinds of rock prove less visibly distinct from each other than the books would suggest. Similarly the classificatory schemata of geologists, which like all taxonomies assume that everything has a place and aims to put everything in its place, do not map neatly on to the natural world, in which everything lies higgledy-piggledy: 'les feuillets de couches s'entremêlent, s'embrouillent'. This jumbledness is the condition for a multiplicity of classificatory systems, itself a source of consternation for the two copy-clerks, tireless seekers after objective order.

Bouvard's and Pécuchet's irritation with the apparent arbitrariness of geological nomenclature speaks of their desire for a discourse that would be perfectly isomorphic to reality. The question that they ask of geological

---

6   Françoise Gaillard, '*Bouvard et Pécuchet*, un conte sur la folie ordinaire (l'exemple du chapitre III)', in *Flaubert, l'autre*, ed. by F. Lecercle and S. Messina (Lyon: Presses Universitaires de Lyon, 1989), pp. 152–60 (p. 157).

7   Flaubert, p. 229.

nomenclature – why is Devonian rock not found only in Devon? – merits a serious response. After all, geological nomenclature is not arbitrary, but Bouvard and Pécuchet mistake the nature of the relationship between the signifier and the signified that obtains in this instance. Devonian rock is not found only in Devon, but it was first identified and classified in Devon.[8] The name is thus historically determined, and part of the fossil record of the discipline of geology itself, memorializing a significant development therein. It is, as Gaillard has pointed out, a curious feature of the two clerks' epistemological approach that they 'ne peuvent pas penser le savoir, dans son évolution constante, comme une recherche jamais achevée de la vérité, mais comme ce qui se doit d'énoncer à tout moment le vrai'.[9] This is a function of the fact that they see meaning not as an intellectual construct elaborated over time but as an inherent feature of the world. The two clerks' misapprehension of the meaning of the word 'dévonien' is symptomatic of this, as they choose to assume that it is determined by geography rather than by historical contingency.

In their belief that language should map perfectly on to reality, Bouvard and Pécuchet follow in the tradition of natural historians such as Linnaeus, who dreamed, Foucault tells us, of 'calligrammes botaniques': 'Il voulait que l'ordre de la description, sa répartition en paragraphes, et jusqu'à ses modules typographiques reproduisent la figure de la plante elle-même.'[10] The assumption that words should correspond to things in such a perfect fashion underpinned, according to François Dagognet, eighteenth-century botany, which conceived of nomenclature as a 'sorte d'algèbre florale. [...] Il faut nommer, pour pouvoir, savoir ordonner, et inversement d'ailleurs. En effet, dès que la plante a été aperçue dans son essentialité, à travers l'attribut déterminant qui le spécifie, le vocable qui lui conviendra s'inspirera de

---

8   Cambrian rock, however, is named not after Cambridge, but after an ancient Welsh tribe that inhabited the area in which it was first identified. This error, if we can ascribe it to Bouvard and Pécuchet rather than Flaubert, further confirms Gaillard's contention that the two clerks are unable to think diachronically, as they forget that place-names change over time.
9   Gaillard, *'Bouvard et Pécuchet'*, p. 158.
10   Foucault, p. 147.

ce caractère, l'exhibera et le véhiculera. Le mot matérialise cette victoire, l'enracine'.[11] Flaubert's heroes take this idea seriously when they think that Devonian rock should be found only in Devon, but their encounter with natural history in fact serves only to force them to confront once again the gap between word and world that they consistently fail to negotiate over the course of the novel. Their disenchantment flows from the fact that the classificatory schemata established by natural historians are shown to be somehow inadequate to reality. This apparent mismatch between words and things had already been explored in another great narrative of collecting, Jules Verne's *Vingt mille lieues sous les mers*.

Vingt milles lieues sous les mers

Verne's 1869 blockbuster novel tapped into a mid-century public interest in all things oceanographic, created, catered to, and sustained by such diverse phenomena as popular natural history books, Hugo's *Les Travailleurs de la mer* (1866) and Michelet's *La Mer* (1861) – both of which feature in Captain Nemo's library – and the aquarium at the 1867 *Exposition Universelle*.[12] The novel, in keeping with the Hetzel-Verne project of education through recreation,[13] incorporates a mass of oceanographic information into an adventure story. The narrator of the story is an eminent natural historian, Pierre Arronax, 'professeur-suppléant au Muséum d'histoire naturelle',[14]

---

11   François Dagognet, *Le Catalogue de la vie* (Paris: Presses Universitaires de la France, 1970), p. 27.

12   For information about public interest in oceanography in the nineteenth century, and the scientific context in which Verne's work appeared, see *Quand Jules Verne raconte la mer: Vingt mille lieues sous les mers*, texts by Muriel Gout, Jacqueline Goy, Lucien Laubier et al (Paris; Monaco: Institut Océanographique, 2005).

13   See Pierre-Jules Hetzel, 'Avertissement de l'éditeur', in Jules Verne, *Les Voyages et aventures du capitaine Hatteras* (Paris: Hetzel, 1866), pp. 1–2.

14   Jules Verne, *Vingt mille lieues sous les mers*, 2 vols (Paris: Hetzel, 1871), p. 7.

and this focalization clearly acts as a narrative device for transmitting to the reader a corpus of natural historical knowledge, chiefly through the many long catalogues of marine flora and fauna that are among the most striking features of the novel's composition. Apollinaire's oft-quoted remark on Verne's style ('Quel style a Jules Verne! Rien que des substantifs!')[15] seems particularly pertinent in relation to *Vingt mille lieues*: the text is crammed with seemingly endless lists of the creatures glimpsed by the travellers through the giant windows of the *Nautilus* as it travels the deep.

One of the central questions in Verne criticism – are his novels *lisible* or *scriptible?* are they rooted, in other words, in an aesthetics of closure or an aesthetics of the never-ending? – hinges precisely on the effect of such lists. In his seminal article '*Nautilus* et *Bateau Ivre*', Roland Barthes argued that the catalogue is the formal expression of the 'principe existentiel' of Verne's 'cosmogonie', 'le geste continu d'enfermement'.[16] In Barthes' reading the use of the catalogue form is freighted with ideological significance:

> [Verne's] mouvement est exactement celui d'un encyclopédiste du XVIIIᵉ siècle ou d'un peintre hollandais: le monde est fini, le monde est plein de matériaux numérables et contigus. L'artiste ne peut avoir d'autre tâche que de faire des catalogues, des inventaires [...]. Verne appartient à la lignée progressiste de la bourgeoisie: son œuvre affiche que rien ne peut échapper à l'homme, que le monde, même le plus lointain, est comme un objet dans sa main.[17]

According to Barthes, therefore, in Verne's novels the classification of the world is inseparable from the appropriation thereof. The principle of enclosure that functions formally through the use of the catalogue is embedded at the level of representational content in the image of the *Nautilus* itself, an 'intériorité sans fissure' where 'la jouissance de l'enfermement atteint son

---

15   Cited in, for example, Tim Unwin, 'The Fiction of Science, or the Science of Fiction', in *Jules Verne: Narratives of Modernity*, ed. Edmund J. Smyth (Liverpool: University of Liverpool Press, 2000), pp. 46–59 (p. 50).

16   Roland Barthes, '*Nautilus* et *Bateau ivre*', in *Mythologies* (Paris: Seuil, 1957), pp. 90–2 (p. 90).

17   Barthes, '*Nautilus* et *Bateau ivre*', pp. 90–1.

paroxysme'.[18] Barthes' reading resonates with Philippe Hamon's remarks on *Vingt mille lieues* in *Expositions*, in which he suggests that the novel transforms the world into a collection – an ordered representation of a world tamed and mastered.[19] The *Nautilus* is not only a private museum, housing a collection in which are represented 'tous les trésors de la nature et de l'art',[20] it is also a tool which turns the oceans themselves into an aquarium.

There also exists, however, a contestatory tradition of Verne criticism. Thus in the same edited volume in which Sarah Capitanio tells us that 'Verne's texts take to an extreme the nineteenth-century Realist tendency to represent a world that is *a priori* circumscribable, causal and explicable in a way that frequently blurs the boundaries between novel and scientific or technical manual',[21] Tim Unwin claims that in Verne's work 'the classification and taxonomical style end up not by appropriating the aquatic world and reducing it to comprehensible proportions, but by doing the opposite: highlighting its strangeness and its mystery and foregrounding the intoxicating effect of descriptive words'.[22] In stressing the poetic effect of the lists in *Vingt mille lieues*, Unwin follows in the wake of critics such as Butor, who presents Verne as a precursor of Lautréamont, Eluard, and Michaux.[23] For these critics the lists in *Vingt mille lieues* do not serve the drearily instrumental purpose of shoehorning into the text a given quantity of technical vocabulary in accordance with its avowed pedagogical remit, but deserve to be read as prose poems, with a specifically aesthetic purpose.

18   Barthes, '*Nautilus* et *Bateau ivre*', p. 92.
19   Philippe Hamon, pp. 75–6 and pp. 79–80.
20   Verne, *Vingt mille lieues*, p. 77.
21   Sarah Capitanio, '"L'Ici-bas" and "l'Au-delà" … but Not as they Knew it. Realism, Utopianism and Science Fiction in the Novels of Jules Verne', in *Jules Verne: Narratives of Modernity*, ed. Edmund J. Smyth (Liverpool: University of Liverpool Press, 2000), pp. 60–77 (p. 63).
22   Unwin, p. 50.
23   Michel Butor, 'Le Point suprême et l'âge d'or à travers quelques œuvres de Jules Verne', in *Répertoire I* (Paris: Editions de Minuit, 1960) pp. 130–62 (pp. 131–2).

The co-existence of these two traditions of Verne criticism reflects the self-contestatory nature of *Vingt mille lieues* itself, which emerges with particular force in the representation of Nemo's private museum, housed on board the *Nautilus*. Nemo's collection is truly encyclopaedic in scope, offering all the riches of the world rationally rearranged. As Andrew Martin notes, it is the 'matrix of an ideal order, of the chaotic planet rationally rearranged, the *summum bonum* of the cult of classification'.[24] The collection is the pretext for the first of the novel's great catalogues, extending over several pages. The following quotation, inventorying Nemo's conchological specimens, concludes this catalogue, as the word 'enfin' suggests:

> Enfin des littorines, des dauphinules, des turritelles, des janthines, des ovules, des volutes, des olives, des mitres, des casques, des pourpres, des buccins, des harpes, des rochers, des tritons, des cérites, des fuseaux, des strombes, des ptérocères, des patelles, des hyales, des cléodores, coquillages délicats et fragiles, que la science a baptisé de ses noms les plus charmants.[25]

This list of nouns is not typical of the catalogue as a whole, which more normally offers a few descriptive words about each of the specimens cited. By reducing the list to a series of unadorned nouns the text thus undergoes a movement of acceleration before the end, as if it were frantically trying to cram in as many words as possible. The keynote of all the catalogues in *Vingt mille lieues*, impossible to convey through selective quotation, is simply their cornucopian quality, a function of their length and the fact that the text explicitly acknowledges the impossibility of exhaustive inventory. Thus Arronax opens his catalogue of Nemo's conchological collection by stating that: 'Je vis là une collection d'une valeur inestimable, et que le temps me manquerait à décrire tout entière. [...] Je citerai seulement [...]'.[26] All of the lists in *Vingt mille lieues* succumb finally to the temptation of the '&c', which in itself seems to belie the assumptions both of Barthes and Nemo. There is thus an odd split in the text, between the image it offers of the

---

24 Andrew Martin, *The Knowledge of Ignorance: From Genesis to Jules Verne* (Cambridge: Cambridge University Press, 1985), p. 155.
25 Verne, *Vingt mille lieues*, p. 80.
26 Verne, *Vingt mille lieues*, p. 79.

material collection itself – a closed, rationally ordered structure – and the textual account of that collection in the form of an incomplete list.

This split is reinforced by the way in which the list, as in the passage cited above, foregrounds the materiality of the signifier, behind which the referent is somewhat obscured. In the final clause of the quotation the text explicitly acknowledges itself as being in thrall to the signifier, but this is already signaled in the composition of the list itself. Verne's text enacts the same crisis that Bouvard and Pécuchet suffer, the experience of the chasm that separates words from things, but it responds thereto in rather a different way, treating words as things in themselves, exploiting their material properties.[27] The locus of the list's coherence is the signifier, not the signified. Thus the opening three nouns are bound together through alliteration in [l] and [t] and assonance in [i]. 'Ovules', 'volutes' and 'olives' similarly form a trio linked through their phonetic properties. There follow another three nouns forming a set, this time linked through connotation and metonymy. A 'mitre', as a form of headwear, belongs in the same paradigm as 'casque', but it is also linked to 'pourpres', the colour of a bishop's vestments. 'Buccin' and 'harpe' are both musical instruments, and thus form a pair, but 'harpe', placed next to 'rochers' and 'triton', almost seems to morph into Harpie, as the folklore of the sea flickers through the mind. According to Didier Maleuvre, lists in literary texts embody in extreme form the tendencies of objective realism. He suggests that in a list all nouns behave as proper names, referring to a singularity. The inventory 'speaks in the childhood of language, a world that precedes connotation and

---

27 For a stimulating general discussion of the relationship between words and things, see Peter Schwenger, 'Words and the Murder of the Thing', *Critical Inquiry*, 28 (2001), 99–113. Schwenger writes that: 'Whenever words are confronted with things, and the attempt is made to think within the space of their difference [...] Either it is argued that words *are* things, partaking in their solidity and presence, or else material things are hollowed out by an awareness that they can never be seen as anything but signifiers in a psychic space' (p. 102). Verne's text, as argued here, seems to incorporate both positions: sometimes words are used as things, the material properties of the signifier foregrounded, sometimes, as in Conseil's discourse, words seem to float free from material reality, which takes on a spectral quality.

metonymy, that is, literature'.[28] The list offers the hope of a straightforward, unproblematic correspondence between words and things. Within *Vingt mille lieues*, however, the lists operate in a completely different fashion, exploiting the multivalence of the signifier.

This multivalence militates against the basic tenet of taxonomical thought – a place for everything and everything in its place. The representative of taxonomical thought in the text is Conseil, Arronax's valet, a comic figure, whose ersatz erudition is exploited as a source of light relief in the novel. Conseil's language, unlike Arronax's, is a language of closure. Thus, after Conseil has successfully classified a dugong – 'Ordre des siréniens, groupe des pisciformes, sous-classe des monodelphiens, classe des mammifères, embranchement des vertébrés' – Arronax wryly notes that, 'lorsque Conseil avait ainsi parlé, il n'y avait plus rien à dire'.[29] The inclusion of the figure of Conseil in the text clearly does operate as a pretext for Verne to incorporate a quantity of taxonomical data, offered to the reader almost apologetically. During the *compte rendu* of their voyage across the Mediterranean, Arronax interrupts his own catalogue thus: 'Conseil s'était occupé plus particulièrement d'observer les mollusques et les articulés, et bien que la nomenclature en soit un peu aride, je ne veux pas faire tort à ce brave garçon en omettant ses observations'.[30] This acts as plea for forbearance on the part of readers, and clearly anticipates a sigh of boredom on their part when confronted with so much 'nomenclature'. But something else is at stake in this interpolation of Conseil's observations on molluscs into Arronax's catalogue of Mediterranean flora and fauna. Arronax introduces this catalogue thus:

> Des diverses poissons qui l'habitent, j'ai vu des uns, entrevu les autres, sans parler de ceux que la vitesse du *Nautilus* déroba à mes yeux. Qu'il me soit donc permis de les classer d'après cette classification fantaisiste. Elle rendra mieux mes rapides observations.[31]

28   Maleuvre, p. 165.
29   Verne, *Vingt mille lieues*, p. 247.
30   Verne, *Vingt mille lieues*, p. 274.
31   Verne, *Vingt mille lieues*, p. 268.

Arronax therefore explicitly draws attention to the fact that his account of the Mediterranean deviates from the discursive norms of ichthyology. His account is not organized through reference to the classificatory schema of natural history, but rather aims to restore to the reader the experience of his own encounter with nature. This is in contrast to Conseil's approach. His observations are structured around the objective classificatory schema of the textbook, introduced with the words: 'Dans l'embranchement des mollusques'.[32] These two contrasting approaches have a hierarchical relationship in the text, as Conseil's discourse is subordinated to that of Arronax:

> Dans l'embranchement des mollusques, il cite de nombreux pétoncles pectiniformes, des spondyles pieds d'âne qui s'entassaient les uns sur les autres, des donaces triangulaires, des hyales tridentées [...], des anomies que les Languedociens, dit-on préfèrent aux huîtres, des clovis si chers aux Marseillais, des praires doubles, blanches et grasses, quelques-uns de ces clams qui abondent sur les côtes de l'Amérique du Nord et dont il se fait un débit si considérable à New-York, des peignes operculaires de couleurs variées, des lithodomes enfoncés dans leurs trous et dont je goûtais fort le goût poivré.[33]

Over the course of these few lines Conseil's observations are colonized by Arronax, and the valet's discourse squeezed out of the text by that of his master. This process begins with the inclusion of the (taxonomically extraneous) information concerning Languedociens' gustatory preferences, and is complete with the intrusion of the first person subject pronoun in the final line, which restores to the list its subjective dimension.

The reference to the taste of the fish represents a further break with the norms of taxonomical discourse. In his account of natural history in the classical age, Foucault notes:

> Au sens strict, on peut dire que l'âge classique s'est ingénié, sinon à voir le moins possible, du moins à restreindre volontairement le champ de son expérience. L'observation, à partir du XVIIe siècle, est une connaissance sensible assortie de

---

32   Verne, *Vingt mille lieues*, p. 274.
33   Verne, *Vingt mille lieues*, p. 274.

conditions systématiquement négatives. Exclusion, bien sûr, du ouï-dire, mais exclusion aussi du goût et de la saveur, parce qu'avec leur incertitude, avec leur variabilité, ils ne permettent pas une analyse en éléments distincts, qui soit universellement acceptable.[34]

As a quale, the flavour of fish was deemed problematic by classical natural historians. Arronax himself draws attention to the irreducibly subjective quality of the experience of taste when he notes of a certain fish observed at the South Pole that: 'Je goûtai leur chair, mais je la trouvai insipide, malgré l'opinion de Conseil qui s'en accommoda fort.'[35] Nonetheless, the professor often refers to the taste of fish in his lists and catalogues.

Indeed, Arronax's catalogues frequently incorporate far more information than that pertaining to the four variables of description (forms, number, arrangement, magnitude) on which, according to Foucault, classical taxonomy was based.[36] One example is the list of fish he sees when travelling around the Greek archipelago:

Entre autres, je remarquai ces gobies aphyses, citées par Aristote et vulgairement connues sous le nom de 'loches de mer', que l'on rencontre particulièrement dans les eaux salées avoisinant le delta du Nil. Près d'elles se déroulaient des pagres à demi phosphorescents, sortes de spares que les Egyptiens rangeaient parmi les animaux sacrés, et dont l'arrivée dans les eaux du fleuve, dont elles annonçaient le fécond débordement, était fêtée par des cérémonies religieuses. Je notai également des cheilines longues de trois décimètres, poissons osseux à écailles transparentes, dont la couleur livide est mélangée de taches rouges; ce sont de grands mangeurs de végétaux marins, ce qui leur donne un goût exquis [...].

Un autre habitant de ces mers attira mon attention et ramena dans mon esprit tous les souvenirs de l'antiquité. Ce fut le remora qui voyage attaché aux ventre des requins; au dire des anciens, ce petit poisson, accroché à la carène d'un navire, pouvait l'arrêter dans sa marche, et l'un d'eux, retenant le vaisseau d'Antoine pendant la bataille d'Actium, facilita ainsi la victoire d'Auguste. [...] J'observai aussi d'admirables anthias qui appartiennent à l'ordre des lutjans, poissons sacrés pour les Grecs qui leur attribuaient le pouvoir de chasser les monstres marins des eaux qu'ils fréquentaient.[37]

34 Foucault, p. 144.
35 Verne, *Vingt mille lieues*, p. 348.
36 Foucault, p. 280.
37 Verne, *Vingt mille lieues*, pp. 261–2.

Here Arronax includes references to the taste of fish, and to the folklore surrounding various species. Arronax's discourse can be understood as mediating the conflict in the novel between the positions of Ned Land and Conseil, pithily summed up thus by Georges Perec: 'Conseil sait CLASSER les poissons. Ned Land sait CHASSER les poissons.'[38] Arronax is perfectly *au fait* with the classificatory schemata of natural history, but he also consistently draws on non-scientific accounts of the sea, the accounts produced by poets and philosophers, and the labourers of the sea. He is able to position himself in various different ways in relation to the sea and its inhabitants, speaking as a scientist or as a gourmet. Unlike Conseil, who, whatever the situation, 'classait, classait toujours',[39] Arronax is consistently concerned throughout the novel with the lived experience of encounters with the sea. This is clear in the above catalogue, where he notes that 'on rencontre' gobias near the delta of the Nile. The use of the verb 'rencontrer' here places the emphasis not simply on identifying the habitat of the gobias, but on understanding how they are perceived by the human societies that inhabit the same locale. Arronax's language stresses the relationship between humanity and the oceans. In particular, of course, he is concerned with exploring and describing his own relationship with the sea. Thus there is a foregrounding of subjective experience in the list of fish seen off the Greek archipelago. When Arronax notes that the sight of the sucker-fish 'attira mon attention et ramena dans mon esprit tous les souvenirs de l'antiquité', the double use of the first-person possessive adjective underlines the personal perspective that frames his account. This is, as already noted, more fully developed in the account of the Mediterranean, where Arronax produces 'une classification fantaisiste' that stands in contrast to Coseil's more orthodox approach. The conflict between Arronax's and Conseil's language is both a struggle between openness and closure, and between subjectivity and objectivity, in which the latter is defeated by the former, as Conseil's voice is eclipsed by Arronax's.

38   Georges Perec, *Penser/Classer* (Paris: Hachette, 1985), p. 156.
39   Verne, *Vingt mille lieues*, p. 123.

The subjective grounding of Arronax's account of the marvels of the sea seems to refract a conflict in natural history in the first half of the nineteenth century, identified by Dorinda Outram, between the claims of the field naturalist, whose adventurousness and derring-do appealed to the general public, and the sedentary naturalist, such as Cuvier, based in the closed space of the study or laboratory. These two ways of approaching the study of natural history led to rather different results. Outram notes of the field naturalist that: 'His observations are vivid, instantaneous, active, and dramatic [...]. But he has little *over*view of the natural order as a whole, his view of individual beings is fragmented and insecure, in spite of their momentary precision and vividness'.[40] In contrast to the field naturalist, there is the sedentary naturalist, whose basic claim, according to Cuvier (quoted by Outram), is that: 'It is only really in one's study (*cabinet*) that one can roam freely throughout the universe'.[41] Outram glosses Cuvier's comment thus:

> Cuvier is [...] making a claim that mastery over and comprehension of nature come not from *passage over* terrain, but from the steady and immobile *gaze* of the sedentary naturalist. [...] He is thus also saying that knowledge of the order of nature comes not from the whole-body experience of crossing the terrain, but from the very fact of the observer's distance from the actuality of nature. True observation of nature depends on *not* being there.[42]

Outram therefore suggests that sedentary naturalism is underpinned by the assumption that distance between the observer and the observed is the precondition of accurate observation. She further notes that this notion of distance enables the concept of objectivity to emerge, 'meaning precisely

---

40 Dorinda Outram, 'New Spaces in Natural History', in *Cultures of Natural History*, ed., N. Jardine, J. A. Secord and E. C. Spary (Cambridge: Cambridge University Press, 1996), pp. 249–65 (p. 261). According to Outram, Darwin is the last of the prestigious field naturalists.
41 Outram, p. 249.
42 Outram, pp. 261–2.

the placing of 'distance' between the observer and the observed, between the knower and his own responses.'[43]

At first blush, the *Nautilus* seems a device through which the conflict between field naturalism and sedentary naturalism is resolved. It literalizes Cuvier's claim that it is only in one's study that one can roam freely through the universe. It enables Arronax and Nemo to watch the world pass in review before them, safely separated therefrom by a pane of glass. It enables Verne to write an adventure story that taps into the popularity of the field naturalist as a cultural hero, while at the same time it offers an image of the naturalist as distanced from nature and dominating it. Arronax's Mediterranean catalogue, however, seems deliberately to eschew the norms of sedentary natural history for field natural history, as Arronax knowingly chooses to offer us a catalogue based on a 'classification fantaisiste', rooted in his own experience, and explicitly aiming to recreate that experience of visual overload for the reader. The catalogue foregrounds the partial and incomplete nature of Arronax's observations, which are based on fleeting glimpses and flashes of colour. It closes with an enumeration of fish unseen: 'Et si je ne pus observer ni miralets, ni balistes, ni tétrodons, ni hippocampus, ni jouans, ni centrisques, ni blennies, ni surmulets, ni labres, ni éperlans, ni exocets, ni anchois, ni pagels, ni bogues, ni orphes, ni tous ces principaux représentants de l'ordre des pleuronectes, les limandes, les flez, les plies, les soles, les carrelets, communs à l'Atlantique et à la Méditerranée, il faut en accuser la vertgineuse vitesse qui emportait la *Nautilus* à travers ces eaux opulentes.'[44] We have already seen that in the account of Nemo's collection there is a tension between the values of plenitude and totality that attach to the collection, and the notion of incompleteness generated through the use of open-ended lists. Here on the other hand, the catalogue of Mediterranean flora and fauna is more extensive and more complete than warranted by Arronax's partial observations. Rather than generate an illusion of totality, however, this closing sentence introduces a note of longing into the text, longing for a more complete visual possession of

43   Outram, p. 263.
44   Verne, *Vingt mille lieues*, p. 270.

the natural environment than that attainable by the individual travelling through that environment. Again there is a tension in the text between the effort to attain a synoptic overview of nature, through a collection or a classificatory schema, and a realization that this is impossible.

Impossible and ultimately undesirable. If Arronax presents himself as a field natural historian, I would like to suggest that this can be read as an ethical choice. Outram, drawing on Norbert Elias' work, suggests that the sedentary naturalist is the very embodiment of *homo clausus*, a man 'whose identity was based precisely on the maintenance of his own "distance", emotional and physical, from other human beings, with a strong consciousness of himself as separate, walled off from others by invisible barriers'.[45] *Vingt mille lieues* offers, in the figure of Nemo, the quintessence of *homo clausus*. The *Nautilus*, intended as his tomb, is an impermeable membrane sealing Nemo off from the world of men. He is an impenetrable, inscrutable figure for both his prisoners and Verne's readers. Arronax never learns the secret of Nemo's true identity, and the public must read *L'Ile mystérieuse* to sate their curiosity.[46] Nemo thus seems to embody all the qualities that the objective scientist, the sedentary naturalist, should possess. Indeed, Nemo speaks of himself in terms that deny his own subjectivity: his chosen pseudonym erases his individuality, and on his first meeting with Arronax, he explains to the professor: 'je suis mort, monsieur le professeur, aussi bien mort que ceux de vos amis qui reposent à six pieds sous terre!'.[47] The *Nautilus*, which opens up the submarine world to Nemo's gaze, is also his tomb. Throughout the novel, Arronax *qua* scientist is tempted to stay on board the *Nautilus*, precisely because of the opportunities for study it allows him, but to do so would be to renounce his links with the world of men. What he ultimately rejects is a certain way of being in the world, or more properly a way of being out of it, that promises absolute knowledge, but involves maintaining strict barriers between the self and others. Arronax does not maintain

45 Outram, p. 263.
46 For the revelation of Nemo's true identity see Jules Verne, *L'Ile Mystérieuse*, 3 vols (Paris: Hetzel, 1874), III, 219–23.
47 Verne, *Vingt mille lieues*, p. 78.

such barriers. *Vingt mille lieues* is, among other things, a story about male camaraderie, informed by an ethos of mutual dependence and co-operative action. Arronax's substitution of a 'classification fantaisiste' for a more conventional account, one organized according to subjective rather than objective criteria, exemplifies *en abyme*, a discursive move that the novel as a whole makes. Arronax spends his days aboard the *Nautilus* rewriting his chief opus: *Les Mystères des grands fonds sous-marins*. The book that he finally produces, however, could not be described as a natural history book, although it contains much natural historical information. Rather it is an adventure story, a first-person narrative, the story of an encounter with the sea, which is also the story of an encounter with another man, for the real mystery of *Vingt mille lieues* is the mystery of Captain Nemo. Arronax consistently writes about the sea not as someone observing it objectively, but as someone living and labouring within it.

Collecting and Death in Loti's *Le Roman d'un enfant*

In *Le Roman d'un enfant*, Loti recalls his childhood, a childhood in which, according to the text, natural history played a significant role. The young Pierre was a rather ambivalent collector of butterflies: 'Bien que cela me fît de la peine de les tuer, j'en composais des collections, et on me voyait constamment la papillonnette en main'.[48] The context in which this first reference to butterfly collecting occurs in the text is significant. It immediately follows a description of a game that he and his friend Antoinette used to play, in which they would pretend to be caterpillars, then chrysalises, then finally, transformed into butterflies, 'on commençait des courses folles ... on courait, on courait, se poursuivant, se fuyant, se croisant en courbes brusques et fantasques'.[49] The juxtaposition of the description

---

48   Pierre Loti, *Le Roman d'un enfant* (Paris, 1890), p. 66.
49   Loti, p. 65.

of this game with the description of his interest in butterfly collecting sets up a series of binary oppositions, which resonate throughout the text. Most obviously play is contrasted with study, and the shift from a purely ludic activity to a knowledge-producing one speaks of a process of growing up, a process which involves Pierre's painful alienation from nature. The language that characterizes the butterfly game, with the three participles suggesting ongoing action, is the language of movement and vitality; butterfly collecting, on the other hand, brings fixity and death into this world. A further distinction between the two pastimes is that whereas the butterfly game involves two people, collecting is a solitary pursuit, which isolates Pierre from his peers, who tease him about it. In fact, Pierre's nascent interest in natural history will be encouraged by a great uncle, a doctor and keen amateur naturalist, who teaches him classification and predicts that Pierre will grow up to be a 'savant naturaliste'.[50] The shift from the butterfly game to butterfly collecting, the latter under the patronage of a male authority figure, appears, therefore, to be exemplary of the passage from childhood to young adulthood that the text as a whole, which begins with Loti's earliest memory and ends at the moment he is forced to make a decision about his career, recounts.

Natural history collecting, however, plays a more complex role in the text, due to the young Pierre's ambivalent attitude to his own favourite pastime. It is not simply that he dislikes killing butterflies; his objections are more radical. In fact, Pierre is not interested in natural history as conventionally understood, and as practiced by his uncle, unable to understand 'que les froides vitrines, les classifications arides, la science morte, n'avaient rien qui pût me retenir'.[51] Here the crescendo of adjectives clearly associates natural history with deathliness, a link that is made again later in the text. One Shrove Tuesday, while the young Pierre is busy with the specimens in his 'musée', he hears the sound of sailors celebrating outside:

50   Loti, p. 114.
51   Loti, p. 114.

Les cris lointains de masques et le bruit de leurs tambours venaient me poursuivre
jusque dans ma retraite de jeune savant et m'y apportaient une insupportable tristesse.
[...] Confusément je souffrais d'être enfermé, moi, et penché sur des choses arides,
bonnes pour des vieillards, quand dehors les petits garçons du peuple [...], couraient,
sautaient, chantaient à plein gosier.[52]

Once again we find the adjective 'savant' associated with the adjective
'arides', and the sterility of young Pierre's intellectual pursuits is emphasized.
The study of natural history is again associated with death, a pastime suitable only for the senescent. Here Pierre, figured as an old man, is almost
assimilated to the dead objects with which he is surrounded, imprisoned
('enfermé') in his museum as much as the specimens he has collected. And
yet, the text continues: 'Je n'avais aucune envie de les suivre, cela va sans
dire [...]. Et je tenais beaucoup à rester là, ayant à finir de mettre en ordre la
famille multicolores des *Purpurifères*, vingt-troisième des *Gastéropodes*'.[53]

The museum thus acts as a bulwark against a world perceived as alien
and threatening.[54] Rosemary Lloyd, in her reading of the novel (which
focuses largely on the representation therein of another childhood pursuit, the puppet theatre) has stressed this psychic function of the museum,
which testifies to the young Pierre's need to impose order on the world:
'The controlled and ordered world of the museum is [...] only a stage in
the child's development, a means of briefly keeping at bay, through the
strictly delimited representations of the world's multiplicity, the tempta-
tions to participate in it.'[55] The ambivalences that characterize the space
of the museum are a function of this transitional role. If the young Pierre

---

52   Loti, pp. 134–5.
53   Loti, p. 135.
54   The young Pierre's friend, Lucette, teases him about his butterfly collecting by call-
     ing him 'Monsieur Cryptogame', in reference to a Töpffer cartoon (pp. 66–7). This
     cartoon recounts the attempts of a keen lepidopterist to avoid marrying, preferring
     butterfly-colllecting to the prospect of conjugal life. This reference functions within
     Le Roman d'un enfant obliquely to suggest the young Pierre's difficult journey to
     sexual maturity.
55   Rosemary Lloyd, *The Land of Lost Content: Children and Childhood in Nineteenth-
     Century French Literature* (Oxford: Oxford University Press, 1992), p. 164.

sometimes experiences the museum as a locus of captivity, it is also a spring-board for escapist reverie. Its position in the upper-storey of the house offers him a broad view of distant horizons: 'le charme de ce lieu lui venait de sa fenêtre, donnant aussi de très haut sur le couchant, les vieux arbres du rempart; sur les prairies lointaines [...]. Dans ce domaine, je passais des heures seul, tranquille, en contemplation devant des nacres exotiques, rêvant aux pays d'où elle étaient venues, imaginant d'étranges rivages'.[56] In the museum the wide world is kept safely behind glass.

Collecting and travel are therefore closely linked in the text, with the former initially acting as a surrogate for the latter. Both activities are presented as a function of a basic ontological homesickness. Oddly, the young Pierre's dreams of travel to distant climes are presented as memories. Thus the narrator remarks that the first time 'le palmier me fut *rappelé*'[57] (his italics) was through an illustration in the magazine *Jeunes Naturalistes*, and that on seeing the same engraving many years later, 'vraiment je me suis demandé comment elle aurait pu faire naître le moindre rêve en moi, si ma petite âme n'eût été pétrie de ressouvenirs ...'.[58] Earlier it was suggested that the shift from the butterfly game to butterfly collecting suggested a narrative of growing up as an alienation from nature, an expulsion from the garden of childhood innocence. The text is clearly permeated by a nostalgia for childhood, but the idea of anamnesis operates here to suggest that that childhood was itself permeated by nostalgia. Rosemary Lloyd has drawn attention to this feature of the text, writing that:

> What is immediately striking to a reader of this work is the deeply nostalgic nature not just of the telling of the story, a mood that frequently typifies accounts of child-hood, but also of the subject of the story, the experience itself, as though Loti's child were constantly aware of the brevity and fragility of his existence as child and were trying to shore up that existence by accumulating objects that seemed less ephemeral than he.[59]

56   Loti, pp. 112–13.
57   Loti, p. 61.
58   Loti, p. 62.
59   Rosemary Lloyd, *Shimmering in a Transformed Light: Writing the Still Life* (Ithaca: Cornell University Press, 2005), p. 36.

Indeed, many of the specimens in the young Pierre's collection are souvenirs, gathered one summer spent in his uncle's house in the South of France. The museum is not just an educational space, but a *lieu de mémoire*: 'Très nostalgiques à présent, les impressions que me causait mon musée [...]. Nostalgie de l'été, nostalgie du soleil et du Midi, amenée par tous ces papillons du jardin de mon oncle'.[60] Exemplary in this respect is a particularly rare specimen, 'un papillon citron-aurore': 'A certains moments, j'éprouvais un amer plaisir à le fixer, pour approfondir et chercher à comprendre la mélancolie qui me venait de lui'.[61] The use of the word 'fixer' is here slightly unexpected, as the butterfly itself is already fixed, pinned to a piece of cardboard. This metaphorical use of the verb 'fixer' recurs again a few pages later, where the young Pierre's nascent habit of keeping a journal is described: 'J'y inscrivais, moins les événements de ma petite existence tranquille, que mes impressions incohérentes, mes tristesses des soirs, mes regrets des étés passés, mes rêves de lointains pays ... J'avais déjà ce besoin de noter, de fixer des images fugitives, de lutter contre la fragilité des choses et de moi-même'.[62] Lived experience is here described as fleeting and fragile in terms that recall the butterfly evoked a few pages earlier, and the recurrence of the verb 'fixer' invites us to consider writing and collecting as analogous acts of preservation, both informed by a sad sense of nostalgia and an acute awareness of the transience of all things. The very form of the text reinforces this. It consists of a series of very short chapters, never more than a few pages long and often only a few paragraphs, each describing a significant moment in the young Pierre's life. Although the book does follow a broadly linear chronology, the chapters do not cohere into a continuous narrative. The text offers us, rather, a collection of brief, isolated moments.

Collecting, therefore, operates in the text as a metaphor for the act of writing itself, both born of the same acute awareness of mortality. Both practices, in fact, are associated with death. Remembering the summer spent in the south of France, the narrator notes:

60   Loti, p. 228.
61   Loti, p. 229.
62   Loti, p. 238.

Quand il m'arrive de jeter les yeux sur quelqu'un de ces objets que je rapportais de là-bas pour mon musée [...], je sens tout à coup comme du soleil, de l'étrangeté neuve, des odeurs de fruits du Midi, de l'air vif de montagne, et je vois bien alors qu'avec mes longues descriptions, dans ces pages mortes, je n'ai rien su mettre de tout cela.[63]

Thus the text here draws a distinction between the ability of an object magically to resurrect the past, and the inadequacy of language to do so. The 'longues descriptions' offer only the death mask of the narrator's childhood. The 'pages mortes' of the book recall the 'science morte' of Pierre's uncle, concerned with dead things. They recall the image of the young Pierre, figured as a 'vieillard', confined in his museum while outside other children enjoy themselves, assimilated to the objects in his collection. The text invites us to read it as a collection in which the mummified young Pierre is the central exhibit.

Natural history as practised by Pierre's uncle is, therefore, like writing, presented as unable to apprehend the life of things. Yet through his uncle's natural history specimens the young Pierre is nonetheless able to catch a glimpse of living nature: 'ce qui m'attirait si puissamment était derrière ces choses glacées, derrière et au delà ; – était la nature elle-même, effrayante, et aux mille visages, l'ensemble inconnu des bêtes et des forêts ...'.[64] This is, of course, partly a restatement of the young Pierre's fascination with the exotic, a fascination that plays a significant role in determining his choice of career, and in the mature Loti's practice as a writer. But this presentation of nature also resonates with the way in which natural history was transformed in the nineteenth century, by the development of what Foucault calls 'la notion synthétique de vie'.[65] This transformation was ushered in by Cuvier, who rewrote the rules of zoological classification by establishing a hierarchy of functions as the basis on which to establish a classificatory system. Discussing Cuvier's ideas, Foucault writes:

63   Loti, pp. 199–200.
64   Loti, p. 114.
65   Foucault, p. 281.

On mesure l'immense renversement que tout cela suppose par rapport à la *taxonomie* classique. Celle-ci se bâtissait entièrement à partir des quatre variables de description (formes, nombre, disposition, grandeur) qui étaient parcourues, comme d'un seul mouvement, par le langage et par le regard; et dans cet étalement du visible, la vie apparaissait comme l'effet d'un découpage – simple frontière classificatrice. A partir de Cuvier, c'est la vie dans ce qu'elle a de non-perceptible, de purement fonctionnel qui fonde la possibilité d'un classement.[66]

Cuvier's innovations, chiefly his emphasis on comparative anatomy, introduced into the study of nature an opposition between the visible and the concealed, surface and inner depth. According to Foucault, therefore, the space of classical natural history 'est maintenant dissocié et comme ouvert en son épaisseur. Au lieu d'un champ unitaire de visibilité et d'ordre, dont les éléments ont valeur distinctive les uns par rapport aux autres, on a une série d'oppositions, dont les deux termes ne sont pas de même niveau.'[67] Among these oppositions is that between identity and difference:

elles ne sont plus de même grain, elles ne s'établissent plus les unes par rapport aux autres sur un plan homogène; mais les différences prolifèrent à la surface, cependant qu'en profondeur, elles s'effacent, se confondent, se nouent les unes avec les autres, et se rapprochent de la grande, mystérieuse, invisible unité focale, dont le multiple semble dériver comme par une dispersion incessante.[68]

I wish to suggest that the traces of this new conception of natural history, in which life is 'une force fondamentale', 'une valeur radicale', underpins the young Pierre's fascination with the idea of 'la nature elle-même, effrayante, et aux mille visages, l'ensemble inconnu des bêtes et des forêts ...'. This nature is conceived of a single, protean being. It is life itself, what Foucault calls 'la grande, mystérieuse, invisible unité focale', that Pierre imagines existing behind and beyond his uncle's natural history cabinet, in the distant tropics.

66   Foucault, p. 280.
67   Foucault, p. 281.
68   Foucault, p. 281.

Science and Collectomania in Maupassant's 'Au Muséum d'histoire naturelle'

The obsession with death which haunts Loti's memoir also informs a short Maupassant text, 'Au Muséum d'histoire naturelle', first published in *Le Gaulois* in 1881, which recounts a visit to the Jardin des Plantes in Paris. Maupassant is drawn to the Jardin des Plantes not in a spirit of scientific enquiry, but in order to reconnect with his childhood. The account opens thus:

> Dans notre mémoire, ce magasin d'antiquités des sensations et des idées, nous retrou-
> vons parfois, tout à coup, un vieux souvenir oublié, qui nous fait revivre en une seconde
> toute une période lointaine de notre existence. En me levant l'autre jour, j'ai eu une de
> ces visions d'autrefois, [...] qui m'a jeté au cœur un irrésistible besoin de revoir là-bas,
> là-bas, ce bon Jardin des Plantes que j'aimais tant quand j'avais dix ou douze ans.[69]

The return to the Jardin des Plantes is, therefore, a return to a space that belongs to the writer's childhood, a childhood fondly remembered. The inclusion of that most basic of adjectives, 'bon', before 'Jardin des Plantes', suffuses the sentence with nostalgia, by evoking not only goodness, but also the simplicity of childhood – a simplicity that is in marked contrast to the elaborate trope of the 'magasin d'antiquités' used to describe the adult narrator's cluttered memory. Moreover, the adult narrator's inner life is characterized by suddenness and instantaneity – things happen 'tout à coup', 'en une seconde', and desires arise abruptly ('jeté au cœur'). The repetition of 'là-bas', however, functions to slow the text down, and in doing so it not only introduces a more contemplative note, but also serves to demarcate more sharply the narrator's childhood from his adult life. The opening lines of the text, therefore, code childhood positively, but also present it as lost to the adult narrator; the visit to the Jardin des Plantes is an attempt to recover something of that lost childhood.

69   Guy de Maupassant, 'Au Muséum d'histoire naturelle', in *Chroniques inédites*, ed. by Pascal Pia, 2 vols (Paris: Maurice Gonon, 1979), I, 53–9 (p. 53).

This attempt is, however, abruptly derailed: 'j'entrai par la porte en face du pont. Mais je m'arrêtai surpris en apercevant, au milieu de cet antique domaine des bêtes exilées, un vrai palais presque achevé, une grande construction blanche, de noble allure, élégante et simple'.[70] The narrator thus finds himself in unfamiliar territory, as does the reader, for this sentence reconfigures some of the ideas introduced in the opening paragraph, and in doing so it re-orients the text. The opening lines had hinted at the Jardin des Plantes as a kind of Eden, but here it is described as a postlapserian, exilic space, 'cet antique domaine des bêtes exilées'. The use of the word 'antique' recalls the figurative 'magasin d'antiquités' of the opening sentence, and thus undoes the opposition set up in the first paragraph between the curiosity shop and the Jardin des Plantes. In its stead, the text introduces a new opposition between the 'antique domaine des bêtes exilées', belonging to the past, and the 'vrai palais presque achevé', belonging to the future. Confronted with this mysterious building, the narrator fortunately encounters someone well placed to elucidate its purpose, 'un des mes meilleurs amis, M. Georges Pouchet'.[71] Pouchet, a real historical figure, was an eminent naturalist and professor of comparative anatomy at the museum. He informs the narrator that: 'j'avais devant les yeux le nouveau Muséum. Tous les anciens bâtiments tombent en ruine, sont devenus insuffisants. Et on a construit, pour les remplacer, cet élégant palais où les collections tiendront à l'aise'.[72] The salient characteristics of the gleaming new palace of science are simplicity, spaciousness, and rationality of design. In every respect it is opposed to the crabbed, dark antiques shop evoked in the opening sentence, and associated now with the old, dilapidated museum. Yet it is the old museum that Pouchet and the narrator visit as they together embark upon 'un vrai voyage à travers ces curieuses galeries qui renferment les mystères de la vie'.[73] The use of the adjective 'curieuses' once more serves to superimpose on the image of the museum the characteristics of the curi-

---

70 Maupassant, 'Au Muséum', p. 53.
71 Maupassant, 'Au Muséum', p. 53.
72 Maupassant, 'Au Muséum', p. 54.
73 Maupassant, 'Au Muséum', p. 53.

osity shop. This superimposition is an unexpected one, as curiosity shops are a privileged locus of the fantastic in literature,[74] far removed from the scientific order of the museum, but it resonates throughout the text. Although the narrator visits the museum in the company of a scientist, it is not the scientific elucidation of 'les mystères de la vie' that he finds there, but the experience of mystery itself. The narrator prefaces his account of the tour of the museum by noting that 'les détails que me donnait mon savant compagnon étaient comme des révélations sur les *dessous* inconnus de l'Être'.[75] Thus the narrator apparently finds occult knowledge in the museum, penetrating to the hidden heart of being, but the inclusion of the word 'comme' suggests that the knowledge he finds is still only partial, still only an approximation. There is an irreducible mystery at the heart of being. Moreover, the details with which Pouchet furnishes the narrator are not relayed to the reader; the text offers us little in the way of information about the exhibits at the museum, as opposed to description thereof, and uses those exhibits as props to create a macabre, ghoulish atmosphere. The museum emerges in the text not as a space of rationality and enlightenment, but as a nightmarish, sinister space of monstrous apparitions.

The visit to the museum begins innocuously enough in the zoo, where the narrator encounters a benign nature: 'nos frères les singes', 'de petits animaux aux noms barbares, mais d'une grâce attendrissante', a family of antilopes 'd'une élégance inoubliable', and 'un jeune rhinocéros [qui] devint mon ami'.[76] Animals and humans are here presented as able to share affective bonds; they are kith and kin to each other. The keynotes of the description of the zoo are friendliness, sentimentalism, and prettiness. Nature here

---

74 One thinks, for example of Balzac's *La Peau de chagrin*, in *La Comédie humaine*, ed. by Pierre-Georges Castex, Bibliothèque de la Pléiade, 12 vols (Paris: Gallimard, 1776–1781), X (1979), 47–294 or Théophile Gautier, *Le Pied de momie*, in *Romans, contes et nouvelles*, ed. by Pierre Laubriet, Bibliothèque de la Pléiade, 2 vols (Paris: Gallimard, 2002), I, 855–66. See also Emile de La Bédollière and P. Bernard, *Les Aventures de M. de Bric-à-Brac: roman zoologique, archéologique et paléontologique* (Paris: Curmer, 1842).
75 Maupassant, 'Au Muséum', p. 54.
76 Maupassant, 'Au Muséum', p. 54.

is a diverting spectacle that obligingly offers itself up for the amusement of humanity. Such an image is disturbed when one of the keepers tells the narrator that recently, while he was cleaning out the rhinoceros' enclosure, 'celui-ci, par farce peut-être, ou seulement par gentillesse, l'avait d'un seul coup de son nez montagneux, lancé, comme une balle dans l'espace'.[77] The eruption of violence in the text – as sudden as the gunshot alluded to by the image of the bullet in space – offers us a glimpse of a threatening and dangerous nature. This nature is not actively malignant, as it is made clear that the rhinoceros acted 'par farce peut-être, ou seulement par gentillesse', but the inability of the keeper to interpret the animal's actions, and the violent results that followed from what was perhaps an affectionate gesture, suggest a chasm that exists between the world of man and the world of beasts, a basic incompatibility.

When the narrator and his guide arrive at the aquarium the tone of the text shifts, through the inclusion of an anecdote about an elderly couple visiting the aquarium at Le Havre. Exhausted after a long day, the couple fell asleep in the aquarium:

> Les deux vieilles gens dormaient toujours, [...] quand une sensation singulière, des frôlements, des caresses de plume, puis des coups aigus, les réveillèrent en sursaut. Le pélican les avait découverts. Hideux, ouvrant le gouffre de sa gorge et battant des ailes, il les piquait de son bec immense pour leur demander quelque chose à manger. Ils se dressèrent dans une indicible épouvante. L'horreur de ce lieu qu'ils ne reconnaissaient pas, les monstres diaboliques qui nageaient de tous les côtes de la vie, la lueur infernale qui les éclairait, cette grotte horrible, habitée par cet être épouvantable, c'était l'enfer avec le diable! Ils étaient morts! C'était le diable.[78]

The aquarium is here transformed into a vision of hell. The pelican, conventionally used as an image of self-sacrifice and a symbol of the Passion in Christian iconography, because it was believed to feed its young with its own blood, is here demanding to be fed, its gaping mouth suggesting its insatiability. The birds and fish become 'monstres diaboliques'. Despite the horror to which they awaken, the elderly couple are treated with a mocking

---

77   Maupassant, 'Au Muséum', p. 54.
78   Maupassant, 'Au Muséum', p. 55.

nonchalance. But if this seems to be a joke at their expense, their experience of a diabolical nature nonetheless anticipates the trajectory of the text. Increasingly, the museum offers the narrator not an encounter with a familiar and benign nature, but an encounter with the unnatural – the monstrous, the abnormal and the freakish. This shift coincides with a move away from living nature, towards dead or inert matter: 'Après avoir salué la Vénus hottentote et callipyge, brune rivale de la Vénus de Milo, parcouru la salle des monstres à deux têtes et l'avenue couverte où des baleines sont suspendues, nous sommes entrés dans le pavillon de la minéralogie'.[79] The mineralogical exhibit that most fascinates the narrator is a block of metal that perspires in the heat: 'Oui, il sue, il fond; des gouttes d'eau rougeâtre sortent du métal qui se ronge, comme s'il maigrissait'.[80] A block of iron, an element synonymous with hardness in French as in English, here appears to be weeping. Its 'travail mystérieux' blurs the line between the organic and the inorganic, between the mineral and the living, but also between life and death. For the rock appears to be living only in so far as it is decaying. The keynote characteristic of life is that it contains within it the processes of its own destruction. The processes of life and the processes of death are interchangeable.

This decadent topos is developed considerably in the following section of the text. After visiting the mineralogical galleries the narrator and his guide leave the public museum, and enter into Pouchet's laboratory:

> Le cabinet du professeur est vaste, orné d'ossements de toute espèce, tapissé de carcasses, de débris d'êtres. Sur la table immense, des livres des papiers, des microscopes, des instruments de dissection, de vivisection, des mâchoires et une quantité de petits morceaux carrés de verre. En regardant ceux-ci de près, on s'aperçoit qu'ils sont formés de deux lames fort minces, appliquées l'une sur l'autre et enfermant une chose presque imperceptible, une tache jaunâtre, une ligne brune; et on lit sur le verso: 'Fibres musculaires de la baleine!'[81]

---

79 Maupassant, 'Au Muséum', p. 56.
80 Maupassant, 'Au Muséum', p. 56.
81 Maupassant, 'Au Muséum', pp. 56–7.

The laboratory thus offers a macabre spectacle, crammed with tokens of death and decay. The language of interior design ('orné', 'tapissé') is here incongruously yoked to the image of the charnel house, but such language recalls once more the curiosity shop evoked in the opening section of the text. Just as a curiosity shop displays the debris of civilizations, so Pouchet's laboratory displays 'débris d'êtres'. Instruments of scientific research appear as clutter to the lay eyes of the narrator, unable to see in a yellow smear on a slide the muscular tissue of a whale. The text does not seek to explain the work of Pouchet and his colleagues; on the contrary it mystifies it, presenting scientific knowledge as arcane and occult. The scientific context in which the grotesque specimens are displayed, far from neutralizing their macabre qualities, itself becomes suffused with this macabre quality. Thus Pouchet himself, displaying to the narrator macerated whales, 'se frotte les mains à la façon des collectionneurs monomanes en ouvrant l'armoire aux bibelots introuvables'.[82] By likening Pouchet to a collectomaniac, cackling over his specimens, the text divests him of scientific authority, and represents him as a madman. His laboratory appears not as the site of serious scientific research, but as a chamber of horrors, and Pouchet is both curator and exhibit.

In Pouchet's laboratory, therefore, the narrator encounters biological decomposition and death; upon leaving the laboratory he encounters another image of decay:

> Je me trouve au bord d'une rivière, d'une petite rivière en putréfaction, noire, infecte, la vraie rivière qui doit couler en ce royaume de charognes. C'est la Bièvre, la triste Bièvre, ce ruisseau jadis charmant [...], devenu égout putride, souillé par les industriels, condamné par les ingénieurs; la Bièvre honteuse de ses fanges, cachée sous terre aujourd'hui, n'osant plus se montrer au soleil.[83]

The description of the Bièvre contrasts a lost pastoral idyll with a grubby industrial reality, and thus maps on to the vision of biological decay offered by Pouchet's laboratory a vision of social degeneration. At the same time,

82   Maupassant, 'Au Muséum', p. 57.
83   Maupassant, 'Au Muséum', p. 58.

this paragraph also recalls the opening of the article. There too, the text evoked a lost golden age, in that case the narrator's own childhood. The description of the Bièvre therefore knits together three different narratives: the language of putrefaction links the contamination of the river through industrial pollution to the spectacle of biological decay staged in Pouchet's laboratory, but the idea of the river's lost innocence also recalls the narrator's own craving to reconnect with his childhood. The world image sketched in Maupassant's text is a thoroughly entropic one.

There is also an allusion to the Styx in the description of the Bièvre, an underground river that flows through a 'royaume de charognes'. The text thus invites us to read the narrator's visit to the museum as a descent to the underworld. Pouchet is the Sibyl who offers the narrator 'des révélations sur les *dessous* inconnus de l'Etre'.[84] This notion of the 'dessous inconnu' recurs in the antepenultimate paragraph of the text, this time in more literal fashion:

> Par le vitrage crevé d'une espèce de serre, un amas d'ossements m'apparaît. Ils semblent pêle-mêle, jetés là comme après une farouche bataille, et des places noires indiquent des vestiges de sang. Ce sont les *doubles*, le grenier aux débarras de l'*anatomie*. Dans ce cimetière viennent puiser avec joie les savants de province qui complètent ainsi leurs collections. Au dessus est la galerie des carcasses à conserver, bondée jusqu'aux portes de tous les échantillons et de toutes les espèces, numérotés, classés, rangés dans un ordre admirable. On se croirait dans l'étrange et sinistre musée de quelque boucher collectionneur et fantaisiste.[85]

Here the calm, rational organization of the museum display is contrasted with the violent chaos of the *grenier*,[86] where the blood and bones conjure up images of war and destruction. The contrast between the 'grenier' and the 'galerie' inscribes the notion of the 'double' into the text, for the space Maupassant describes has a double nature, both museum and charnel-house, and the doubling of the adjectives in the final sentence ('étrange et sinistre',

---

84 Maupassant, 'Au Muséum', p. 54.
85 Maupassant, 'Au Muséum', p. 58.
86 This description of the museum's *grenier* seems in many ways to parallel the description of the Goncourts' *grenier* in *La Maison d'un artiste*, as discussed above, pp. 161–6.

'collectionneur et fantaisiste') further enacts the notion of doubling. The spatial indices, positioning the museum gallery 'au-dessus', resonate with the discourse of the 'dessous' that is present throughout the text, and function to suggest that the orderly organization of samples, if 'admirable', is none-theless somehow factitious. It is not in the space of the museum, with its orderly displays that the truth of being is located, but rather down below, in the ossuary. The privileged inhabitant of this ossuary is the private col-lector, who is once more invoked as a sinister, maniacal figure. Throughout the text the world of *curiosité*, the world of the collector and the curiosity shop, is placed in contrast to the world of conventional natural history, as represented in the gleaming white galleries of the unfinished museum, and the display cases where all the exhibits are 'numérotés, classés, rangés dans un ordre admirable'. Pouchet himself, although a scientist, belongs not to the latter realm but to the former. He does not offer explanations for the mysterious phenomena on display. The only words he speaks directly in the text are, in response to the narrator's query as to why the alcohol in a test-tube containing a foetus has turned red: 'Je n'en sais rien; il se produit dans tout cela une foule de réactions plus inconnues les unes que les autres.'[87] Akin to a 'collectionneur monomane', he is himself one of the curiosities the text exhibits, a crazed, unsettling figure, revelling in decay.

Maupassant's portrait of the naturalist seems less startling, however, if read alongside Foucault's comments on biology in *Les Mots et les choses*. Central to Foucault's argument is that, in the shift from classical natural history to biology that occurred in the nineteenth century, the notion of life as a merciless and destructive force emerged:

> L'expérience de la vie se donne donc comme la loi la plus générale des êtres, la mise au jour de cette force primitive à partir de quoi ils sont; elle fonctionne comme une ontologie sauvage, qui chercherait à dire l'être et le non-être indissociables de tous les êtres. Mais cette ontologie dévoile moins ce qui fonde les êtres que ce qui les porte un instant à une forme précaire et secrètement déjà les mine de l'intérieur pour les détruire. Par rapport à la vie, les êtres ne sont que des figures transitoires et l'être qu'ils maintiennent, pendant l'épisode de leur existence, n'est rien de plus que

---

87   Maupassant, 'Au Muséum', p. 59.

leur présomption, leur volonté de subsister. Si bien que, pour la connaissance, l'être des choses est illusion, voile qu'il faut déchirer pour retrouver la violence muette et invisible qui les dévore dans la nuit.[88]

Foucault's remarks resonate with Maupassant's presentation of Pouchet, steeped in blood and gore, dissecting, vivisecting, cutting open bodies to find the secret of life, which is death. The contrasting images in the text of the museum display and the ossuary resonate with Foucault's comment that 'l'être des choses est illusion'. The carefully reconstructed skeletons of the taxonomical museum display are merely a mirage: the *dessous* of life, its essential truth, is of processes of dissolution and destruction which tend to undo differentiation. Maupassant's text can be read as a statement of the intellectual bankruptcy of classical natural history, once the fundamental intuition of the pitiless destructiveness of life is grasped, but it still uses the discourse of collecting to talk about science. It is the discourse of pathological, rather than rational collecting, however, that is deployed here, in a narrative of morbid curiosity.

Collecting is often conceptualized as being about mastery – both self-mastery and mastery of the world. The activities of collecting and classifying can be a means of bringing order to the world, of imposing structures on it. Nowhere is this drive to order more apparent than in natural history collecting. All of the texts studied here, however, undermine the notion that collecting can function to establish order. In all these texts, the natural world is refractory to the collector's attempts rationally to reorganize it in the space of the collection. I have argued that this is partly a function of changes in the way the study of nature was conceptualized in the nineteenth century, but it is also a function of an experience of the gap between words and things that is one of the hallmarks of modernist literature. The texts studied here range from the canonical to the popular, from the serious to the slight, but all of them are concerned with negotiating the relationship between the word and the world.

---

88   Foucault, p. 291.

CHAPTER 6

To Create or To Collect?

'Le génie de l'admiration, de la compréhension', according to the narrator of *Le Cousin Pons*, '(est) la seule faculté par laquelle un homme ordinaire devient le frère d'un grand poète'.[1] From his first entrance into French literature, therefore, the connoisseur collector, as a result of his highly developed aesthetic sensibility, was conceived of as having a privileged relationship with the artist. But if the connoisseur collector was, as Balzac's narrator suggests, the artist's brother, he was clearly a younger brother. Pons himself is a failed musician, for whom collecting provides 'vives compensations à la faillite de la gloire'.[2] He is a second-rate artist pursuing a second-rate destiny. Edmond Bonnaffé, in his *Physiologie du curieux*, would later express a similar view of the relationship between the artist and the connoisseur. Bonnaffé acknowledges that the *amateur* and the artist, both engaged in 'la recherche exclusive du beau', 'sont la conséquence l'un de l'autre: l'artiste dépend de l'amateur, c'est pour lui qu'il travaille de son vivant, c'est sur lui qu'il compte après sa mort; l'amateur dépend de l'artiste, sans lui quelle serait sa raison d'être?'.[3] The two figures are thus in a relationship of mutual dependency, but not, as Bonnaffé goes on to explain, one of equality: 'l'artiste a toute la supériorité du génie créateur; il est le père, le générateur du beau; l'autre n'a qu'une paternité secondaire: il ne crée pas de chefs-d'œuvre, il adopte ceux des autres'.[4] The connoisseur is thus clearly distinguished in Bonnaffé's formulation from the creative artist, the latter a figure of productivity, the former one of sterility. The

1   Balzac, *Le Cousin Pons*, p. 489.
2   Balzac, *Le Cousin Pons*, p. 489.
3   Bonnaffé, *Physiologie*, p. 5.
4   Bonnaffé, *Physiologie*, p. 5.

fact that collectors are conventionally childless bachelors clearly functions discursively to ascribe to them a sterility which is not merely reproductive, but also artistic.

The distinction between collecting and creating appeared to Bonnaffé's gloomier contemporaries, however, to be one that the nineteenth century had disregarded. In Albert Robida's sketch, 'Un homme de goût qui n'en avait pas', the painter Jobic explains to the eponymous collector: 'Ce n'est pas votre faute si vous n'avez pas de goût […], c'est la faute du siècle! […] Renonçant définitivement à faire quelque chose lui-même, il se dépouille de toute personnalité et s'installe en garni dans le mobilier des autres siècles Et il a raison! Collectionnez, collectionnez, entourez-vous d'un entassement de vieilles jolies choses, pour tâcher de ne pas voir les platitudes toutes neuves'.[5] Jobic presents the nineteenth century as the century style forgot, in which an excessive fondness for pretty old things has stymied the development of an authentic contemporary style. Antique collecting reflects this taste for pretty old things, and is thus part of the problem, but it also offers a palliative solution, masking the ugliness of modern life, with its 'rangées de boîtes carrées qui constituent nos villes, habitées par des gens qui passent des tuyaux de drap aux jambes, s'enfournent dans un sac noir, se mettent encore un tuyau sur la tête et se croient habillés'.[6] Paul Bourget, in his celebrated essay on the Goncourt brothers, echoed this view, developing a critique of late-nineteenth-century French literature in which contemporary bricabracomania was profoundly implicated, claiming that 'une grande portion de notre littérature actuelle demeure inintelligible sans l'aspect d'un magasin de bric-à-brac, habituel à nos installations'.[7] For Bourget, the late nineteenth century was characterized by a profound lack of originality: 'notre XIXᵉ siècle, à force de colliger et de vérifier tous les styles aura oublié de s'en fabriquer un!'.[8] For both Bourget and Robida, the collector

5   Robida, pp. 237–8.
6   Robida, p. 238.
7   Bourget, p. 381.
8   Bourget, p. 380.

appears to have usurped the role of the creative artist as the principal agent of cultural development, with consequences both disparage.

The relationship between the collector and the artist is thus one that shifts across the nineteenth century, and this shift is a function of both changing conceptions of the collector and changing conceptions of the artist. In this chapter I wish to explore two moments at which the distinction established by Balzac and Bonnaffé between the creative artist and the collector was challenged: in the late nineteenth century by the emergence of an aesthetic grounded in a sense of creative exhaustion, and in the mid-nineteenth century, by the emergence of anti-idealist realism. At both moments it is the very notion of 'le génie créateur' that is called into question. First, however, I wish to examine further what is at stake in maintaining an absolute distinction between collector and creator, and nowhere is this distinction more sharply drawn than in the work of Marcel Proust.

Proust Reads Nodier:
Bibliophilia and the Idealist Critique of Collecting

The distinction between the collector and the creative artist is central to *A La Recherche*, embodied in the figures of Swann and Marcel. To collect art, rather than produce it, is the fate of Swann, who, although gifted with taste, erudition and a passion for art, and although he dreamed of becoming a writer, remains always a dilettante, 'qui avait gaspillé dans les plaisirs frivoles les dons de son esprit,'[9] unable even to compose his projected monograph on Vermeer. Moreover, the private collector in the Swann mould is presented within the text as obsolescent. In the final scene of the novel, at the Guermantes' matinée, meditating on the twilight of the aristocracy, Marcel claims that the 'tableaux anciens réunis par Swann dans un arrangement de

9   Marcel Proust, *A La Recherche*, I, 188.

"collectionneur" [...] achevait le caractère démodé, ancien, de cette scène".[10]
Swann is ultimately an irrelevancy, historically and artistically. It is this fate
that Marcel manages to escape, thanks ostensibly to the moment of grace
vouchsafed him when he serendipitously dips his madeleine into a cup
of tea. But the distinction between the collector and the artist is neither
a function of the former's laziness nor the latter's good fortune; it points
rather to the essential underpinnings of Proustian aesthetics. The collector
and the artist each subscribe to a different ontology of the art object. This
difference is established by the narrator in the course of his description of
Swann's passion for Odette:

> Et quand il était tenté de regretter que depuis des mois il ne fît plus que voir Odette,
> il se disait qu'il était raisonnable de donner beaucoup de son temps à un chef-
> d'œuvre inestimable, coulé pour une fois dans une matière différente et particulière-
> ment savoureuse, en un exemplaire rarissime qu'il contemplait tantôt avec l'humilité,
> la spiritualité et le désintéressement d'un artiste, tantôt avec l'orgeuil, l'égoïsme et la
> sensualité d'un collectionneur.[11]

This statement revolves around a dualist axis, which distinguishes sharply
between the realm of the material and the realm of the ideal. The notion of
Odette as 'un chef-d'œuvre inestimable, coulé pour une fois dans une matière
différente et particulièrement savoureuse' is underpinned by strongly idealist aesthetic assumptions, as the essence of the work of art, of the masterpiece, is presented as somehow distinct from its realization in the material
realm. The collector, however, is presented as being concerned precisely
with the materiality of the art object, possession of which is necessary to
confer status upon him, to gratify his egoism and his pride. The collector
here stands in sharp contrast to the artist, whose attitude is characterized
by disinterestedness, who is unconcerned with material possession. This
distinction is elaborated over the course of the novel, as Marcel emerges
as a creative artist.

10   Proust, *A La Recherche*, IV, 596.
11   Proust, *A La Recherche*, I, 221.

The discourse of collecting within *A La Recherche* is consistently folded into the discourse of love, from the moment that Swann discovers in Odette a resemblance to Botticelli's Zipporah, and thus falls in love with her. The desire for possession is central to both passions, with the difference that the collector desires a material object, and the lover desires another subject. Where the collector's passion can therefore be satisfied, the lover's cannot. Through the course of his relationship with Albertine, Marcel is repeatedly confronted with the impossibility of possessing her as he desires:

> Je pouvais bien prendre Albertine sur mes genoux, tenir sa tête dans mes mains, je pouvais la caresser, passer longuement mes mains sur elle, mais, comme si j'eusse manié une pierre qui enferme la salure des océans immémoriaux ou le rayon d'une étoile, je sentais que je touchais seulement l'enveloppe close d'un être qui par l'intérieur accédait à l'infini.[12]

This quotation brings into play a series of oppositions between exterior and interior, proximity and distance, surface and depth. The physical contact between Albertine and Marcel is a surface contact only; Marcel continues to experience Albertine's interiority as inaccessible to him. The image of 'la pierre qui enferme la salure des océans immémoriaux' presents her as unfathomable, with the idea of depth suggested both by the reference to the oceans and by the inclusion of the adjective 'immémoriaux', suggestive of deep time.

This unfathomability is presented not only as frustrating Marcel's desire, however, but also as the very pre-condition of that desire. Contrasting his love for Albertine with Swann's for Odette, Marcel notes:

> Albertine n'etait nullement pour moi une œuvre d'art. Je savais ce que c'était qu'admirer une femme d'une façon artistique – j'avais connu Swann. De moi-même d'ailleurs, j'étais, de n'importe quelle femme qu'il s'agit, incapable de le faire, n'ayant aucune espèce d'esprit d'observation extérieure, ne sachant jamais ce qu'était ce que je voyais [...]. Même, pour dire vrai, quand je commençais à regarder Albertine comme un ange musicien merveilleusement patiné et que je me félicitais de posséder, elle ne tardait pas à me devenir indifférente, je m'ennuyais bientôt auprès d'elle, mais ces instants-là

---

12   Proust, *A La Recherche*, III (1988), 888.

duraient peu. On n'aime que ce en quoi on poursuit quelque chose d'inaccessible, on n'aime que ce qu'on ne possède pas, et bien vite je me remettais à me rendre compte que je ne possédais pas Albertine.[13]

Here again, the text's rhetoric of desire is structured by an opposition between exterior and interior, and between surface and depth, oppositions which are exemplified in the contrasting attitudes of Swann and Marcel. The reference to Swann in this quotation harks back to 'Un Amour de Swann', reminding the reader of the genesis of Swann's passion for Odette, which grew out of and was sustained by her resemblance to a painted image. Under Swann's gaze, the gaze of the collector, Odette was reduced to a surface, a representation. Marcel's passion for Albertine, however, rather than flatten her out in such a fashion, is sustained by an awareness of her depth.[14]

This rejection of the collector's gaze has aesthetic implications. Marcel's comment that he has 'aucune espèce d'esprit d'observation extérieure' is presented in the above quotation as a lack, a fault that disqualifies him from the pleasures of collecting. Later, however, it will be re-interpreted as a positive quality, and one that allows Marcel to emerge as a writer. One of the crucial moments in *A La Recherche* consists of Marcel coming across an account in the Goncourt journal of a dinner party hosted by the Verdurins. Reading Edmond de Goncourt's description of the party allows Marcel, in an Œdipal gesture, to define his own literary project through rejecting a prior and influential model. Marcel identifies as the essence of the Goncourts' style an attention lavished on external details, on appearance, an extraordinary acuity of observation, and notes that he himself is concerned with something rather different:

13   Proust, *A La Recherche*, III (1988), 885–6.
14   For an examination of the concept of depth in relation to affectivity in the novel, see Katja Haustein, 'Proust's Emotional Cavities: Vision and Affect in *A La Recherche du temps perdu*', *French Studies* 63 (2009), 161–73. Haustein argues that in fact, in those scenes describing the sleeping Albertine, Marcel's gaze does turn her into a petrified surface, on to which he can project his images of ideal love. According to Haustein these scenes exemplify a tension in the novel between a commitment to a Romantic conception of affectivity and a modernist experience of emotional atrophy.

Il y avait en moi un personnage qui savait plus ou moins bien regarder, mais c'était un personnage intermittent, ne reprenant vie que quand se manifestait quelque essence générale, commune à plusieurs choses, qui faisait sa nourriture et sa joie. Alors le personnage regardait et écoutait, mais à une certaine profondeur seulement, de sorte que l'observation n'en profitait pas. [...] J'avais beau dîner en ville, je ne voyais pas les convives, parce que, quand je croyais les regarder, je les radiographiais.[15]

Again this comment seems to be a statement of Marcel's limitations, another admission of artistic failure. In the light of *Le Temps retrouvé*, however, it can be seen as a programmatic statement of artistic purpose: Marcel's novel will be a work of moral radiography, penetrating the superficial to arrive at a subjacent truth. The idea that the function of the artwork is to apprehend an 'essence générale', disregarding the apparent in favour of the essential, resonates with the difference the text sets up between the collector and the artist, presenting the former as bound to the material realm. The collector is concerned with surface rather than depth, the apparent rather than the essential, the material rather than the ideal. In setting up the figures of the artist and the collector in opposition to one another, and in associating the latter with materiality, Proust's text resonates with and reformulates a long-established idealist critique of collecting.

The collector's materialism is a frequent topos of the discourse surrounding collecting. Bonnaffé notes that the collector was viewed with contempt in ancient Rome, because of the baseness of his passion. Thus Seneca 'déplore mélancholiquement cette passion pour des objets, poids matériel auquel ne saurait s'attacher une âme pure et qui se rappelle son origine'.[16] Champfleury, in *L'Hôtel des commissaires-priseurs*, proclaims the futility of the collector's passion in the final chapter, 'Le Collectionneur de ciels'. This chapter is a monition against worldly ambition, against the folly of a society in which 'l'homme se torture le cœur et le cerveau pour arriver à s'élever entre quelques-uns, à être sifflé par beaucoup d'autres'.[17] The eponymous collector is a man who lost a fortune but finally found

---

15 Proust, *A La Recherche*, IV, 296–7.
16 Edmond Bonnaffé, *Les Collectionneurs de l'ancienne France* (Paris: Aubry, 1888), p. ii.
17 Champfleury, *L'Hôtel*, pp. 287–8.

happiness, in a small house outside Paris where, like more celebrated literary predecessors, he cultivates his garden, all the while enjoying the spectacle of nature, collecting skies in lieu of the paintings he had previously
sought: 'Son cerveau contient une galerie de ciels. Il les aime tous avec une
égale passion, les ciels radieux et pluvieux, les ciels gris et les ciels clairs.
[...] Pas une heure qui ne change l'aspect du ciel, pas un jour qui n'amène
de nouveaux tableaux dans le musée'.[18] Champfleury's text therefore offers
a narrative of the collector ascending from the kingdom of necessity to
the kingdom of freedom, renouncing a material collection in favour of a
superior, immaterial one.

A similar critique of collecting was frequently advanced in the discourse
surrounding bibliophilia, which had a somewhat vexed relationship with
other forms of collecting. In his essay, 'L'Amateur de livres', Charles Nodier,
the doyen of nineteenth-century bibliophilia, distinguished between the
'bibliophile' and the 'bibliomane'. The former 'est un homme doué de
quelque esprit et de quelque goût, qui prend plaisir aux œuvres du génie,
de l'imagination et du sentiment. [...] De l'amour de cet auteur absent dont
l'artifice de l'écriture lui a rendu le langage, il est arrivé sans s'en apercevoir
à l'amour du symbole matériel qui le représente'.[19] Bibliophilia originates
in a love of reading, with the love of books as material objects developing
as a consequence of this primary love. In stark contrast to the bibliophile
is the 'bibliomane': 'Le bibliophile sait choisir les livres; le bibliomane les
entasse. [...] Le bibliophile apprécie le livre; le bibliomane le pèse ou le
mesure. Le bibliophile procède avec une loupe, et le bibliomane avec une
toise'.[20] Whereas the bibliophile's passion is first and foremost an intellectual one, the bibliomaniac's passion is grounded in the material. This idea
is given a comic twist in the sketch 'Le Bibliomane', in which the eponymous bibliomaniac, Théodore, falls gravely ill after discovering in a rival's
collection a 1676 edition of Virgil which is physically bigger than his own

---

18   Champfleury, *L'Hôtel*, p. 286.
19   Charles Nodier, 'L'Amateur de livres', in *Les Français peints par eux-mêmes*, 8 vols
       (Paris: Curmer, 1840–1842), III (1841), 201–9 (p. 202).
20   Nodier, 'L'Amateur de livres', p. 205.

edition, hitherto believed to be the biggest, by a third of a line in height. When a priest is sent to attend to the dying Théodore, a *dialogue de sourds* ensues. In response to the question whether he believes in the Trinity, the book collector replies: 'Comment ne croirais-je pas au fameux volume *De Trinitate* de Servet [...] ?'.[21] The priest is wholly bemused by Théodore's response, but as the narrator explains, 'le cher homme avait poussé trop loin dans les livres la vaine étude de la lettre, pour prendre le temps de s'attacher à l'esprit.'[22] Thus the taxonomy of book-lovers that Nodier establishes is organized around a dualist axis, with bibliophiles privileging the word, and bibliomaniacs the flesh. Nodier further suggests in 'L'Amateur des livres', that bibliomania is an expression of 'l'instinct de la collectivité', and likens the bibliomaniac to a gentleman of his acquaintance who collected corks.[23] He thus assimilates the bibliomaniac to the broader category of the collectomaniac, driven by an insatiable urge to material accumulation, in contrast to the discriminating, intellectual bibliophile.

Henri Rochefort's *Les Petits Mystères de l'hôtel des ventes* also uses the figure of the bibliophile as a foil for the collector. The bibliophile is initially set up as the positive counterpart to the fine art collector, for whereas the latter 'tend complaisamment son porte-monnaie à tous les industriels en quête de pigeons, et qu'il se trouve livré pieds et poings liés à toutes les fantaisies d'un expert souvent aussi ignorant que lui, l'autre, le bibliophile, sait ce qu'il fait, où il va et ce qu'il achète.'[24] Rochefort goes on to nuance this, however, as he introduces the canonical distinction between the 'bibliophile', motivated by a love of reading, and the 'bibliomane', 'une espèce d'amateur', in terms that recall Nodier's: 'Le bibliomane ne lit pas, il entasse; il ne s'occupe pas du sens des pages dont se composent les ouvrages, qu'il achète, il s'inquiète de la qualité du papier et de la forme des caractères.'[25] Thus he distinguishes between those who value a book for its contents,

21 Charles Nodier, 'Le Bibliomane', in *Paris: ou Le Livre des Cent-et-Un*, 15 vols (Paris: Ladvocat, 1831–1834), I, 87–108 (p. 103).
22 Nodier, 'Le Bibliomane', p. 104.
23 Nodier, 'L'Amateur des livres', p. 206.
24 Rochefort, p. 192.
25 Rochefort, p. 203.

and those who value it for its material perfections, again distinguishing the former from the figure of the collector, while assimilating the latter to that very category.

Jules Janin's book of bibliophile lore, *Le Livre*, similarly considers the relationship between bibliophilia and other forms of curiosity. The text purports to be the minutes of the meetings of a society of bibliophiles. This society is founded during, and in response to, the *Exposition universelle* of 1869:

> Dans cet immense tohu-bohu de la curiosité la plus niaise et des plus grands efforts de l'industrie humaine, et voyant qu'en dépit de toute prudence nous étions envahis par le vulgaire des cinq parties du monde: – Non certes, disions-nous, nous ne resterons pas sans défense, et, puisqu'ils ont oublié dans leur Champ de Mars notre chère et douce passion [...], nous aurons, nous aussi, notre Champ de Mars de douze cents mètres carrés; nous nous ferons à nous-mêmes une humble et chère exposition des plus belles choses.[26]

Bibliophilia is thus contrasted favourably with the degraded form of curiosity represented by the *Exposition universelle*. The exhibition is presented as vulgar and populist, and bibliophilia, in implicit contrast to this, as an élite and refined pastime. Where the exhibition is presented as chaotic and tumultuous, 'un tohu-bohu', bibliophilia is coded as orderly, both through the chiastic structure of the bibliophiles' response to the threat posed by the exhibition, and through the precision with which the space in which the bibliophiles meet is measured and delimited. Books, as 'belles choses', are presented as superior to the objects of industrial manufacture on display at the exhibition. The text thus seems to establish an axiology based on a distinction between popular curiosity and connoisseurship, a distinction that implies some objects merit the attention of collectors, and some do not. Later on in the book, however, in one of the conversations of which the text consists, this distinction is called into question, as it is suggested that bibliophilia is also distinct from other forms of connoisseur collecting. In response to the claim that bibliophilia is a variety of connoisseur

26   Jules Janin, *Le Livre* (Paris: Plon, 1870), pp. 13–14.

collecting, one of the interlocutors argues that it is clearly distinct from and superior to fine art collecting:

> Il appartient à peu d'hommes de posséder dans un coin de leur maison ces bronzes et ces marbres [...]. Au contraire, le livre appartient à tout le monde. Il va de main en main, sans cesse et sans fin, parfait, superbe, plein de clémence. Il tient peu de place, et chacun le peut emporter dans sa tête et dans son cœur. [...] En vérité, quand nous parlons ainsi, préférant la matière à la pensée et le statuaire à l'orateur, au livre exquis le faiseur d'ornements, nous ne parlons pas comme des sages.[27]

Thus the speaker offers an idealist and democratic critique of connoisseur collecting, dismissing it as a worthless, mindless pursuit, precisely because it wrongly prefers 'la matière' to 'la pensée'. Implicit in Janin's text is the distinction Rochefort draws between two kinds of book-collecting, a materialist variety and an idealist variety, effectively love of reading. The internecine debate staged in Janin's text continued into the fin-de-siècle and Belle Epoque, as bibliophiles sought to distinguish book-collecting from mere *bibelotage*, from the crass materialism with which other kinds of collecting were tainted.[28]

Proust's essay 'Journées de lecture' reformulates the distinction between a materialist and idealist approach to books in a way which significantly intersects with his representation of the collector in *A La Recherche*. The essay, which was originally published as the introduction to Proust's translation of Ruskin's *Sesame and Lilies*, is concerned, like its English pretext, with the value of reading, rather than book-collecting, but it couches its discussion of this topic in the language of idealism and materialism that had long shaped the discourse around bibliophilia. Proust posits two distinct ways of reading, one of which acts as a stimulus to the creative development of the individual, and one of which in fact blocks that creative development. According to Proust:

27 Janin, *Le Livre*, p. 43.
28 See Willa Z. Silverman, *The New Bibliopolis: French Book Collectors and the Culture of Print, 1880–1914* (Toronto: University of Toronto Press, 2008), pp. 10–11.

> [Le rôle de la lecture] devient dangereux [...] quand, au lieu de nous éveiller à la vie personnelle de l'esprit, la lecture tend à se substituter à elle, quand la vérité ne nous apparaît plus comme un idéal que nous ne pouvons réaliser que par le progrès intime de notre pensée et par l'effort de notre cœur, mais comme une chose matérielle, déposée entre les feuillets des livres.[29]

Proust here uses the language of the ideal and the material, mapped on to an opposition between the subjective and the objective, to discuss two different ways of reading, one of which is productive and one of which is ultimately sterile. Sterile reading is a dangerously reifying tendency to imagine that truth exists as a thing in the world, that we have merely to seize hold of to possess. Proust refers to this kind of attitude as 'un respect fétichiste pour les livres'.[30] Although Proust is talking about a kind of reading practice, describing it as fetishistic serves to elide it with the kind of bibliomania described by Nodier and Rochefort, a cult of the material. It is the kind of reading practice that Swann imagines engaging in when he loiters jealously outside Odette's apartment block one night, spying on her. The narrator describes his need to know whether Odette is faithful to him or not in the following terms:

> Il savait que la réalité de circonstances qu'il eût donné sa vie pour restituer exactement, était lisible derrière cette fenêtre striée de lumière, comme sous la couverture enluminée d'or d'un de ces manuscrits précieux à la richesse artistique elle-même desquels le savant qui les consulte ne peut rester indifférent. Il éprouvait une volupté à connaître la vérité qui le passionnait dans cet exemplaire unique, éphémère et précieux, d'une matière si translucide, si chaude et si belle.[31]

Here there is an odd slippage in the way in which the figure of the illuminated manuscript operates. When it is first introduced the cover of the book is the window separating Odette from Swann, and the contents of the book is the 'réalité de circonstances'. The simile is a comforting one for the jealous lover, suggesting that it is a fairly straightforward matter for

29 Marcel Proust, 'Journées de lecture', in *Contre Sainte-Beuve*, ed. by Pierre Clarac, Bibliothèque de la Pléiade (Paris: Gallimard, 1971), pp. 160–94 (pp. 180–1).
30 Proust, 'Journées de lecture', p. 183.
31 Proust, *A La Recherche*, I, 270.

Swann to discover the truth that will set his mind at ease, a matter merely of opening a book. In the second sentence, however – picking up on the earlier reference to Odette as 'un exemplaire rarissime' cited above – Odette herself seems to become the manuscript, as 'matière [...] si chaude et si belle' is more apt to refer to warm flesh than a pane of glass. This reworking of the simile entails a second shift, as it is no longer 'la réalité de circonstances' that Swann hopes to discover but 'la vérité', in this case implicitly the truth of Odette's feelings for him. There is thus a crescendo of the question occupying Swann's mind, which is implicitly transformed from, 'Is Odette sleeping with someone else?', to 'Does Odette love me?', as his attention shifts from the circumstantial to the absolute, from the external fact to the inner experience, from the objective to the subjective. This shift is effected covertly, however, smuggled into the text under cover of the double use of the figure of the illuminated manuscript. It is as if the text, here inflected by Swann's point of view, seeks to suggest that the facts and the truth are the same thing, and can be found in the same place – between the pages of a book one has merely to seize hold of and open. Swann here is akin to those readers reproached by Proust in 'Journées de lecture', who think that the truth is 'une chose matérielle, déposée entre les feuillets des livres'.

Swann's error here does not merely have consequences for his love-life, but is also pertinent to his failure as an artist. In 'Journées de lecture' Proust insists on the fact that excessive fondness for reading blocks creativity. The individual afflicted with 'un respect fétichiste pour les livres' has an essentially unproductive relationship with what he reads:

> Son esprit sans activité originale ne sait pas isoler dans les livres la substance qui pourrait les rendre plus fort; il s'encombre de leur forme intacte, qui, au lieu d'être pour lui un élément assimilable, un principe de vie, n'est qu'un corps étranger, un principe de mort.[32]

Thus Proust suggests that reading is useful only in so far as the reader is able to assimilate what he has read, to absorb it into his own self and thus transform it. His model of creativity is rooted in a monadic conception of the self; it is essentially through the cultivation of that self that the original work, artwork stamped with the artist's personality, is forged. The encounter with a text can strengthen the self only if that text is properly digested. Proust returns to this digestive figure in his description in *Le Temps retrouvé* of the 'célibataires de l'Art' – those *amateurs* whose passion for art is wholly sterile, 'qui ont les chagrins qu'ont les vierges et les paresseux, et que la fécondité ou le travail guérirait', and who, precisely because 'ils n'assimilent pas ce qui dans l'art est vraiment nourricier [...] ont tout le temps besoin de joies artistiques, en proie à une boulimie qui ne les rassasie jamais.'[33] Proust describes such individuals as always reaching for other's words to express their own experiences, fastening on a sentence in La Bruyère and imagining that it perfectly encapsulates their own situation. Thus 'peu à peu, conservée par la mémoire, c'est la chaîne de toutes ces expressions inexactes où rien ne reste de ce que nous avons réellement éprouvé, qui constitue pour nous notre pensée, notre vie, la réalité.'[34] The process that the narrator here describes is analogous to the process of collecting, although it involves collecting ideas and phrases rather than material objects. Rather than a gathering-in through which the collector annexes the world to the self, however, this kind of collecting involves an alienation of the self. Rather than assimilate the artwork, these 'célibataires de l'Art' are assimilated by it. Their own subjectivity is gradually smothered under the weight of imported ideas, expressions and emotional responses, and thus they become incapable of original creation.

Decadent Collecting

Proust's idea of artistic bulimia echoes in fact the views of Octave Uzanne, who diagnosed a crisis in French cultural production a generation earlier, in 1888, surveying the contemporary cultural landscape from the sales rooms

33   Proust, *A La Recherche*, IV, 470 and 471.
34   Proust, *A La Recherche*, IV, 473.

at the hôtel Drouot: 'La passion du bric-à-brac, poussée dans les limites extrêmes de ce temps-ci, est bien un des plus furieux symptômes de la décadence que je connaisse, car elle indique à la fois l'anémie dans le style déco et la *boulimie* occulaire des formes et des perfections du passé.'[35] Uzanne, like Bourget, thus presents late-nineteenth-century French aesthetics as characterized both by excess and deficiency, a clutter of objects and a lack of style. The language of medical pathology – 'l'anémie', 'la boulimie' – serves here to tie his comments about the decline of the arts into a broader, medicalized narrative of social decline, caused by a hereditary degeneration that would, according to its theorists, ultimately lead to sterility.[36] Uzanne here is concerned specifically with the artistic sterility of late-nineteenth-century France, where collecting has superseded creating. But the story of this creative exhaustion, as told by Uzanne, Robida, Bourget and others,[37] in fact entwines two distinct narratives of decline, one of creating and one of collecting itself, for in the late nineteenth century the image of a specifically decadent kind of collecting emerges.

Uzanne, in his essay 'Les Bibliophiles collectionneurs', the pretext for which was the publication of Charles Cousin's *Racontars illustrés d'un vieux collectionneur* (1887), drew attention to the emergence of a new kind of collector, distinct from the old-fashioned kind represented by Cousin Pons. Uzanne describes Cousin as:

> une sorte de *Cousin Pons* très moderne, un Cousin Pons avec apparat, qui n'a rien d'un fouisseur et qui aime *grolièrement* ses raretés pour lui et ses amis. [...] Vaniteux sans doute, mais qui ne l'est point dans la possession, en dehors de l'égoïste ombrageux qui est vanitivore par jouissance occulte. Vaniteux comme un amoureux charmé de la sensation produite par sa maîtresse; et sa maîtresse à lui, le *Toqué*, c'est la démonomanie de la collection.[38]

---

35   Uzanne, *Les Zigzags*, p. 251.
36   See Bénédicte Morel, *Traité des dégénérescences physiques, intellectuelles et morales de l'espèce humaine et des causes qui produisent ces variétés maladives* (Paris: Baillière, 1857), p. 5.
37   Further examples of this topos can be found in Bonnaffé, *Les Collectionneurs*, pp. x–xii and Octave Mirbeau, 'Les Bibelots', *Le Gaulois*, 5 March 1885, p. 1.
38   Uzanne, *Les Zigzags*, p. 215.

Uzanne's notion of the modern collector as 'un Cousin Pons avec apparat' is a telling one. We saw in chapter two that the collection in *Le Cousin Pons* functions both as an affirmation of privacy and as the embodiment of an ideology of the transcendence of art. In both respects it stands in opposition to the *roman feuilleton*, a form shaped by a commercial logic, industrially produced for mass-consumption. The novel, itself originally a *feuilleton* production, instantiates a post-Romantic aesthetics in which the artwork is reduced to the status of a commodity. *Le Cousin Pons* thus offers a narrative of cultural decline, in which it itself is profoundly implicated, but against which the connoisseur collector, distinguished by 'un nez à la Don Quichotte',[39] stands as a figure of valiant but futile resistance. When the novel concludes with the collection falling into the hands of Comte Popinot, for whom the reputation of a connoisseur is effectively a status symbol, the kingdom of art has been annexed to the murky, mercenary kingdom of Louis-Philippe. Uzanne's passing reference to Charles Cousin as 'un Cousin Pons avec apparat', seems to confirm Balzac's pessimistic predictions concerning the fate of the collector in the nineteenth century, for the modern collector described by Uzanne is far closer to Comte Popinot than Cousin Pons. One of the essential features of the Pons collection was precisely that it was a private collection, to which not even Du Sommerard was allowed entry. In complete contrast to this, the collector Uzanne describes revels in exhibiting his objects to his friends. The neologism '*grolièrement*' is presumably a reference to the famous Renaissance bibliophile Jean Grolier de Servières, whose books were inscribed with the legend 'Grolierii et amicorum'. This inscription encapsulates the sociability for which Grolier was renowned, sharing his library with his friends. Thus the modern collector, according to Uzanne, far from jealously guarding his collection as does Pons, flaunts it. At stake in the transition from Pons to Popinot is what Rémy Saisselin has identified as the *bibelotization* of art in the nineteenth century, a process by which the distinction between the *objet d'art* and the industrially produced luxury good was dismantled. For Comte Popinot, as for Uzanne's

---

39   Balzac, *Le Cousin Pons*, p. 485.

putative modern collector, the collection is a symbol of wealth and distinction, no longer the object of a disinterested and gratuitous cult of beauty. Uzanne's comparison of the collection to a man's mistress clearly points to this process of bibelotization, for as Saisselin notes in *The Bourgeois and the Bibelot*, women were the most expensive of all the luxury items that nineteenth-century men could buy.[40]

Seen from within the aesthetic paradigm described by *Le Cousin Pons*, therefore, the modern collector as described by Uzanne is an agent of cultural decline. But the bibelotization of art, a process in which domestic interiors came to resemble bric-a-brac shops, crammed with knickknacks, can be described as a phenomenon of decadence in another sense, in which the aesthetic experience is linked to a certain conception of history. Saisselin insists, like the nineteenth-century cultural critics who first grappled with this phenomenon, that:

> The bibelotization of art implies too much of anything from anywhere in the same space, and hence it is a bourgeois style, rather than a true style, namely the creation of artists and architects, of mind disciplining imagination, such as Louis XV, Louis XVI, or Directoire, the style which supposes a harmony and unity. The bourgeois style, in contrast is an economic and psychological style that at worst might be called the accumulative, or museum, style, or, at best, the eclectic.[41]

This negative view of eclecticism resonates with Uzanne's account of the modern collector. Although we have seen in chapter three that the discourse of collecting often valorizes eclecticism, as in *A Rebours* for example, presenting it as a means through which the collector can imagine himself to have escaped from the order of time,[42] for Uzanne the collection seems to function in a very different fashion, offering a spectacle of scatter and historical contingency. He writes that, in 'toute collection multiforme

---

40 Rémy G. Saisselin, *The Bourgeois and the Bibelot* (New Brunswick: Rutgers University Press, 1984), pp. 53–62.

41 Saisselin, p. 68.

42 See above, pp. 102–6. On the euphoria of eclecticism see also Dominique Pety, *Les Goncourt et la collection: de l'objet d'art à l'art d'écrire* (Geneva: Droz, 2003), pp. 114–15.

moderne, on sent la déroute des arts battus et dispersés par le temps'.[43] Eclecticism seems to function here not to offer an escape from time, but rather to foreground the effects of its wasteful action. 'La passion du bric-à-brac' was, therefore, both an expression of a decadent, twilit sensibility, and a factor in cultural decline, as the 'boulimie' of the bricabracomaniac went hand in hand with 'l'anémie dans le style déco'. In a world crammed with bits of the past, originality becomes impossible.[44]

The Uses and Disadvantages of History for Life in
Le Crime de Sylvestre Bonnard

The question of how to find the living kernel in the rubble of past civilizations is precisely the question posed by Anatole France's novel, Le Crime de Sylvestre Bonnard. The eponymous hero and narrator of this first-person text in journal form is a sexagenarian antiquarian and bibliophile, living a quiet and rather empty life as a bachelor, his books his closest companions. The text mobilizes a pre-existing stereotype of the antiquarian collector as a musty, dusty, decrepit and dessicated figure living an emotionally impoverished life.[45] Bonnard himself experiences his life as an empty and unfulfilled one, largely loveless save for one romantic episode in his youth:

> J'ai pourtant, comme un autre, senti la beauté; j'ai pourtant éprouvé le charme mys-
> térieux que l'incompréhensible nature a répandu sur des formes animées; une vivante
> argile m'a donné le frisson qui fait les amants et les poètes. Mais je n'ai su aimer ni

---

43   Uzanne, Les Zigzags, p. 220.
44   Similar concerns were widespread in Europe in this period. The most famous critique of historicist thought is articulated by Friedrich Nietzsche in 'On the Uses and Disadvantages of History for Life', in Untimely Meditations, ed. by Daniel Breazeale (Cambridge: Cambridge University Press, 1997), pp. 58–123.
45   See for example, 'Collectionneur' in Grand Dictionnaire, p. 601.

chanter. Dans mon âme, encombrée d'un fatras de vieux textes et de vieilles formules, je retrouve, comme une miniature dans un grenier, un clair visage avec deux yeux de pervenche.[46]

This quotation is the first reference in the text to an unhappy love affair in Bonnard's youth. The substance of the plot concerns Bonnard's serendipitous encounter with Jeanne, a young woman whom he discovers to be the orphaned grand-daughter of his lost love, whom he rescues from a life of forced claustration in a convent school and adopts, finally selling his beloved books to provide her with a dowry. The novel thus traces the transformation of Bonnard from lonely antiquarian to *père de famille*. The initial reference to the great love affair of Bonnard's life serves to establish what is at stake in his story, by setting up an opposition between the antiquarian on the one hand, and the lover and the poet on the other, and between living nature and moribund texts. These antitheses structure the development of the novel.

The springboard for the novel's main narrative thread is a visit Bonnard makes to the ancestral home of the de Gabry family, where he meets Jeanne, a family friend. Paul de Gabry has recently inherited the title and estate of his uncle, and employs Bonnard to organize the family archives, which, like the château itself, have been long neglected. Indeed, on arriving at the château, Bonnard finds a chestnut-tree growing in the reception room. This fact solicits further reflection on the sterility of antiquarianism:

> Je ne pus m'empêcher d'admirer la vigueur magnifique de la nature et l'irrésistible force qui pousse tout germe à se développer dans la vie. Par contre, je m'attristai à songer que l'effort que nous faisons, nous autres savants, pour retenir et conserver les choses mortes est un pénible et vain effort. Tout ce qui a vécu est l'aliment nécessaire de nouvelles existences.[47]

The fecundity of nature, ceaselessly creative, is starkly contrasted with a historical science that privileges the dead over the living. Here again, as in the work of Proust and Uzanne, we find a digestive figure used to trope

46 France, *Sylvestre Bonnard*, p. 170.
47 France, *Sylvestre Bonnard*, p. 205.

the process of creation. In Proust's account of creativity, the writer feeds on the work of other writers, absorbing and transforming it. Here the past is consumed in the present, and feeds the development of the future. The antiquarian's work serves only to inflict on society a painful cultural indigestion, obstructing the creation of 'de nouvelles existences'.

The consequences of the idea that 'Tout ce qui a vécu est l'aliment nécessaire de nouvelles existences' are worked out in the novel at the level both of representational content and of formal textual practices. At the level of plot, the development of the novel serves as a warning against the kind of excessive affective investment in the past, the privileging of the dead over the living, which characterizes the antiquarian attitude. The novel ends on a melancholy note, with the death of Jeanne's infant son, named Sylvestre in honour of the antiquarian. As Bonnard remarks, 'c'est un mystère douloureux que la mort d'un enfant',[48] but in the economy of the novel as a whole the death of the child seems in an obscure way to play a retributive role. *Le Crime de Sylvestre Bonnard* is an ambiguous title, for there are two acts in the text that can be construed as criminal. One is the abduction of Jeanne from the convent school by Bonnard, which although illegal is presented in the novel as unambiguously a morally justified act. The second is one that, although perfectly licit, is presented as criminal within the moral economy of the novel. As mentioned above, Bonnard sells his library to provide a dowry for Jeanne, thus abandoning the past in favour of the future, facilitating marriage and the establishment of a new family unit. In fact, however, Bonnard keeps a secret hoard of books: 'C'est alors que je connus le crime. [...] Je volais la dot de Jeanne'.[49] Within the book, the death of baby Sylvestre (the tragic dimension of which is very much tempered by the text, which foregrounds the expectation that Jeanne will have more children) thus reads almost as an expiation of Bonnard's guilt.

At the formal level, the text seems to exemplify the digestive conception of creativity to which Bonnard alludes. In her notes to the Pléiade edition, Marie-Claire Bancquart draws attention to France's extensive

48   France, *Sylvestre Bonnard*, p. 313.
49   France, *Sylvestre Bonnard*, pp. 309–10.

borrowings from other authors. For example, the account of a voyage to Sicily undertaken by Bonnard 'juxtapose des morceaux du guide Joanne, lui-même empli de citations et d'emprunts à d'autres descriptions de voyage, et des morceaux du récit publié par Renan dans *La Revue des Deux Mondes* de son propre voyage en Sicile, avec là encore, citations ou allusions à des textes antiques'.[50] Bancquart goes on to describe the effect of such borrowings within the text thus: 'C'est la bibliothèque de Babel, le renvoi au renvoi, sans crier gare'.[51] Bancquart's reference to the library of Babel is particularly telling in the light of the ending of the novel. Bonnard's trajectory from bachelorhood to family life is complemented by changes in his professional life, as he abandons antiquarianism in favour of the study of natural history, addressing himself particularly to the relationship between plants and insects. The final chapter of the novel incorporates the final paragraph of Bonnard's book on this subject, but footnotes this with a 'note de l'éditeur', which states:

> M. Sylvestre Bonnard ne savait pas que de très illustres naturalistes avaient fait avant lui des recherches sur les rapports des insectes et des plantes. Il ignorait les travaux de M. Darwin, ceux du docteur Hermann Müller, ainsi que les observations de Sir John Lubbock. Il est à remarquer que les conclusions de M. Sylvestre Bonnard se rapprochent très sensiblement de celles de ces trois savants.[52]

This footnote makes clear that Bonnard approaches the study of nature not through the prism of other scholars' work on the subject, but in more direct fashion, seeking to achieve a direct contact with living nature. Earlier in the novel he claims that: 'par une habitude de plus de soixante ans, je ne sente plus les choses que par les signes qui le représentent. Il n'y a pour moi dans le monde que des mots, tant je suis philologue!'.[53] His work on natural history, however, is grounded in direct, empirical observation. Bonnard's trajectory over the course of the novel is thus ostensibly from

---

50   Marie-Claire Bancquart, '*Le Crime de Sylvestre Bonnard*: Notice', in France, *Œuvres*, Bibliothèque de la Pléiade, 4 vols (Paris: 1984–1991), I, 1109–29 (p. 1119).
51   Bancquart, pp. 1119–20.
52   France, p. 311.
53   France, p. 201.

the library to the field, from the dusty archive to living nature. In fact, however, there is a sly irony woven into the final pages of the novel, which suggests that there is no escape from the library. As Bancquart makes clear in her notes to the text, the paragraph of Bonnard's book cited in the text is in fact plagiarized from the French translation of John Lubbock's *Les Insectes et les fleurs sauvages. Leurs rapports réciproques*. Indeed, the 'note d'éditeur' itself is based on a note in Lubbock's introduction, in which he acknowledges his debt to other writers. France thus seems to insist on the citational nature of language. As Bancquart argues,[54] this view compromises a Romantic, demiurgic view of creativity, but it enables the emergence of a literary practice that, far from disavowing the citational nature of language, exploits it, creating new texts out of bits and pieces of old ones. This practice elides the distinction between the creator and the collector, turning the writer into a collector of other people's words, cutting and pasting them to produce a new work.

Creative Collecting in Champfleury's *La Mascarade de la vie parisienne*

How to create something new out of second-hand materials is a question that also underpins another novel of collecting, Champfleury's *La Mascarade de la vie parisienne*. Originally published in *feuilleton* form, this novel is very much an example of the kind of anti-idealist realism that Champfleury championed in the culture wars of the mid-nineteenth century.[55] Such realism was often denounced by its detractors as a kind

54   See Bancquart, pp. 1120–2.
55   My understanding of these culture wars in general, and of the emergence of anti-idealist realism, is very much shaped by Toril Moi, *Henrik Ibsen and the Birth of Modernism: Art, Theater, Philosophy* (Oxford: Oxford University Press, 2006), pp. 67–104.

of anti-aesthetics, which seemed, in its supposed slavish fidelity to reality, to leave no room for the artist's own individual imagination.[56] This was certainly the view of Uzanne, who tended to view it as a symptom of the same creative exhaustion that led to the proliferation of pastiche in the decorative arts. Thus in *Le Miroir du Monde*, he writes: 'Ce qui entrave principalement le libre essor de l'Art moderne, c'est l'étude constante du passé [...]. La science et l'érudition momifient tous les Arts, les déssèchent et les pédantisent. Nous sommes empêtrés dans le document, alors que l'idéal ne connaît point de dossiers documentaires.'[57] Here Uzanne once more begins by identifying an inordinate love of the past as blocking the development of new forms, but here this cultural necrophilia is expressed not through the relentless accumulation of antique objects, but through the relentless accumulation of knowledge, in the form of prodigious 'dossiers documentaires'. The reference to such 'dossiers' also, however, invites us to read these comments as a critique of documentary realism. Elsewhere Uzanne's hostility to naturalist aesthetics is much more explicit. In a short-story co-authored and illustrated by Albert Robida, 'La Fin des Livres', a symbolist artist called Arthur Blackcross condemns the late nineteenth century as the age of the copy: 'Nous ne voyons que des copies de toute sorte: copies des vieux maîtres accommodés au goût moderne, reconstitutions toujours fausses d'époques à jamais disparues, copies banales de la nature vue avec un œil de photographe [...], rien qui nous sorte de notre humanité! Le devoir de l'art cependant [...] est de nous en sortir à tout prix et de nous faire planer un instant dans des sphères irréelles où nous puissions faire comme une cure d'aérothérapie idéaliste.'[58] Uzanne therefore presents naturalism as a betrayal of idealism in art, too closely tied to base matter. Indeed, *La Mascarade de la vie parisienne* very much fits into this anti-idealist paradigm. Like Uzanne, Champfleury ties together the

---

56   See David Baguley, *Naturalist Fiction: The Entropic Vision* (Cambridge: Cambridge University Press, 1990), pp. 40–70, for the postulates of natural fiction, and specifically its commitment to materialism, objectivity and mimesis.

57   Octave Uzanne, *Le Miroir du monde* (Paris: Quantin, 1885), p. 27.

58   Albert Robida and Octave Uzanne, 'La Fin des Livres', in *Contes pour les bibliophiles* (Paris: May et Metteroz, 1895), pp. 123–45 (pp. 129–30).

collecting, materialism and a certain kind of literary practice, but he does so in a productive mode, to bury idealism not to praise it.

La Mascarade de la vie parisienne largely concerns the self-inflicted misfortunes of Claire Couturier. Seduced by frippery, she leaves her father's house and suffers variously predictable degradations, before finally finding redemption in marriage to a good and constant man. The novel is crucially concerned with the meretricious lures of consumerism, and explores the seamy side of Parisian life. Claire's father earns a gruesome living killing cats, whose fur is then used in the production of fashion items, and his brother, Topino, works as a *chiffonnier*. If the name Couturier points ironically to Claire's father's role in the fashion industry, the latter's name, a diminutive of the Italian word for 'mouse', suggests both his status as a scavenger, living off refuse, and also the affection with which he is universally regarded within the novel. Topino is a successful and conscientious rag-picker. In the courtyard of his apartment building he sorts his rags into different piles: 'Ces produits étaient rangés avec un art infini et faisaient plaisir à voir [...]. Le goût se remarque dans l'arrangement des choses les plus basses. Topino était un artiste en matière de chiffons: aussi vendait-il ses produits un tiers plus cher que ses confrères, grâce à la conscience de son triage.'[59] The essence of Topino's work lies not in the accumulation of rags, but in their classification and arrangement. This classification is based primarily on industrial criteria, but the above quotation makes clear that aesthetic judgement is also in operation. Topino's work as a rag-picker is thus closely linked to his hobby, the collection and display of advertising bills. He is the proud proprietor of 'un musée unique dans son genre':[60]

> Topino logeait au rez-de-chaussée et il avait loué une grande pièce, dont toute la décoration primitive consistait en trois fenêtres par lesquelles entrait un jour clair. De cette pièce unique, Topino fit un appartement complet, en la divisant en quatre parties égales par des affiches qu'il détachait adroitement des murailles de Paris, et qui, collées les unes sur les autres, avaient fini par former des entrefends solides.

59 Champfleury, *La Mascarade de la vie parisienne* (Paris: Librairie Nouvelle, 1861), pp. 77–8.
60 Champfleury, *La Mascarade*, p. 69.

C'étaient des affiches de théâtres, mêlées à des affiches de marchands de nouveau-
tés, des affiches de dentistes, d'eau pour les cheveux à côté d'affiches de marchands
d'habits confectionnés, d'affiches de bains et d'affiches de remèdes que Topino savait
varier avec goût.[61]

Thus Topino has amassed an impressive collection of advertising bills,
which serve a practical purpose, reorganizing the space in which he lives,
but which also have an aesthetic value: '[il] aimait les affiches à cause des
figures et des images fortement coloriées'.[62]

The novel thus superimposes on the features of the rag-picker those
of the connoisseur collector, which is an innovative discursive move. For
a number of reasons, the collector and the rag-picker might appear to be
diametrically opposed figures. The connoisseur collector is a member of
the cultural elite; the rag-picker was a figure of abject poverty. The collector
has a highly developed faculty of discrimination; a keynote of representations of the rag-picker in the July Monarchy and Second Empire is the
indiscriminate nature of their work. The article 'Chiffonnier' in Larousse's
Grand Dictionnaire Universel du XIXè siècle offers two figurative uses of the
word: 'Personne qui recueille de tout côté des nouvelles vraies ou fausses,
et les répète sans discernement. || Celui à qui tout est bon, qui ramasse
sans choix tout ce qu'il rencontre'.[63] The collector, to cite Benjamin, 'strips
objects of the drudgery of being useful'.[64] The rag-picker works to find
new uses for refuse. Collecting is normally conceptualized as being about
taking objects out of circuits of distribution and exchange; thus Krzysztof
Pomian defines the collection as 'un ensemble d'objets naturels ou artifi-
ciels, maintenu temporairement ou définitivement hors du circuit d'activité
économiques, soumis à une protection spéciale et exposés au regard dans

---

61   Champfleury, *La Mascarade*, p. 69.
62   Champfleury, *La Mascarade*, p. 69.
63   'Chiffonnier', in *Grand Dictionnaire universel du XIXᵉ siècle français, historique, géo-
      graphique, bibliographique, littéraire, artistique, scientifique etc.*, ed. by Pierre Larousse,
      17 vols (Paris: Librairie classique Larousse et Boyer, 1866–1877), IV (1869), 96–8
      (p. 96).
64   Walter Benjamin, 'Paris, 1939', p. 19.

un lieu clos aménagé à cet effet.'⁶⁵ This is in complete contrast to the rag-
picker, who, as Irving Wohlfarth comments, is 'so abjectly dependent on
the laws of exchange-value that he can reproduce his own existence only
by directly serving the reproductive needs of the capitalist economy'.⁶⁶

If Topino is an unusual collector by virtue of his profession, his choice
of object is also telling. Clearly it is dictated by economic necessity. In his
'Monographie du Rentier' – the text that features the first recorded use
of the word 'collectionneur' – Balzac had already offered the example of
advertising bills as a cheap collectable. According to Balzac, the collector,
whom he identifies as a sub-species of *rentier*:

> se recommande par des idées bizarres. Son peu de fortune lui interdit les collections
> d'objets chers, mais il trouve à satisfaire sur des riens le goût de la collection, passion
> réelle, définie, reconnue chez les anthropomorphes qui habitent les grandes villes.
> J'ai connu personnellement un individu de cette variété qui possède une collec-
> tion de toutes les affiches affichées ou qui ont dû l'être. Si, au décès de ce rentier, la
> Bibliothèque royale n'achetait pas sa collection, Paris y perdrait ce magnifique herbier
> des productions originales venues sur ses murailles.⁶⁷

The tone of this is mocking but indulgent. The collector is presented as
an eccentric figure, motivated by a mysterious instinct (rather than a lofty
love of art), and the activity of collecting advertising bills is offered as an
example of this eccentricity. The use of the adjective 'personnellement'
('J'ai connu personnellement …') suggests the improbability of anyone
bothering to collect advertising bills. Having introduced this collection,
Balzac goes on to generate humour by discussing it in language that is more
normally used to describe fine art collections: it is a 'magnifique' trove,
which deserves to be housed in the Bibliothèque royale. The use of the word
'originales' is particularly loaded. Of course the term is an important one
in the discourse of art, capable of conferring value on a painting, but it is
here used in a slightly different sense. Posters are precisely not 'original' in
the sense used in art criticism (and art commerce); they are not authentic

65   Pomian, 'Collections: une typologie historique', p. 9.
66   Wohlfarth, p. 152.
67   Balzac, 'Monographie', p. 14.

works attributable to a particular artist. Rather, they are anonymous and mass-produced. In this context, the word 'originales' carries connotations of novelty, which seem to apply not only to the posters but also to the idea of collecting them. The humourous effect of this passage depends precisely upon the incongruity of the language of fine art being applied to posters. The poster collection thus functions as a burlesque of the traditional fine art collection. Almost forty years later, Albert Robida used the notion of the poster collection in a similar mode. His 'homme de goût qui n'en avait pas' is forced to collect posters after he has bankrupted himself collecting more traditional objects, and is almost immediately imprisoned for a month for vandalism. Again the idea of the poster collection is used in a parodic mode, as a kind of *reductio ad absurdum* of the activity of collecting.[68]

The figure of Topino, therefore, a rag-picker who collects posters, appears in many ways to stand outside the standard paradigm of the collector. In fact, the figure of Topino is a dialectical image, in which collector and *chiffonnier* collide to form a specific kind of collector, who recycles his objects, but no longer to serve the needs of the capitalist economy. For Topino is not a passive consumer of the images he collects; his museum is a productive space, as through the posters Topino teaches local children to read, and at the same time furthers his own education. His method is inductive. When we are first introduced to Topino he is engaged in puzzling out the meaning of an unfamiliar word, 'humanitaire', which features on two of his latest acquisitions, an advertisement for a chemist, and a campaign poster urging electors to vote Dumoulin, 'candidat humanitaire':

> Un député et une pharmacie qui sont tous les deux humanitaires, voilà quelque chose d'étonnant ... Il y a de l'humanité là-dessous; je comprends que l'apothicaire aime l'humanité qui lui achète des drogues, mais le député ... ah! que je suis sot! c'est la même chose ... Le député aussi aime l'humanité qui lui donne des voix ... Ce Dumoulin est un intrigant.[69]

68 Robida, pp. 242–4.
69 Champfleury, *La Mascarade*, p. 74.

Thus Topino generates new meanings through collage. Disparate images and scraps of language signify differently when brought into contact with each other. Just as the bits of rubbish Topino collects are recycled and turned into new goods, so odds and ends of discourse serve new purposes once they are rearranged and reconfigured in the Topino museum. At first blush, the posters that do not simply decorate the walls of Topino's home, but actually constitute them, would seem to bring the market into the domestic interior. But in fact, when they enter the Topino collection, the posters no longer function as advertisements, but have a new use value conferred upon them. Through reconfiguring the words and images on the poster, Topino generates a contestatory discourse.

Thus in Champfleury's text the convergence of rag-picker and collector rehabilitates both figures. By stressing the discriminate nature of Topino's work, his good taste and aesthetic judgement, Champfleury ennobles the figure of the rag-picker and thus furthers the progressive and democratic agenda which underpinned his work. At the same time, however, the collector, so often a figure of sterility in nineteenth-century literature, is here a creative, productive figure. Whereas in *Le Cousin Pons* the collection and the narrative are antagonistic principles, Topino's collection plays an instrumental role in the development of the narrative in Champfleury's novel, as an advertisement for a mesmerist that hangs in Topino's gallery ultimately leads to the reunion of Claire and her father. Far from obstructing narrative, collecting in *La Mascarade* acts in its interest. If in *Le Cousin Pons* the collection stands in opposition to the realist novel, embodying an alternative aesthetic, albeit one that is presented as obsolescent, within *La Mascarade*, Topino's museum can be read as instantiating, *en abyme*, the realist aesthetics of the novel itself. In *Le Réalisme*, Champfleury described the work of the realist novelist in the following terms: 'Le romancier choisit un certain nombre de faits saisissants, les groupe, les distribue et les encadre'.[70] According to Champfleury, therefore, the novelist's role is essentially one of selection and arrangement. Like the rag-picker he does not create anything from scratch; the secret of his art is knowing how to make use of the

70   Champfleury, *Le Réalisme* (Paris: Michel Lévy, 1857), p. 96.

bits and pieces he picks up in the street. Realism, for Champfleury, was necessarily a popular art form:

> L'art n'est-il pas la communication à la foule de mes sensations personnelles?
> Je dois remuer, échauffer des cœurs, faire sourire ou pleurer des individus que je ne connais pas.
> L'art sert de trait d'union entre eux et moi.
> Longtemps j'ai étudié les aspirations, les désirs, les joies, les chagrins des classes qui me sont sympathiques, et je m'applique à rendre ces sentiments dans toute leur sincérité.
> J'écris ce qu'ils ne sauraient écrire: je ne suis que leur interprète.[71]

Thus for Champfleury, art is doubly tied to the popular classes: it is both for and about them that he writes, describing them and speaking on their behalf. Champfleury's conception of the artist is a modest one; far from a Promethean figure, a creative genius, he is presented as mere interpreter. Thus it is in the lowly figure of the rag-picker who collects mass-produced, anonymous images that Champfleury found an appropriate image of the artist.

The relationship between the collector and the artist has often been presented as an unequal one, in which sterility is placed in contrast to creativity. We have seen, however, that at two moments this relationship was reconfigured. In the late nineteenth century, an aesthetics of exhaustion led writers to find in the figure of the collector an appropriate figure for the artist, precisely because of the collector's traditional association with sterility. At the same time, however, anti-idealist realism used the figure of the colletor in a far more positive way, developing the notion that collecting could itself be a creative practice. Of the many images salvaged by Topino, not the least is that of the collector himself, transformed from figure of sterility to the harbinger of a new aesthetics.

71 Champfleury, *Le Réalisme*, p. 8.

Conclusion

In his essay 'Eduard Fuchs: Collector and Historian', Walter Benjamin mused: 'The figure of the collector, more attractive the longer one observes it, has not been given its due attention so far. [...] The type is motivated by dangerous though domesticated passions'.[1] Benjamin's formulation points to the seeming innocuousness of the collector. After all, the collector's activity is simple: he accumulates objects, and then scrutinizes them. To those immune to the collector's disease, this activity can be somewhat bemusing; it seems to be almost entirely pointless, a dead end. This bemusement echoes through accounts of collecting produced throughout the nineteenth century, in which the collector is routinely treated as a figure of ridicule.

But let us, like Benjamin, follow the collector's lead, and take the time properly to look at the figure of the collector. Suddenly, it seems less banal, and we can begin to make sense of Benjamin's reference to 'dangerous though domesticated passions'. Domesticated and domestic. The popularity of collecting was closely linked to the rise of the domestic sphere, as Edmond de Goncourt, the doyen of *haute curiosité*, suggested. Describing life in the nineteenth century, he wrote: 'Dans cette vie assise au coin du feu, renfermée, sédentaire, la créature humaine [...] a été poussé à vouloir les quatre murs de son *home* agréables, plaisants, amusants aux yeux'.[2] The collection, an affirmation of privacy, provided a refuge for the collector, a space segregated from the dreary workaday world. The domestic interior was also closely tied to the concept of interiority. The collection was a space within which the collector could fashion an image of himself.

But towards the end of the century the clutter of the domestic interior became threatening. No longer did the collection function as a private

1   Benjamin, 'Eduard Fuchs', p. 241.
2   Goncourt, *La Maison d'un artiste*, I, 2.

refuge. The domestic interior was no longer segregated from the public sphere. Rather the public sphere invaded the domestic interior, which came to resemble a museum or a bric-a-brac shop. Bourget referred disparagingly to 'l'aspect de magasin de bric-à-brac, habituel à nos installations'.[3] Nordau, writing of the interiors of the degenerates he studied, wrote: 'Here are at once stage properties and lumber-rooms, rag-shops and museums.'[4] The domestic interior became a confused and confusing space. At the same time, the collection came to be seen no longer as a process of gathering in through which the self could annexe the other, but as a process through which the self was alienated, scattered through the collection.

The failure of collecting to produce coherent, autonomous, self-determined subjects is linked to its increasing failure to produce knowledge. We noted in the introduction that the nineteenth-century concept of collecting displaced an earlier one, in which collecting was closely linked to curiosity and in which it had a pre-eminently epistemological function. Over the course of the nineteenth century, the epistemological function of collecting was increasingly called into question. We saw in chapter five how this occurred in the sub-field of natural history collecting, when classical natural history gave way to modern biology. Although the fate of natural history collecting in the nineteenth century must be understood in terms of significant epistemological shifts in the natural sciences, it must also be understood in the context of a remapping of the discursive field of collecting. At stake in accounts of natural history collecting are concepts of mastery and control that resonate throughout the entire field of collecting, and that unite epistemological concerns with aesthetic ones. The four texts studied in chapter five all challenge the notion that the natural history collection could provide a controlled, ordered, but adequate representation of reality. Verne, Flaubert and Loti all tie this concern to their own practice as writers, to question the relationship between language and lived experience. In this respect their work resonates with the concerns of other writers discussed in this book, and with specific kinds of literary

3   Bourget, p. 381.
4   Nordau, p. 10.

practice. In particular, accounts of natural history collecting can usefully be read alongside the examples of sketch-writing we examined in chapter one. Sketch-writers, the natural historians of nineteenth-century Paris, ostensibly promised to make sense of the teeming, multifarious reality of the metropolis, to produce an exhaustive taxonomy of its different types. As we saw, however, this promise is never fulfilled by the texts. In both sketch-writing and accounts of natural history collecting, therefore, the limitations of taxonomical thought are exposed. Accounts of natural history collecting also raise questions about the literary uses of the list, which are pertinent to debates around realism. Verne's work demands to be read alongside texts by Balzac and Huysmans as an exploration of the list as literary form. In the work of all three writers, the list is used to force the reader to confront the distance between words and things, although to very different ends. In *La Muse du département*, the inventory of Dinah de La Baudraye's collection is, as we have seen, a kind of anti-inventory, in which language swallows up the objects in her collection. By placing Dinah de La Baudraye firmly on the side of the signifier, Balzac mocks her ersatz connoisseurship. In *A Rebours* and in *Vingt mille lieues*, however, the problem of the gap between signifer and signified is generalized, and it is objective realism itself that is called into question, as the list form seems to expose the extent to which language is autonomous of material reality.

The relationship between words and things has been a recurrent concern throughout this book, concerned with the relationship between material culture and writing in the nineteenth century. As we saw in chapter six, this relationship was very much influenced by idealist aesthetic assumptions. Although for some writers, such as Champfleury, it was precisely because the collector had a privileged relationship with material objects that he was a potentially creative figure, for most of the writers whose work we have examined, the collector's materialism places him in opposition to the artist. The relationship between materiality and discursivity was also of central importance in accounts of historical collecting, haunted by the fear that objects asked to bear witness to the past can in reality offer only silence. In chapter four we saw that the historical collector was an ambivalent figure: dedicated to preservation, he was nonetheless an agent of destruction; concerned with the formation and transmission of cultural memory, his very existence was evidence of historical disjunction. The collection could be a locus of loss, or give rise to an experience of timelessness, in which the self seemed to escape from history. We saw in chapter two that in *Le Cousin Pons* this experience of timelessness places the collection in opposition to the narrative demands of the realist novel. But the collector's insatiable desire to acquire new objects can also elicit narrative, a fact to which the vast corpus of narratives of collecting in nineteenth-century France attests.

Thus the collection is an ambivalent construct, and this ambivalence is partly what makes the collector a 'dangerous' figure. The collector straddles different worlds. We might recall Balzac's comment on collectors: 'Ils n'appartiennent ni à la Tribu remuante des Artistes, ni à celles des Savants, ni à celle des Écrivains, mais ils tiennent de tous.'[5] The collector is a marginal figure, but he is also a mobile one. He is always on the move, both physically and conceptually: roaming across Paris on the hunt for new objects, he moves between the spheres of art and commerce. There is something inherently transgressive about the collector.

This apparently rather simple figure thus turns out, upon closer examination, to be rather more complex than we might have thought. In this respect, the collector holds the same appeal as nineteenth-century realist novels. For such books are deceptively straightforward. Their project is apparently a simple one: to observe and transcribe reality. Of course, this apparent simplicity is illusory; realist novels are more complex, more fraught than they appear at first glance. This, for me, is a source of fascination, and the source too of the fascination of the collector. For while the collector seems like a harmless eccentric, his way of being in the world in fact poses a basic challenge to the society in which he lives. Hence the hostility which the collector routinely provokes, for he is not merely an object of ridicule but frequently one of contempt, mockery, and scorn.

5   Balzac, 'Monographie', p. 14.

This challenge is to the phenomenon Giorgio Agamben has described in *Stanzas: Word and Phantasm in Western Culture* as one 'increasingly familiar to the modern age: a bad conscience with respect to objects'.[6] Agamben finds this bad conscience expressed by Grandville in his *Petites Misères de la vie humaine*, a series of illustrations produced in 1843, in which objects seem to wreak an obscure revenge on man: 'In a leaky faucet that cannot be turned off, in an umbrella that reverses itself, in a boot that can be neither completely put on nor taken off and remains tenaciously stuck on the foot, in the sheets of paper scattered by a breath of wind, in a coverlet that does not cover, in a pair of pants that tears, the prophetic glance of Grandville discovers, beyond the simple fortuitous incident, the cipher of new relation between humans and things.'[7] This new relation is a result of commodification: 'the degeneration implicit in the transformation of the artisanal object into the mass-produced article is constantly manifest to modern man in the loss of his own self-possession with respect to things. The degradation of objects is matched by human clumsiness, that is the fear of their possible revenge, to which Grandville lends his pen'.[8]

Agamben finds in the figure of the dandy a possible way out of this impossible situation: 'To men who had lost their self-possession, the dandy, who makes of elegance and the superfluous his raison d'être, teaches the possibility of a new relation to things, which goes beyond both the enjoyment of their use-value and the accumulation of their exchange value.'[9] The collector and the dandy are in many respects opposed figures (the collector is shabby rather than elegant, and eccentric rather than effortlessly at ease), but like the dandy the collector too teaches a new relation to objects, which cannot be made sense of through reference to either use or exchange value. Unlike the unfortunate individuals in Grandville's illustrations, the collector

6   Giorgio Agamben, *Stanzas: Word and Phantasm in Western Culture*, trans. by Ronald L. Martinez (Minneapolis: University of Minnesota Press, 1993), p. 47.
7   Agamben, p. 47.
8   Agamben, p. 47.
9   Agamben, p. 48.

is at home in the world of things, bound to it by a mysterious sympathy. He resists the degradation of objects, simply through his reverence for them, and his intense focus on the individual object as an individual object. Like the dandy, he is 'the redeemer of things'.[10]

10   Agamben, p. 48.

Bibliography

Primary Texts

Asselineau, Charles, *Mélanges curieux et anecdotiques tirés d'une collection de lettres autographes et de documents historiques* (Paris: Techener, 1861)

Balzac, Charles, 'L'Hôtel des commissaires-priseurs' in *La Grande Ville*, ed. by Paul de Kock, 2 vols (Paris: Marescq, 1844), II, 275–92

Balzac, Honoré de, 'Monographie du rentier', in *Les Français peints par eux-mêmes*, 8 vols (Paris: Curmer, 1840–1842), III (1841), 1–16

——, *La Muse du département*, in *La Comédie humaine*, ed. by Pierre-Georges Castex, Bibliothèque de la Pléiade, 12 vols (Paris: Gallimard, 1976–1981), IV (1976), 629–791

——, *Pierre Grassou*, in *La Comédie humaine*, ed. by Pierre-Georges Castex, Bibliothèque de la Pléiade, 12 vols (Paris: Gallimard, 1976–1981), VI (1977), 1091–1111

——, *Le Cousin Pons*, in *La Comédie humaine*, ed. by Pierre-Georges Castex, Bibliothèque de la Pléiade, 12 vols (Paris: Gallimard, 1976–1981), VII (1977), 483–765

——, 'L'Avertissement quasi-littéraire', in *La Comédie humaine*, ed. by Pierre-Georges Castex, Bibliothèque de la Pléiade, 12 vols (Paris: Gallimard, 1976–1981), VII (1977), 1388–9

——, *La Peau de chagrin*, in *La Comédie humaine*, ed. by Pierre-Georges Castex, Bibliothèque de la Pléiade, 12 vols (Paris: Gallimard, 1976–1981), X (1979), 47–294

Bernard, P., and Louis Couailhac, *Le Jardin des plantes: description complète, historique et pittoresque du Muséum d'histoire naturelle, de la menagerie, des serres, des galeries de minéraolgie et d'anatomie* (Paris: Curmer, 1842)

Blanc, Charles, *Le Trésor de la curiosité tiré des catalogues de vente avec diverses notes et notices historiques & biographiques etc.* (Paris: Jules Renouard, 1857)

Blondel, Spire, *L'Art intime et le goût en France* (Paris: Rouveyre & Blond, 1884)

Bonnaffé, Edmond, *Causeries sur l'art et la curiosité* (Paris: Quantin, 1878)

——, *Physiologie du curieux* (Paris: Martin, 1881)

——, *Les Collectionneurs de l'ancienne France* (Paris: Aubry, 1888)

Bourget, Paul, Edmond et Jules de Goncourt', in *Œuvres complètes: Critique I. Essais de psychologie contemporaines* (Paris: Plon, 1899), pp. 371–414

Champfleury, *Le Réalisme* (Paris: Michel Lévy, 1857)

——, *La Mascarade de la vie parisienne* (Paris: Librairie Nouvelle, 1861)

——, *Le Violon de faïence* (Paris: Hetzel, 1862)

——, *L'Hôtel des commissaires-priseurs* (Paris: Dentu, 1867)

Charcot, Jean-Martin, and Valentin Magnan, 'Inversion du sens génital', *Archives de Neurologie*, 3:7 (January–February 1882), 53–60 and 4:10 (July 1882), 296–322

'Chiffonnier', in *Grand Dictionnaire universel du XIXè siècle français, historique, géographique, bibliographique, littéraire, artistique, scientifique etc.*, 17 vols (Paris: Librairie classique Larousse et Boyer, 1866–1877), IV (1869), 96–8

Clarétie, Jules, *Un Assassin* (Paris: Faure, 1866)

——, 'Préface', in Paul Eudel, *L'Hôtel Drouot en 1881*(Paris: Charpentier, 1882), pp. vii–xv

——, *La vie à Paris*, 21 vols (Paris: Havard, 1881–1885, 1895–1913), II (1882)

Clément de Ris, Louis Torterat, Comte de, *La Curiosité: collections françaises et étrangères, cabinets d'amateurs, biographies* (Paris: Librairie Ve Jules Renouard, 1864)

——, *Les Amateurs d'autrefois* (Paris: Plon, 1877)

'Collectionneur', in *Grand Dictionnaire universel du XIXè siècle français, historique, géographique, bibliographique, littéraire, artistique, scientifique etc.*, 17 vols (Paris: Librairie classique Larousse et Boyer, 1866–1877), IV (1869), 601–2

Cousin, Charles, *Racontars illustrés d'un vieux collectionneur* (Paris: La Librairie de l'Art, 1887)

'Curieux', in *Grand Dictionnaire universel du XIXè siècle français, historique, géographique, bibliographique, littéraire, artistique, scientifique etc.*, 17 vols (Paris: Librairie classique Larousse et Boyer, 1866–1877), V (1869), 679–80

Daudet, Alphonse, *L'Immortel*, in *Œuvres*, ed. by Roger Ripoll, Bibliothèque de la Pléiade, 3 vols (Paris: Gallimard, 1986–1994), III, 682–845

De La Bédollière, Emile, and P. Bernard, *Les Aventures de M. de Bric-à-Brac: roman zoologique, archéologique et paléontologique* (Paris: Curmer, 1842)

De La Bruyère, Jean, *Les Caractères ou les mœurs de ce siècle*, in *Œuvres complètes*, ed. by Julien Benda, Bibliothèque de la Pléiade (Paris: Gallimard, 1951), pp. 59–478

Descuret, Jean Baptiste Félix, *La Médecine des passions* (Paris: Béché jeune et Labé, 1841)

Eudel, Paul, *L'Hôtel Drouot en 1881* (Paris: Charpentier, 1882)

——, *Collections et collectionneurs* (Paris: Charpentier, 1885)

——, 'A l'Hôtel Drouot', in *Balades dans Paris*, ed. by E. R., Paul Eudel, B-H. Gausseron, and Adolphe Retten (Paris: Société des Bibliophiles Contemporains, 1897), pp. 33–70

Flaubert, Gustave, *Bouvard et Pécuchet*, in *Œuvres Complètes*, ed. by Bernard Masson, 2 vols (Paris: Seuil, 1964), pp. 201–301

Les Français peints par eux-mêmes, 8 vols (Paris: Curmer, 1840–1842)

France, Anatole, *Le Crime de Sylvestre Bonnard*, in *Œuvres*, ed. by Marie-Claire Bancquart, Bibliothèque de la Pléiade, 4 vols (Paris: Gallimard, 1984–1991), I, 149–313

——, *Le Lys Rouge*, in *Œuvres*, ed. by Marie-Claire Bancquart, Bibliothèque de la Pléiade, 4 vols (Paris: Gallimard, 1984–1991), II (1987), 329–562

Gautier, Théophile, *Le Pied de momie*, in *Romans, contes et nouvelles*, ed. by Pierre Laubriet, Bibliothèque de la Pléiade, 2 vols (Paris: Gallimard, 2002), I, 855–66

Goncourt, Edmond and Jules de, *Histoire de la société française pendant la révolution*, 2nd edn (Paris: Dentu, 1854)

Goncourt, Edmond de, *La Maison d'un artiste*, 2 vols (Paris: Charpentier, 1881)

Grégoire, Henri, *Troisième Rapport sur le vandalisme*, in *Œuvres de l'Abbé Grégoire*, 14 vols (Nendeln, Liechtenstein: Kraus-Thomson; Paris: Editions d'Histoire Sociale, 1977), II, 335–57

Havard, Henry, *L'Art dans la maison* (Paris: Rouveyre & Blond, 1884)

Hetzel, Pierre-Jules, 'Avertissement de l'éditeur', in Jules Verne, *Les Voyages et aventures du capitaine Hatteras* (Paris: Hetzel, 1866), pp. 1–2

Huysmans, Joris-Karl, *A Rebours*, ed. by Rose Fortassier (Paris: Imprimerie Nationale, 1981)

'Introduction', in *Le Cabinet de l'amateur et de l'antiquaire*, I (1842), 5–13

Janin, Jules, 'M. Dusommerard', *Le Cabinet de l'amateur et de l'antiquaire*, 1 (1842), 324–33

——, *The American in Paris* (London: Longman, Brown, Green and Longmans, 1843)

——, *Le Livre* (Paris: Plon, 1870)

Kock, Paul de, ed., *La Grande Ville*, 2 vols (Paris: Marescq, 1844)

Larousse, Pierre, ed., *Grand Dictionnaire universel du XIXè siècle français, historique, géographique, bibliographique, littéraire, artistique, scientifique etc.*, 17 vols (Paris: Librairie classique Larousse et Boyer, 1866–1877)

Leblanc, Maurice, *Arsène Lupin, Gentleman-Cambrioleur* (Paris: Lafitte, 1907)

——, *L'Aiguille Creuse* (Paris: Lafitte, 1909)

Lorrain, Jean, *Monsieur de Phocas* (Paris: La Table Ronde, 1992)

Maupassant, Guy de, 'Au Muséum d'histoire naturelle', in *Chroniques inédites*, ed. by Pascal Pia, 2 vols (Paris: Maurice Gonon, 1979), I, 53–9

——, 'Vieux Pots', in *Chroniques inédites*, ed. by Pascal Pia, 2 vols (Paris: Maurice Gonon, 1979), II, 15–19

——, 'Bibelot', in *Chroniques inédites*, ed. by Pascal Pia, 2 vols (Paris: Maurice Gonon, 1979), II, 27–32

——, 'Les Amateurs d'artistes', in *Chroniques inédites*, ed. by Pascal Pia, 2 vols (Paris: Maurice Gonon, 1979), II, 299–304

Mirbeau, Octave, 'Les Bibelots', *Le Gaulois*, 5 March 1885, p. 1

Montesquiou, Robert de, *Les Pas effacés: mémoires*, 3 vols (Paris: Emile-Paul Frères, 1923)

Morel, Bénédicte, *Traité des dégénérescences physiques, intellectuelles et morales de l'espèce humaine et des causes qui produisent ces variétés maladives* (Paris: Baillière, 1857)

'M. Du Sommerard', in *L'Artiste: Beaux-Arts et Belles-Lettres*, 3rd Series, vol. 2 (1842–1844), 148–50

'Musée des Thermes et de l'hôtel de Cluny', in *Le Cabinet de l'amateur et de l'antiquaire*, 2 (1843), 385–99

Nodier, Charles, 'Le Bibliomane', in *Paris: ou Le Livre des Cent-et-Un*, 15 vols (Paris: Ladvocat, 1831–34), I, 87–108

——, 'L'Amateur de livres', in *Les Français peints par eux-mêmes*, 8 vols (Paris: Curmer, 1840–1842), III (1841), 201–9

Nordau, Max, *Degeneration* (London: Heinemann, 1895)

Paris: ou Le Livre des Cent-et-Un, 15 vols (Paris: Ladvocat, 1831–1834)

Proust, Marcel, 'Journées de lecture', in *Contre Sainte-Beuve*, ed. by Pierre Clarac, Bibliothèque de la Pléiade (Paris: Gallimard, 1971)

——, *A La Recherche du temps perdu*, ed. by Jean-Yves Tadié, Bibliothèque de la Pléiade, 4 vols (Paris: Gallimard, 1987–1989)

Quatremère de Quincy, Antoine-Chrysostome, *Considérations morales sur la destination des ouvrages d'art* (Paris: Fayard, 1989)

——, *Lettres à Miranda sur le déplacement des monuments de l'art et de l'Italie*, ed. by Edward Pommier (Paris: Macula, 1989)

R., E., Paul Eudel, B-H. Gausseron, and Adolphe Retten, eds, *Balades dans Paris* (Paris: Société des Bibliophiles Contemporains, 1897)

Robida, Albert, *Le XIXᵉ siècle* (Paris: Decaux, 1888)

——, and Octave Uzanne, *Contes pour les bibliophiles* (Paris: May et Metteroz, 1895)

Rochefort, Henri, *Les Petits Mystères de l'hôtel des ventes* (Paris: Dentu, 1862)

Rochoux, Armand-Ambroise, *Les Moutons de Panurge: chapitres émouvants et drolatiques sur les estampes, les experts, les catalogues et les collectionneurs* (Paris: Delion, 1861)

Roehn, Charles, *Physiologie du commerce des arts* (Paris: Lagny, 1841)

Rosny, J.-H., *Le Testament volé* (Paris: Fontemoing, 1905)

Uzanne, Octave, *Le Miroir du monde* (Paris: Quantin, 1885)

——, *Les Zigzags d'un curieux: causeries sur l'art des livres et la littérature d'art* (Paris: Quantin, 1888)

——, 'Notes sur le goût intime et la décoration personnelle de l'Habitation Moderne', *L'Art et l'idée*, 2 (1892), 257–76

Verne, Jules, *Les Voyages et aventures du capitaine Hatteras* (Paris: Hetzel, 1866)

——, *Voyage au centre de la terre* (Paris: Hetzel, 1864)

——, *Vingt mille lieues sous les mers*, 2 vols (Paris: Hetzel, 1871)

——, *L'Ile mystérieuse*, 3 vols (Paris: Hetzel, 1874)

Viel-Castel, Horace de,'Les Collectionneurs' in *Les Français peints par eux-mêmes*, 8 vols (Paris: Curmer, 1840–1842), I, 121–8

Viollet-le-Duc, Eugène Emmanuel, *Habitations Modernes*, 2 vols (Paris: Morel, 1875–1877)

Secondary Texts

Abbas, Ackbar, 'Walter Benjamin's Collector: The Fate of Modern Experience', *New Literary History* 20 (1988), 217–37

Abélès, Luce, 'La Fin du siècle', in *Les Français peints par eux-mêmes: panorama social du XIXe siècle*, ed. by Ségolène Le Men and Luce Abélès (Paris: Editions de la Réunion des musées nationaux, 1993), pp. 68–83

Agamben, Giorgio, *Stanzas: Word and Phantasm in Western Culture*, trans. by Ronald L. Martinez (Minneapolis: University of Minnesota Press, 1993)

Apter, Emily, *Feminizing the Fetish: Psychoanalysis and Narrative Obsession in Turn-of-the-Century France* (Ithaca: Cornell University Press, 1991)

——, and William Pietz, eds, *Fetishism as Cultural Discourse* (Ithaca: Cornell University Press, 1993)

Arato, Andrew, and Eike Gebhardt, eds, *The Essential Frankfurt School Reader* (New York: Urizen Books, 1978)

Auslander, Leora, *Taste and Power: Furnishing Modern France* (Berkeley: University of California Press, 1996)

Baguley, David, *Naturalist Fiction: The Entropic Vision* (Cambridge: Cambridge University Press, 1990)

Bal, Mieke, 'A Narrative Perspective on Collecting', in *The Cultures of Collecting*, ed.
    by John Elsner and Roger Cardinal (London: Reaktion, 1994), pp. 97–115

Bancquart, Marie-Claire, '*Le Crime de Sylvestre Bonnard*: Notice', in France, *Œuvres*, ed.
    by Marie-Claire Bancquart, Bibliothèque de la Pléiade, 4 vols (Paris: Gallimard,
    1984–1991), I, 1109–29

Bann, Stephen, *The Clothing of Clio: a study of the representation of history in nineteenth-
    century Britain and France* (Cambridge: Cambridge University Press, 1984)

Barbéris, Pierre, *Mythes Balzaciens* (Paris: Armand Colin, 1972)

Barthes, Roland, '*Nautilus* et *Bateau ivre*', in Mythologies (Paris: Seuil, 1957)

——, *S/Z* (Paris: Seuil, 1970)

Baudrillard, Jean, *Le Système des objets* (Paris: Gallimard, 1968)

Belk, Russell W., *Collecting in a Consumer Society* (London: Routledge, 1995)

Benjamin, Walter, 'Edward Fuchs: Collector and Historian', in *The Essential Frankfurt
    School Reader*, ed. by Andrew Arato and Eike Gebhardt (New York: Urizen
    Books, 1978), pp. 225–53

——, 'Unpacking my Library: A Talk about Book Collecting', in *Illuminations*, ed. by
    Hannah Arendt, trans. by Harry Zorn (London: Pimlico, 1999), pp. 61–9

——, 'Convolute H: The Collector', in *The Arcades Project*, trans. by Howard Eiland
    and Kevin McLaughlin (Cambridge, MA: Belknap, 1999), pp. 203–27

——, 'Paris: Capital of the Nineteenth Century. Exposé of 1935', in *The Arcades Project*,
    trans. by Howard Eiland and Kevin McLaughlin (Cambridge, MA: Belknap,
    1999), pp. 3–13

——, 'Paris: Capital of the Nineteenth Century. Exposé of 1939', in *The Arcades Project*,
    trans. by Howard Eiland and Kevin McLaughlin (Cambridge, MA: Belknap,
    1999), pp. 14–26

Bernheimer, Charles, in 'Fetishism and Decadence: Salomé's Severed Heads', in
    Fetishism as Cultural Discourse, ed. by Emily Apter and William Pietz (Ithaca:
    Cornell University Press, 1993), pp. 62–83

Biasi, Pierre-Marc de, 'La Collection Pons comme figure du problématique', in *Balzac
    et les parents pauvres*, ed. by Françoise van Rossum-Guyon and Michiel van
    Brederode (Paris: Société d'édition d'enseignement supérieur, 1981), pp. 61–73

Bordas, Eric, 'Le rôle de la peinture dans *Le Cousin Pons*', *Australian Journal of French
    Studies*, 32 (1995), 19–37

Bourdieu, Pierre, *La Distinction: critique sociale du jugement* (Paris: Editions de Minuit,
    1979)

Brown, Bill, ed., *Things*, Critical Inquiry 28 (2001)

Brown, Frederick, *Flaubert: A Biography* (Cambridge. MA: Harvard University Press,
    2007)

Butor, Michel, 'Le Point suprême et l'âge d'or à travers quelques œuvres de Jules Verne', in *Répertoire I* (Paris: Editions de Minuit, 1960), pp. 130–62

Cabanne, Pierre, *Les Grands Collectionneurs*, 2 vols (Paris: Editions de l'amateur, 2003–2004)

Capitanio, Sarah, '"L'Ici-bas" and "l'Au delà" … but Not as they Knew it. Realism, Utopianism and Science Fiction in the Novels of Jules Verne', in *Jules Verne: Narratives of Modernity*, ed. by Edmund J. Smyth (Liverpool: University of Liverpool Press, 2000), pp. 67–77

Clifford, James, *The Predicament of Culture: Twentieth-Century Ethnography, Literature, and Art* (Cambridge, MA: Harvard University Press, 1988)

Dagognet, François, *Le Catalogue de la vie* (Paris: Presses Universitaires de la France, 1970)

——, *Le Musée sans fin* (Lyon: Champ Vallon, 1984)

Donato, Eugenio, 'The Museum's Furnace: Notes Toward a Contextual Reading of *Bouvard et Pécuchet*', in *Textual Strategies: Perspectives in Post-Structuralist Criticism*, ed. by Josué V. Harari (Ithaca: Cornell University Press, 1979), pp. 213–38

Du Plessis, Michael, 'Unspeakable Writing: Jean Lorrain's *Monsieur de Phocas*', *French Forum* 27 (2002), 65–98

Elsner, John, and Roger Cardinal, eds, *The Cultures of Collecting* (London: Reaktion, 1994)

——, 'Introduction', in *The Cultures of Collecting*, ed. by John Elsner and Roger Cardinal (London: Reaktion, 1994), pp. 1–6

Fernbach, Amanda, *Fantasies of Fetishism: from Decadence to the Post-Human* (Edinburgh: Edinburgh University Press, 2002)

Foucault, Michel, *Les Mots et les choses: une archéologie des sciences humaines* (Paris: Gallimard, 1966)

Freedgood, Elaine, *The Ideas in Things: Fugitive Meaning in the Victorian Novel* (Chicago: University of Chicago Press, 2006)

Gaillard, Françoise, '*A Rebours*: une écriture de la crise', *Revue des sciences humaines*, 43.170–1 (April–September 1978), 111–22

——, '*Bouvard et Pécuchet*, un conte sur la folie ordinaire (l'exemple du chapitre III)', in *Flaubert, l'autre*, ed. by F. Lecercle and S. Messina (Lyon: Presses Universitaires de Lyon, 1989), pp. 152–60

Georgel, Chantal, 'Moderne ou Ancien: *Le Cousin Pons*', in *Balzac et la peinture*, ed. by Roger Pierrot and Philippe Le Leysour (Tours: Farrago, 1999), pp. 181–5

Goetz, Adrien, '"De si vives compensations à la gloire": les collectionneurs au centre de *La Comédie Humaine*', in *Balzac et la peinture*, ed. by Roger Pierrot and Philippe Le Leysour (Tours: Farrago, 1999), pp. 187–92

Gout, Muriel, Jacqueline Goy, Lucien Laubier et al, *Quand Jules Verne raconte la mer: Vingt mille lieues sous les mers* (Paris; Monaco: Institut Océanographique, 2005)

Guichardet, Jeannine, *Balzac: 'Archéologue' de Paris* (Paris: Sedes, 1986)

Hamon, Françoise, 'Collections: ce que disent les dictionnaires', *Romantisme* 112 (2001), 55–70

Hamon, Philippe, *Expositions: littérature et architecture au XIXe siècle* (Paris: José Corti, 1989)

Harari, Josué V., ed., *Textual Strategies: Perspectives in Post-Structuralist Criticism* (Ithaca: Cornell University Press, 1979)

Haustein, Katja, 'Proust's Emotional Cavities: Vision and Affect in *A La Recherche du temps perdu*', *French Studies* 63 (2009), 161–73

Jardine, N., J. A. Secord, and E. C. Spary, eds, *Cultures of natural history* (Cambridge: Cambridge University Press, 1996)

Kingcaid, Renée A., *Neurosis and Narrative: The Decadent Short Fiction of Proust, Lorrain, and Rachilde* (Carbondale: Southern Illinois University Press, 1992)

Knight, Diana, *Balzac and the Model of Painting: Artist Stories in 'La Comédie Humaine'* (London: Legenda, 2007)

Lauster, Martina, *Sketches of the Nineteenth Century: European Journalism and its Physiologies, 1830–1850* (Basingstoke: Palgrave Macmillan, 2007)

Le Brun, Jean-Baptiste-Pierre, *Réflexions sur le Muséum national: 14 janvier 1793* (Paris: Réunion des musées nationaux, 1992)

Le Men, Ségolène, and Luce Abélès, eds, *Les Français peints par eux-mêmes: panorama social du XIXe siècle* (Paris: Editions de la Réunion des musées nationaux, 1993)

Lecercle, F., and S. Messina, eds, *Flaubert, l'autre* (Lyon: Presses Universitaires de Lyon, 1989)

Lloyd, Rosemary, *The Land of Lost Content: Children and childhood in Nineteenth-Century French Literature* (Oxford: Clarendon Press, 1992)

——, *Shimmering in a Transformed Light: Writing the Still Life* (Ithaca: Cornell University Press, 2005)

Lucey, Michael, *The Misfit of the Family: Balzac and the Social Forms of Sexuality* (Durham, NC: Duke University Press, 2003)

Maleuvre, Didier, *Museum Memories: History, Technology, Art* (Stanford: Stanford Universtiy Press, 1999)

Marcus, Sharon, *Apartment Stories: city and home in nineteenth-century Paris and London* (Berkeley: University of California Press, 1999)

Martin, Andrew, *The Knowledge of Ignorance: From Genesis to Jules Verne* (Cambridge: Cambridge University Press, 1985)

Moi, Toril, *Henrik Ibsen and the Birth of Modernism: Art, Theater, Philosophy* (Oxford: Oxford University Press, 2006)

Muensterberger, Werner, *Collecting: An Unruly Passion. Pyschological Perspectives* (Princeton: Princeton University Press, 1994)

Nicholson, Jane A., 'Discourse, Power, and Necessity: Contextualising *Le Cousin Pons*', *Symposium* 42/1 (Spring, 1998), 48–61

Nietzsche, Friedrich, 'On the Uses and Disadvantages of History for Life', in *Untimely Meditations*, ed. by Daniel Breazeale (Cambridge: Cambridge University Press, 1997), pp. 58–123

Nora, Pierre, ed., *Les Lieux de mémoire*, 3 vols (Paris: Gallimard, 1984–1992)

——, 'Entre Mémoire et Histoire', in *Les Lieux de mémoire*, ed. by Pierre Nora, 3 vols (Paris: Gallimard, 1984–1992), I, pp. xvii–xlii

Nye, Robert A., 'The Medical Origins of Sexual Fetishism', in *Fetishism as Cultural Discoure*, ed. by Emily Apter and William Pietz (Ithaca: Cornell University Press, 1993), pp. 13–30

Outram, Dorinda, 'New Spaces in Natural History', in *Cultures of Natural History*, ed. by N. Jardine, J. A. Secord, and E. C. Spary (Cambridge: Cambridge University Press, 1996), pp. 249–65

Pearce, Susan M., *On Collecting: An Investigation into Collecting in the European Tradition* (London: Routledge, 1995)

Perec, Georges, *Penser/Classer* (Paris: Hachette, 1985)

Pety, Dominique, 'Le Personnage du collectionneur au XIXᵉ siècle: de l'excentrique à l'amateur distingué', *Romantisme* 112 (2001), 71–81

——, *Les Goncourt et la collection: de l'objet d'art à l'art d'écrire* (Geneva: Droz, 2003)

Pierrot, Roger, and Philippe Le Leysour, eds, *Balzac et la peinture* (Tours: Farrago, 1999)

Pomian, Krzysztof, *Collectionneurs, Amateurs et Curieux: Paris, Venise: XVIᵉ – XVIIIᵉ siècle* (Paris: Gallimard, 1987)

——, 'Collections: une typologie historique', *Romantisme* 112 (2001), 9–22

Reed, John R., *Decadent Style* (Athens, Ohio: Ohio University Press, 1985)

Rheims, Maurice, *La Vie étrange des objets: histoire de la curiosité* (Paris: Plon, 1959)

Rossum-Guyon, Françoise van and Michiel van Brederode, eds, *Balzac et les parents pauvres* (Paris: Société d'édition d'enseignement supérieur, 1981)

Pommier, Edward, 'Postface', in Jean-Baptiste-Pierre Le Brun, *Réflexions sur le Muséum national: 14 janvier 1793* (Paris: Réunion des musées nationaux, 1992), pp. 51–94

Poulot, Dominique, 'Alexandre Lenoir et les musées des monuments français', in *Les Lieux de mémoire*, ed. by Pierre Nora, 3 vols (Paris: Gallimard, 1984–1992), II(2) (1986), 497–531

Preiss-Basset, Nathalie, 'Les Physiologies, un miroir en miettes', in *Les Français peints par eux-mêmes: panorama social du XIXe siècle*, ed. by Ségolène Le Men and Luce Abélès (Paris: Editions de la Réunion des musées nationaux, 1993), pp. 62–7

Saisselin, Rémy G., *The Bourgeois and the Bibelot* (New Brunswick: Rutgers University Press, 1984)

Schuerewegen, France, '*Muséum* ou *Croutéum?* Pons, Bouvard, Pécuchet et la collection', *Romantisme* 55 (1987), 41–84

Schwenger, Peter, 'Words and the Murder of the Thing', *Critical Inquiry*, 28 (2001), 99–113

Secord, James A., 'The Crisis of Nature', in *Cultures of Natural History*, ed. by N. Jardine, J. A. Secord, and E. C. Spary (Cambridge: Cambridge University Press, 1996), pp. 227–59

Sieburth, Richard, 'Same Difference: The French *Physiologies*, 1840–2,' *Notebooks in Cultural Analysis*, 1 (1984), 163–200

Silverman, Debora, *Art Nouveau in Fin-de-Siècle France: Politics, Psychology, and Style* (Berkeley: University of California Press, 1989)

Silverman, Willa Z., *The New Bibliopolis: French Book Collectors and the Culture of Print, 1880–1914* (Toronto: University of Toronto Press, 2008)

Smyth, Edmund J., ed., *Jules Verne: Narratives of Modernity* (Liverpool: University of Liverpool Press, 2000)

Spoelberch de Lovenjoul, Charles de, *Histoire des œuvres de Honoré de Balzac: troisième édition entièrement revue et corrigée à nouveau* (Geneva: Slatkine Reprints, 1968)

Stammers, Tom, 'The Bric-a-Brac of the Old Regime: Collecting and Cultural History in Post-Revolutionary France', *French History* 22 (September 2008), 295–315

Stewart, Susan, *On Longing: Narratives of the Miniature, the Gigantic, the Souvenir, the Collection* (Baltimore: Johns Hopkins University Press, 1984)

Terdiman, Richard, *Present Past: Modernity and the Memory Crisis* (Ithaca: Cornell University Press, 1993)

Things, ed. by Bill Brown, *Critical Inquiry* 28 (2001)

'"Unless you do these crazy things ...": An Interview with Robert Opie, in *The Cultures of Collecting*, ed. by John Elsner and Roger Cardinal (London: Reaktion, 1994), pp. 25–48

Unwin, Tim, 'The Fiction of Science, or the Science of Fiction', in *Jules Verne: Narratives of Modernity*, ed. by Edmund J Smyth (Liverpool: University of Liverpool Press, 2000), pp. 46–59

Vouilloux, Bernard, 'Le Discours sur la collection', *Romantisme* 112 (2001), 95–108
Watson, Janell, *Literature and Material Culture from Balzac to Proust: The Collection and Consumption of Curiosities* (Cambridge: Cambridge University Press, 1999)
Wohlfarth, Irving, 'Et Cetera? The Historian as Chiffonnier', *New German Critique* 39 (1986), 142–68

Index

French Studies of the Eighteenth and Nineteenth Centuries

Edited by Robin Howells, Emeritus Professor of French at Birkbeck, University of London, and James Kearns, Emeritus Professor of French at the University of Exeter

This series publishes the latest research by teachers and researchers working in all the disciplines which constitute French studies in this period, in the form of monographs, revised dissertations, collected papers and conference proceedings. Adhering to the highest academic standards, it provides a vehicle for established scholars with specialised research projects but also encourages younger academics who may be publishing for the first time.

The Editors take a broad view of French studies and intend to examine literary and cultural phenomena of the eighteenth and nineteenth centuries, excluding the Romantic movement, against their historical, political and social background in all the French-speaking countries.

Volume 1   Malcolm Cook and Annie Jourdan (éds.):
            Journalisme et fiction au 18ᵉ siècle.
            241 pages. 1999.
            ISBN 3-906761-50-9 / US-ISBN 0-8204-4221-6

Volume 2   Paul Rowe: A Mirror on the Rhine?
            The Nouvelle revue germanique, Strasbourg 1829–1837.
            340 pages. 2000.
            ISBN 3-906762-39-4 / US-ISBN 0-8204-4233-X

Volume 3   Rachael Langford: Jules Vallès and the Narration
            of History. Contesting the French Third Republic in the
            Jacques Vingtras Trilogy.
            271 pages. 1999.
            ISBN 3-906762-99-8 / US-ISBN 0-8204-4249-6

Volume 32   Emma Bielecki:
The Collector in Nineteenth-Century French Literature.
Representation, Identity, Knowledge.
242 pages. 2012.
ISBN 978-3-0343-0757-4